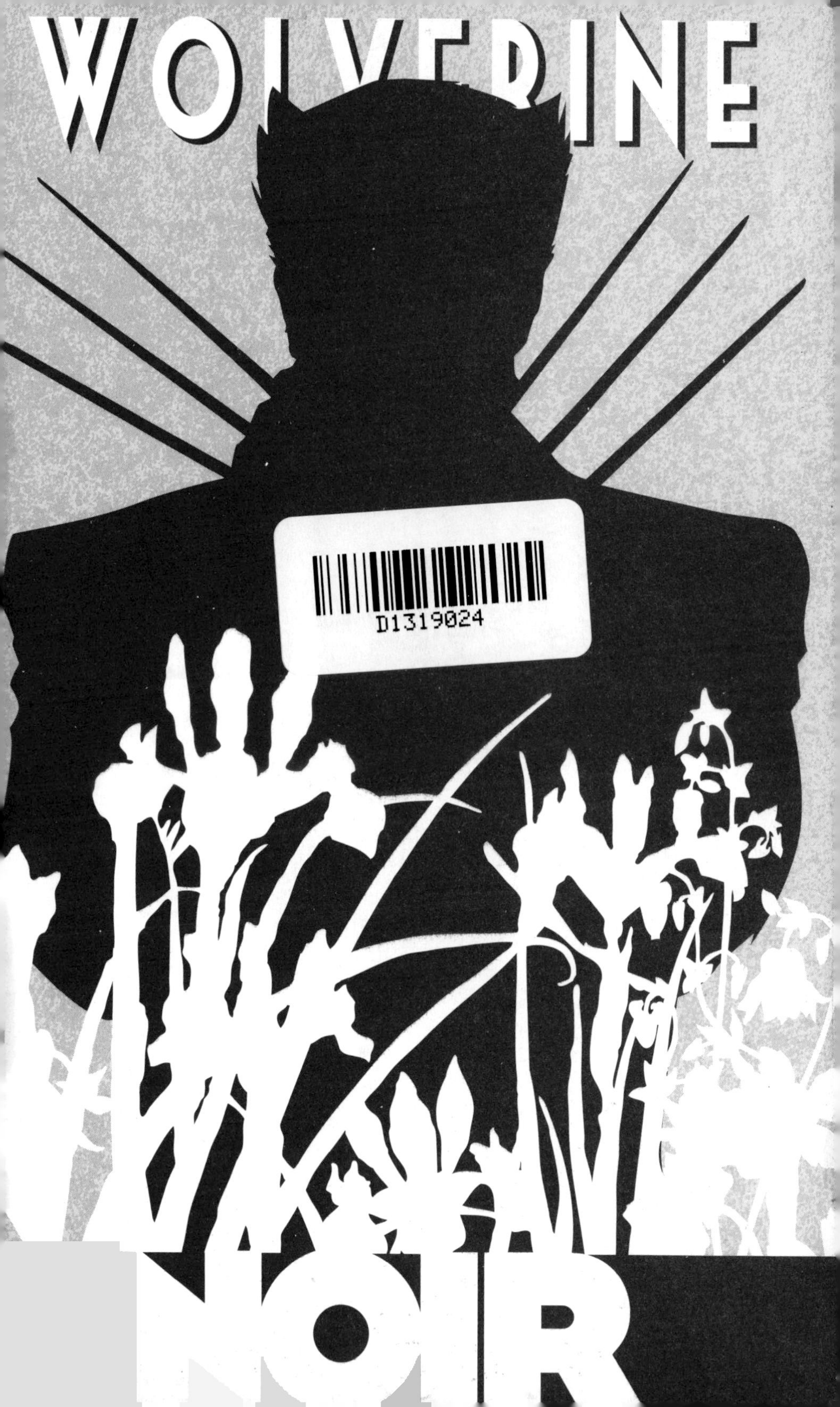
WOLVERINE
NOIR

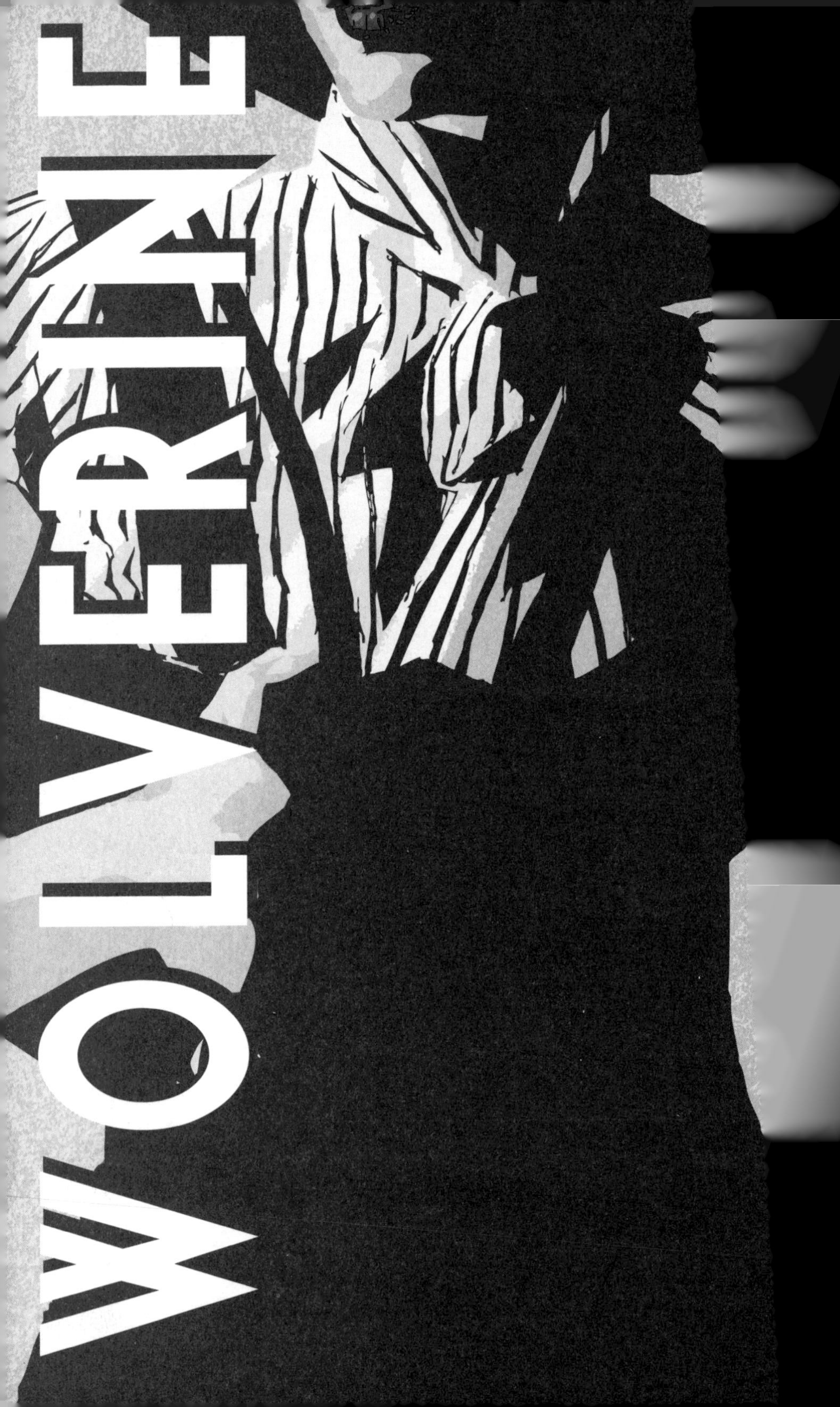
WOLVERINE

WRITER
STUART MOORE

ART
C.P. SMITH

COLORIST
RAIN BEREDO

LETTERER
JEFF ECKLEBERRY

EDITOR
DANIEL KETCHUM

EXECUTIVE EDITOR
AXEL ALONSO

COLLECTION EDITOR
JENNIFER GRÜNWALD
ASSISTANT EDITOR
ALEX STARBUCK
ASSOCIATE EDITOR
JOHN DENNING
EDITOR, SPECIAL PROJECTS
MARK D. BEAZLEY
SENIOR EDITOR, SPECIAL PROJECTS
JEFF YOUNGQUIST
SENIOR VICE PRESIDENT OF SALES
DAVID GABRIEL
BOOK DESIGN
JEFF POWELL

EDITOR IN CHIEF
JOE QUESADA
PUBLISHER
DAN BUCKLEY
EXECUTIVE PRODUCER
ALAN FINE

WOLVERINE NOIR. Contains material originally published in magazine form as WOLVERINE NOIR #1-4. First printing 2010. ISBN# 978-0-7851-3547-0. Published by MARVEL WORLDWIDE, INC., a subsidiary of MARVEL ENTERTAINMENT, LLC. OFFICE OF PUBLICATION: 417 5th Avenue, New York, NY 10016. Copyright © 2009 and 2010 Marvel Characters, Inc. All rights reserved. $14.99 per copy in the U.S. (GST #R127032852); Canadian Agreement #40668537. All characters featured in this issue and the distinctive names and likenesses thereof, and all related indicia are trademarks of Marvel Characters. Inc. No similarity between any of the names, characters, persons, and/or institutions in this magazine with those of any living or dead person or institution is intended, and any such similarity which may exist is purely coincidental. **Printed in the U.S.A.** ALAN FINE, EVP - Office of the President, Marvel Worldwide, Inc. and EVP & CMO Marvel Characters B.V.; DAN BUCKLEY, Chief Executive Officer and Publisher - Print, Animation & Digital Media; JIM SOKOLOWSKI, Chief Operating Officer; DAVID GABRIEL, SVP of Publishing Sales & Circulation; DAVID BOGART, SVP of Business Affairs & Talent Management; MICHAEL PASCIULLO, VP Merchandising & Communications; JIM O'KEEFE, VP of Operations & Logistics; DAN CARR, Executive Director of Publishing Technology; JUSTIN F. GABRIE, Director of Publishing & Editorial Operations; SUSAN CRESPI, Editorial Operations Manager; ALEX MORALES, Publishing Operations Manager; STAN LEE, Chairman Emeritus. For information regarding advertising in Marvel Comics or on Marvel.com, please contact Ron Stern, VP of Business Development, at rstern@marvel.com. For Marvel subscription inquiries, please call 800-217-9158. **Manufactured between 3/26/10 and 4/14/10 by R.R. DONNELLEY INC. (CRAWFORD), CRAWFORDSVILLE, IN, USA.**

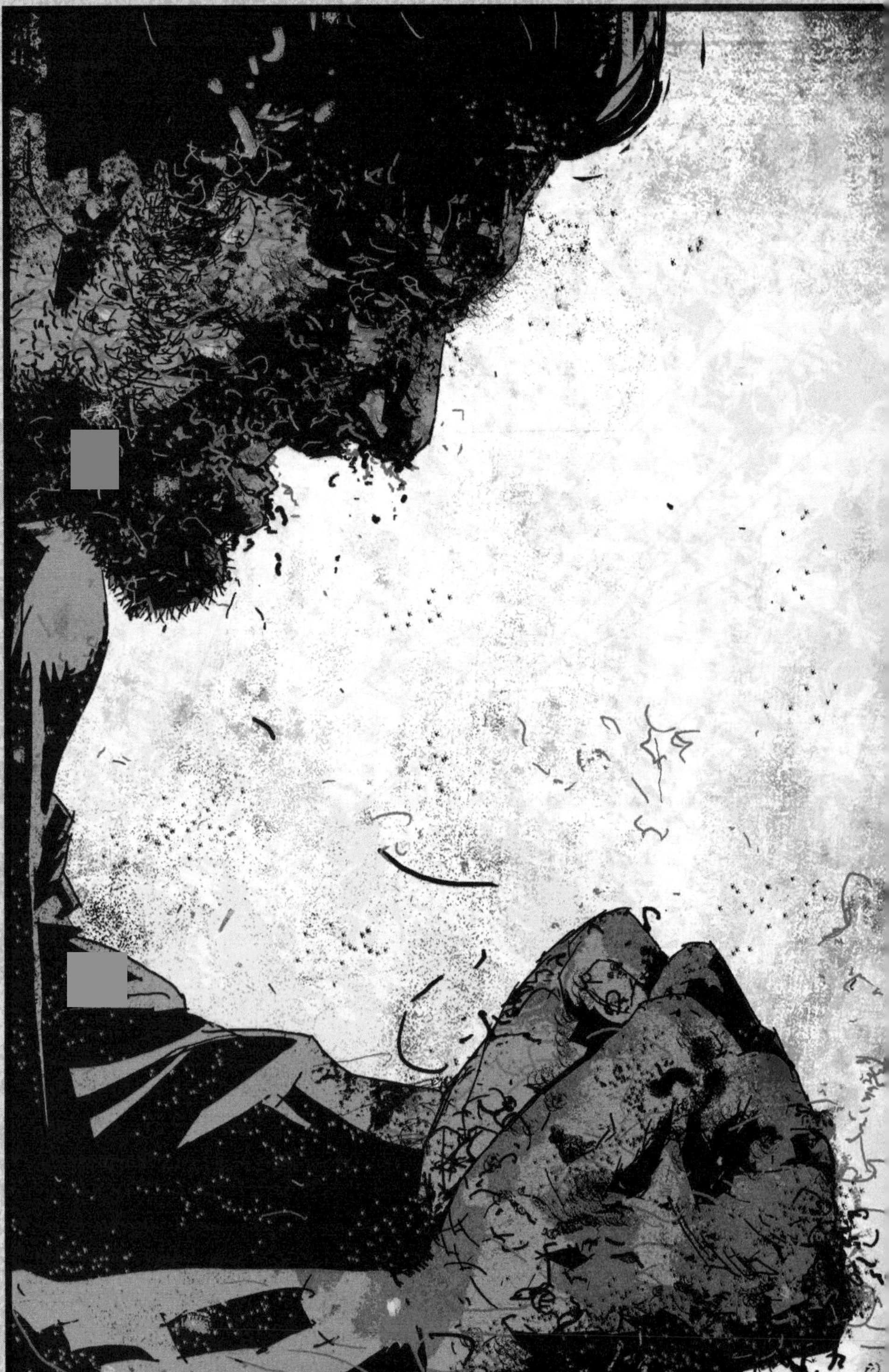

ONE

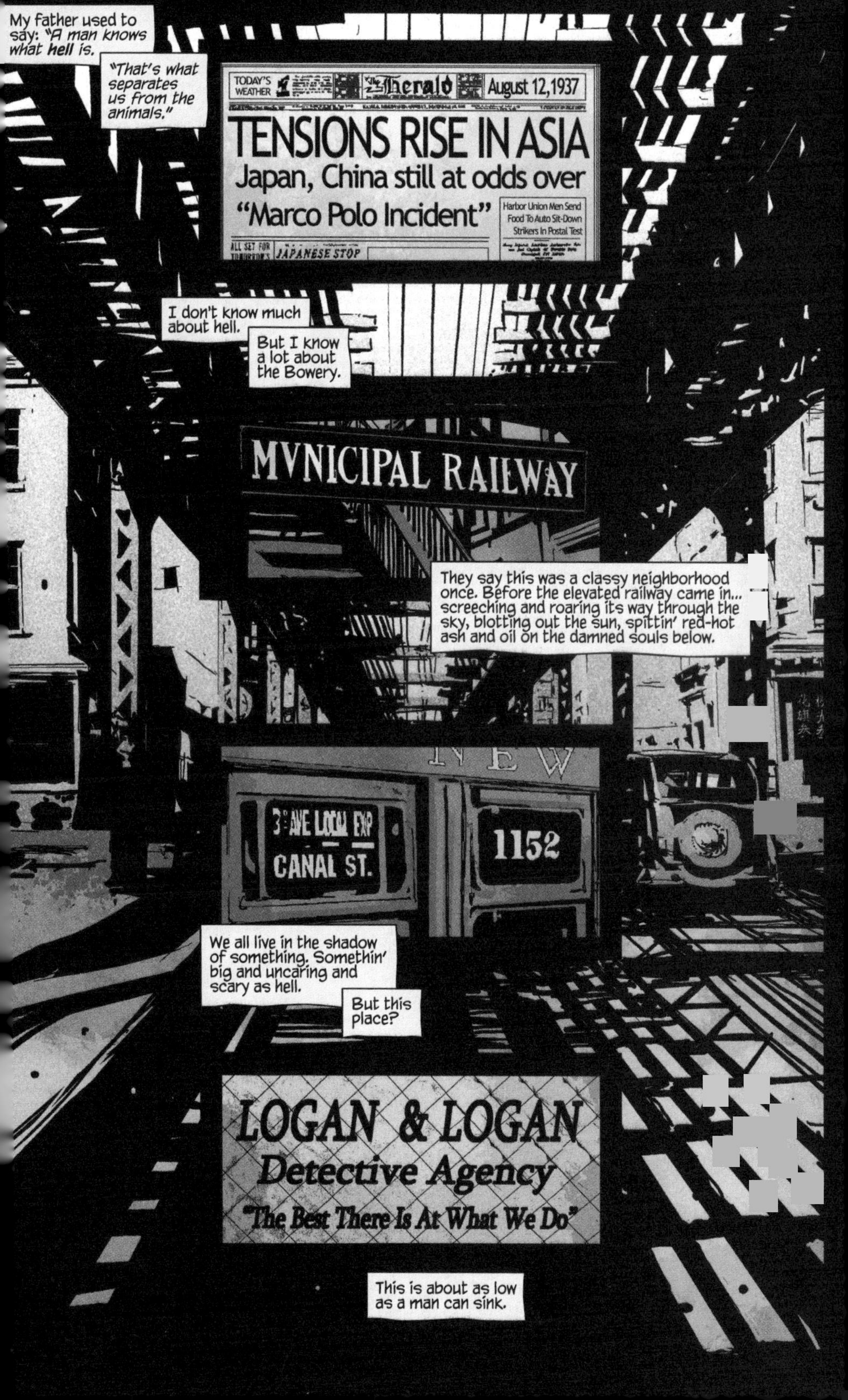

My father used to say: "A man knows what hell is.
"That's what separates us from the animals."
TODAY'S WEATHER
Herald
August 12,1937
TENSIONS RISE IN ASIA
Japan, China still at odds over "Marco Polo Incident"
Harbor Union Men Send Food To Auto Sit-Down Strikers In Postal Test
JAPANESE STOP
I don't know much about hell.
But I know a lot about the Bowery.
MVNICIPAL RAILWAY
They say this was a classy neighborhood once. Before the elevated railway came in... screeching and roaring its way through the sky, blotting out the sun, spittin' red-hot ash and oil on the damned souls below.
NEW
3rd AVE LOCAL EXP
CANAL ST.
1152
We all live in the shadow of something. Somethin' big and uncaring and scary as hell.
But this place?
LOGAN & LOGAN
Detective Agency
"The Best There Is At What We Do"
This is about as low as a man can sink.

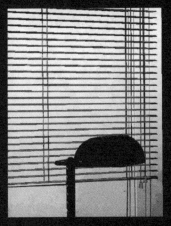

My name's Jim Logan. I'm a private detective.

And for about the eightieth time today...

WOLVERINE NOIR

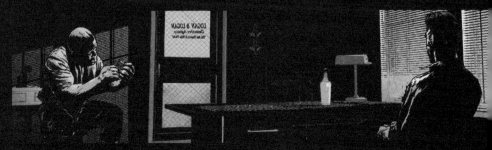

1: JACK ROLLER

...I'm thinkin' about killing my partner.

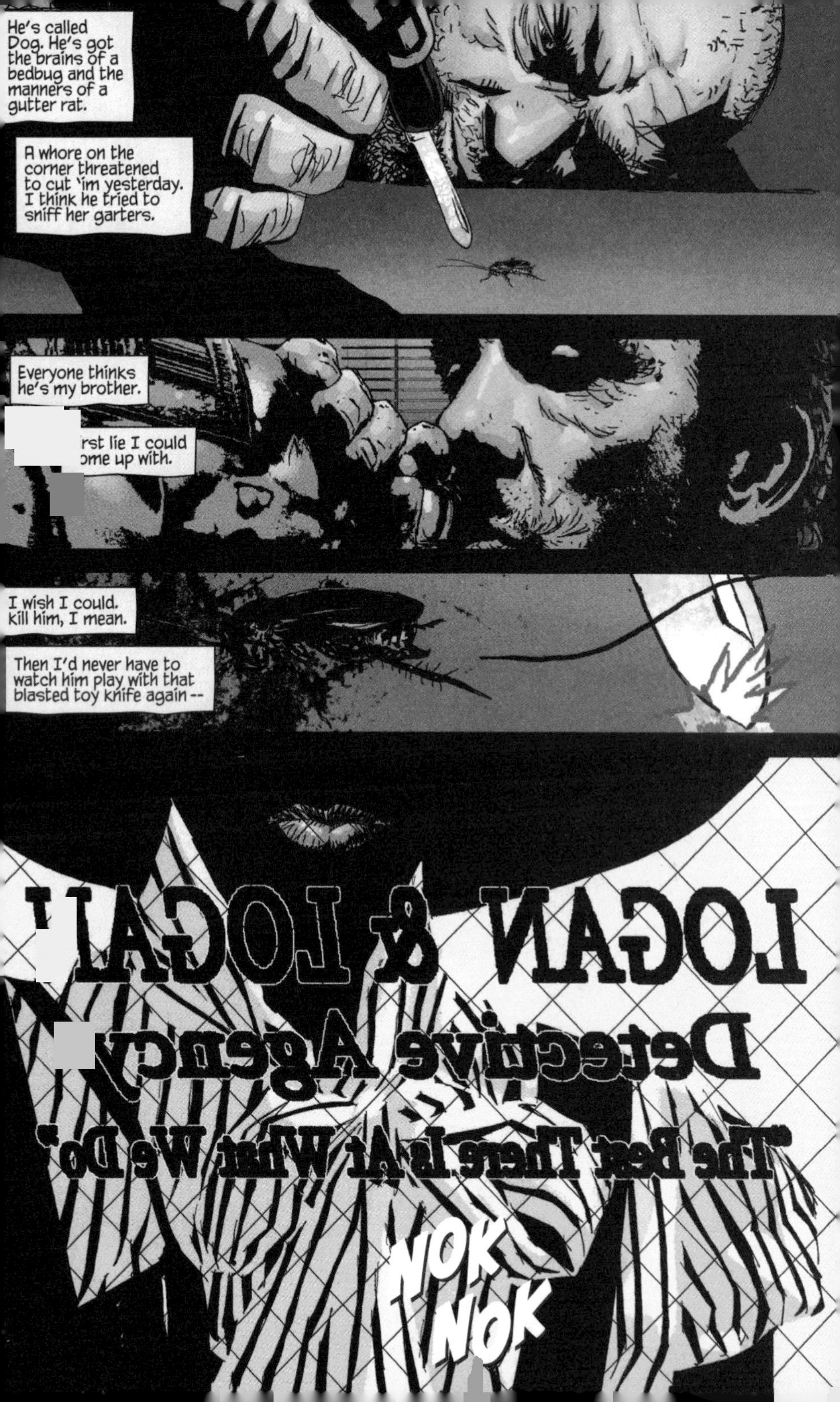
He's called Dog. He's got the brains of a bedbug and the manners of a gutter rat.
A whore on the corner threatened to cut 'im yesterday. I think he tried to sniff her garters.
Everyone thinks he's my brother.
rst lie I could ome up with.
I wish I could. kill him, I mean.
Then I'd never have to watch him play with that blasted toy knife again --
LOGAN & LOGA
Detective Agency
"The Best There Is At What We Do"
NOK NOK

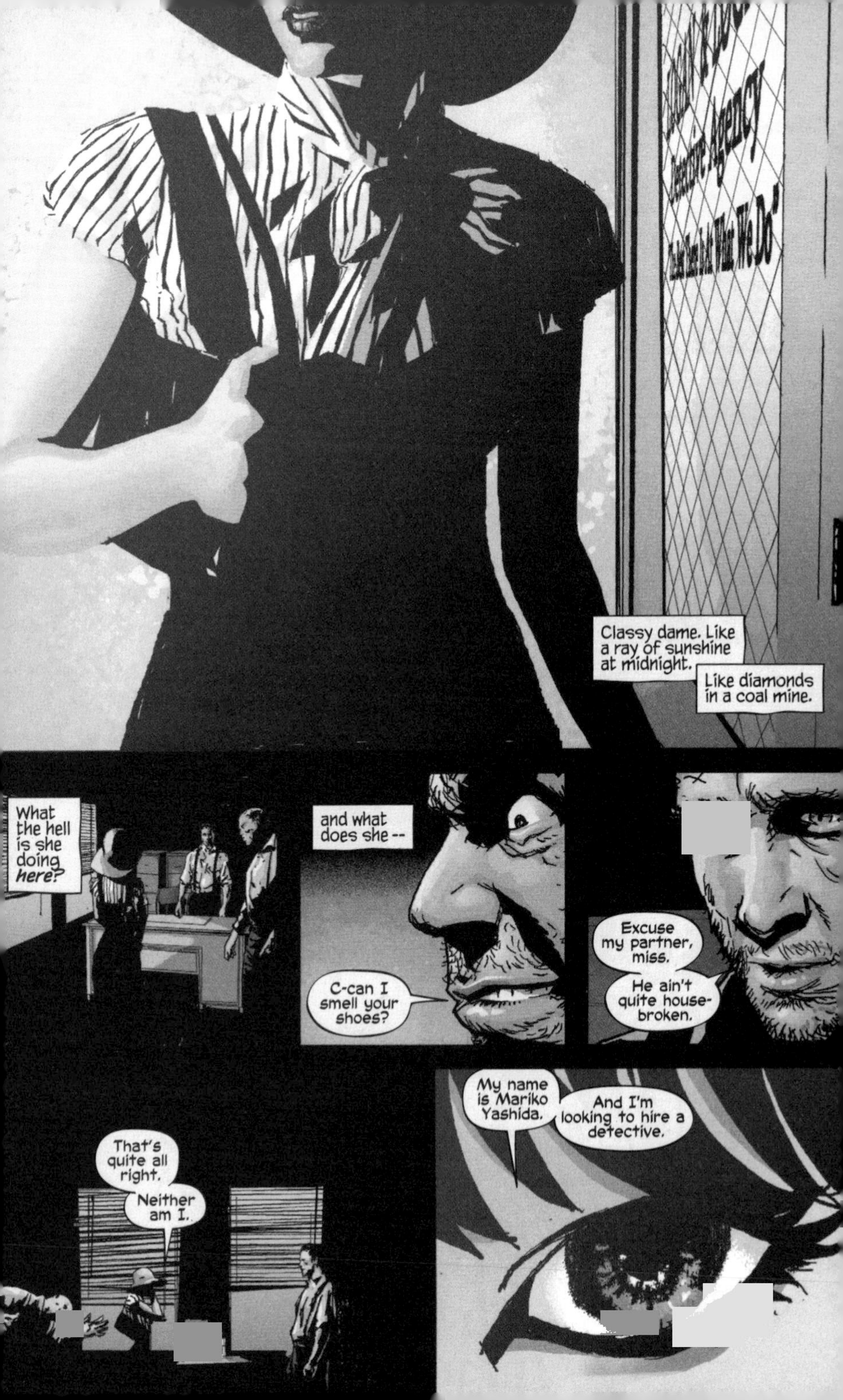

Detective Agency
Classy dame. Like a ray of sunshine at midnight.
Like diamonds in a coal mine.
What the hell is she doing *here?*
and what does she --
C-can I smell your shoes?
Excuse my partner, miss.
He ain't quite house-broken.
That's quite all right.
Neither am I.
My name is Mariko Yashida.
And I'm looking to hire a detective.

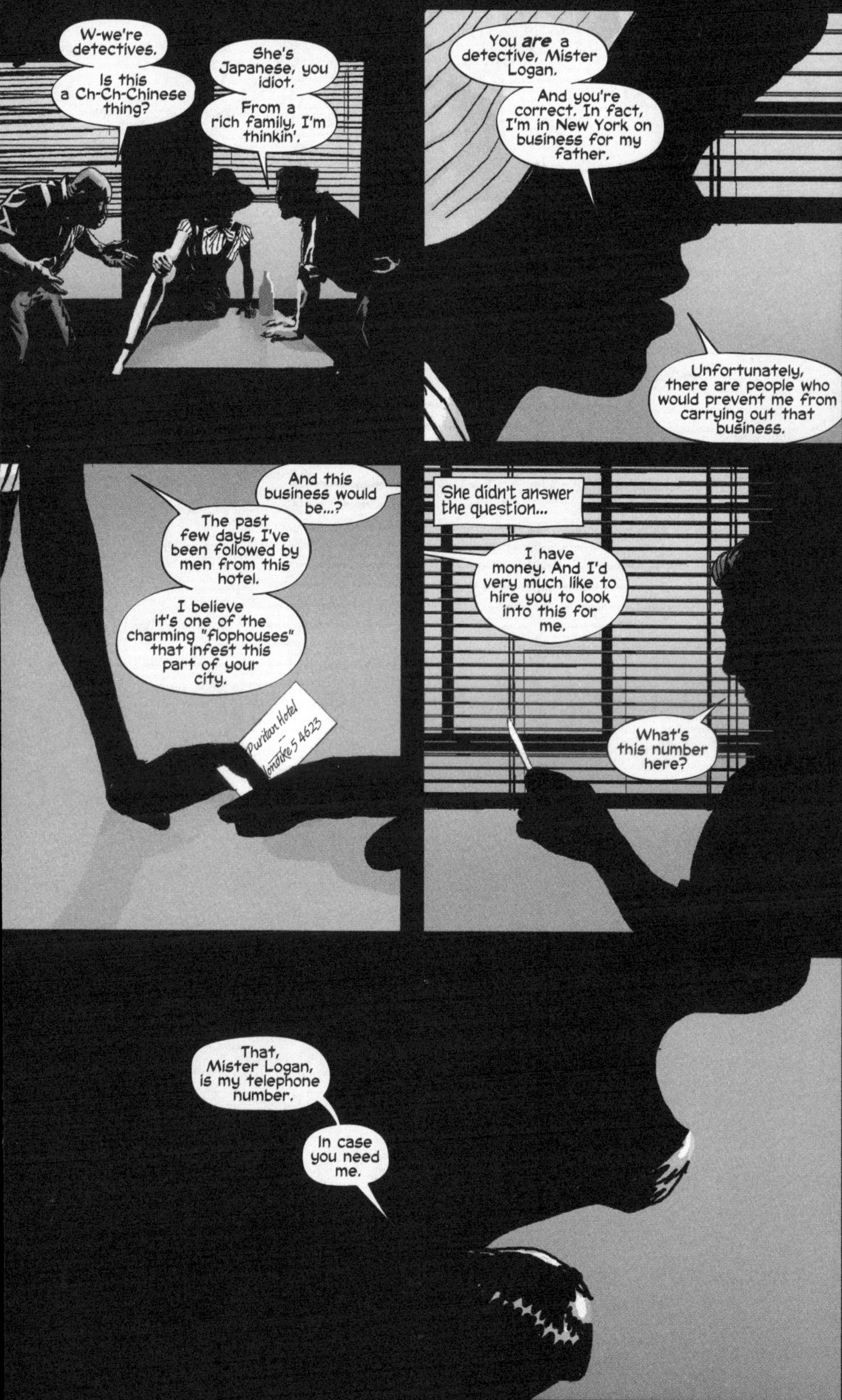

W-we're detectives.
Is this a Ch-Ch-Chinese thing?
She's Japanese, you idiot.
From a rich family, I'm thinkin'.
You *are* a detective, Mister Logan.
And you're correct. In fact, I'm in New York on business for my father.
Unfortunately, there are people who would prevent me from carrying out that business.
And this business would be...?
The past few days, I've been followed by men from this hotel.
I believe it's one of the charming "flophouses" that infest this part of your city.
Puritan Hotel
She didn't answer the question...
I have money. And I'd very much like to hire you to look into this for me.
What's this number here?
That, Mister Logan, is my telephone number.
In case you need me.

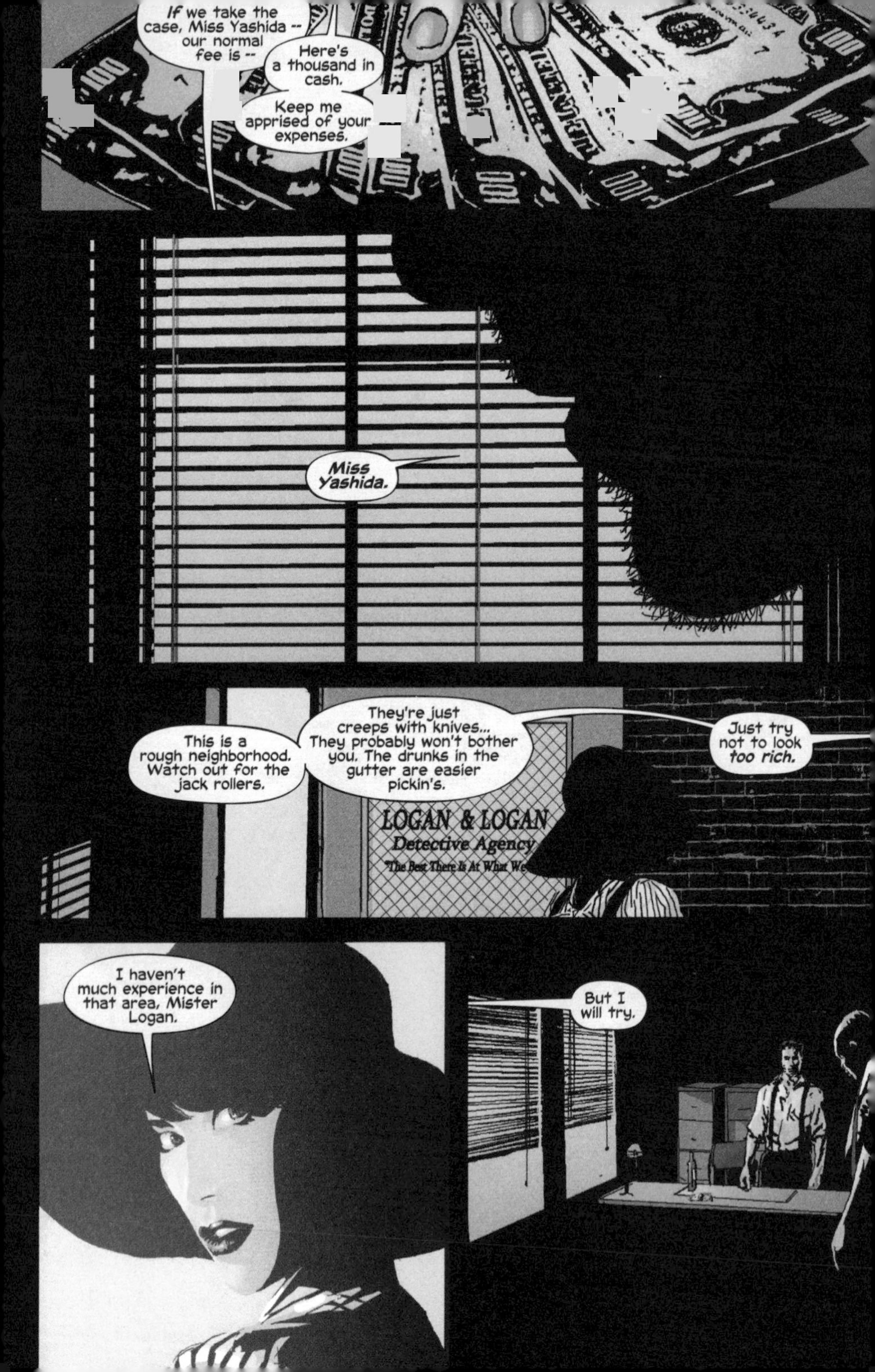
If we take the case, Miss Yashida -- our normal fee is --
Here's a thousand in cash.
Keep me apprised of your expenses.
Miss Yashida.
This is a rough neighborhood. Watch out for the jack rollers.
They're just creeps with knives... They probably won't bother you. The drunks in the gutter are easier pickin's.
Just try not to look too rich.
LOGAN & LOGAN
Detective Agency
"The Best There Is At What We
I haven't much experience in that area, Mister Logan.
But I will try.

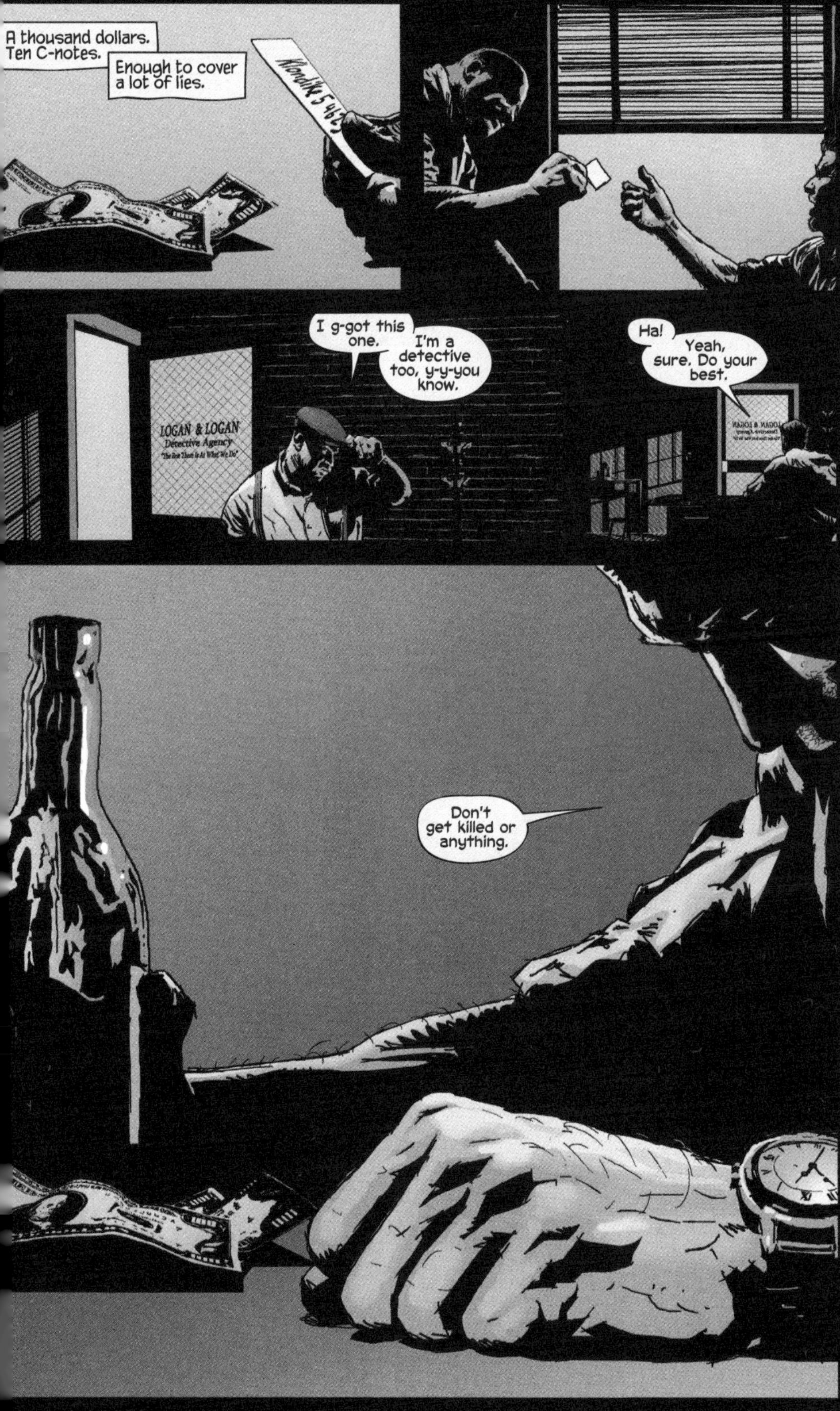
A thousand dollars. Ten C-notes.
Enough to cover a lot of lies.
I g-got this one.
I'm a detective too, y-y-you know.
LOGAN & LOGAN
Detective Agency
Ha!
Yeah, sure. Do your best.
Don't get killed or anything.

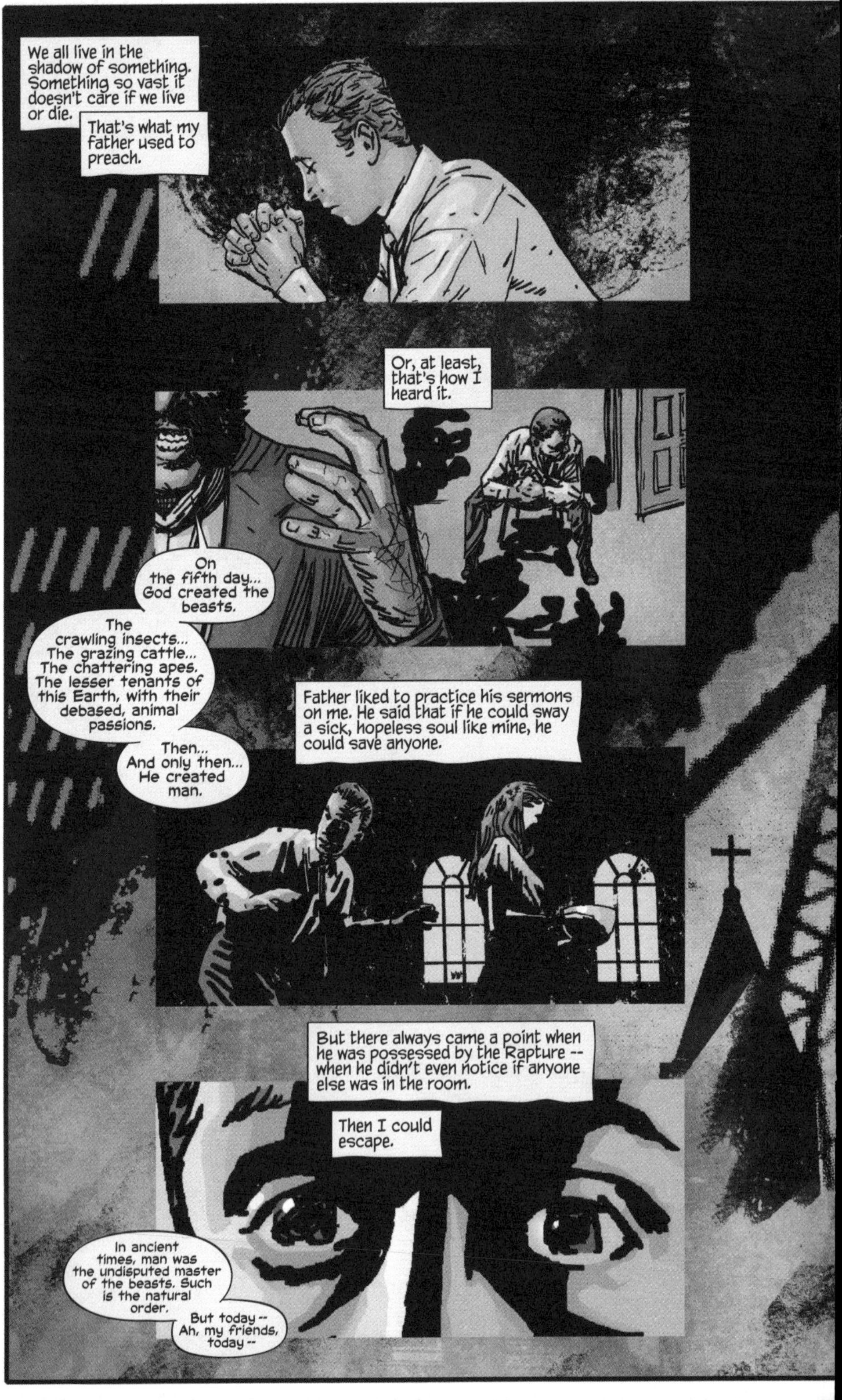

We all live in the shadow of something. Something so vast it doesn't care if we live or die.
That's what my father used to preach.
Or, at least, that's how I heard it.
On the fifth day... God created the beasts.
The crawling insects... The grazing cattle... The chattering apes. The lesser tenants of this Earth, with their debased, animal passions.
Then... And only then... He created man.
Father liked to practice his sermons on me. He said that if he could sway a sick, hopeless soul like mine, he could save anyone.
But there always came a point when he was possessed by the Rapture -- when he didn't even notice if anyone else was in the room.
Then I could escape.
In ancient times, man was the undisputed master of the beasts. Such is the natural order.
But today -- Ah, my friends, today --

-- man has *fallen.*

Aahhh!

Oh!

R-Rose...

Did I startle you, James? I'm dreadfully sorry.

I simply came next door to borrow some ice for my mother.

Oh, James.

Your face is flushed.

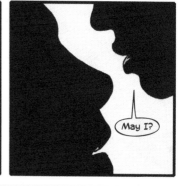

May I?

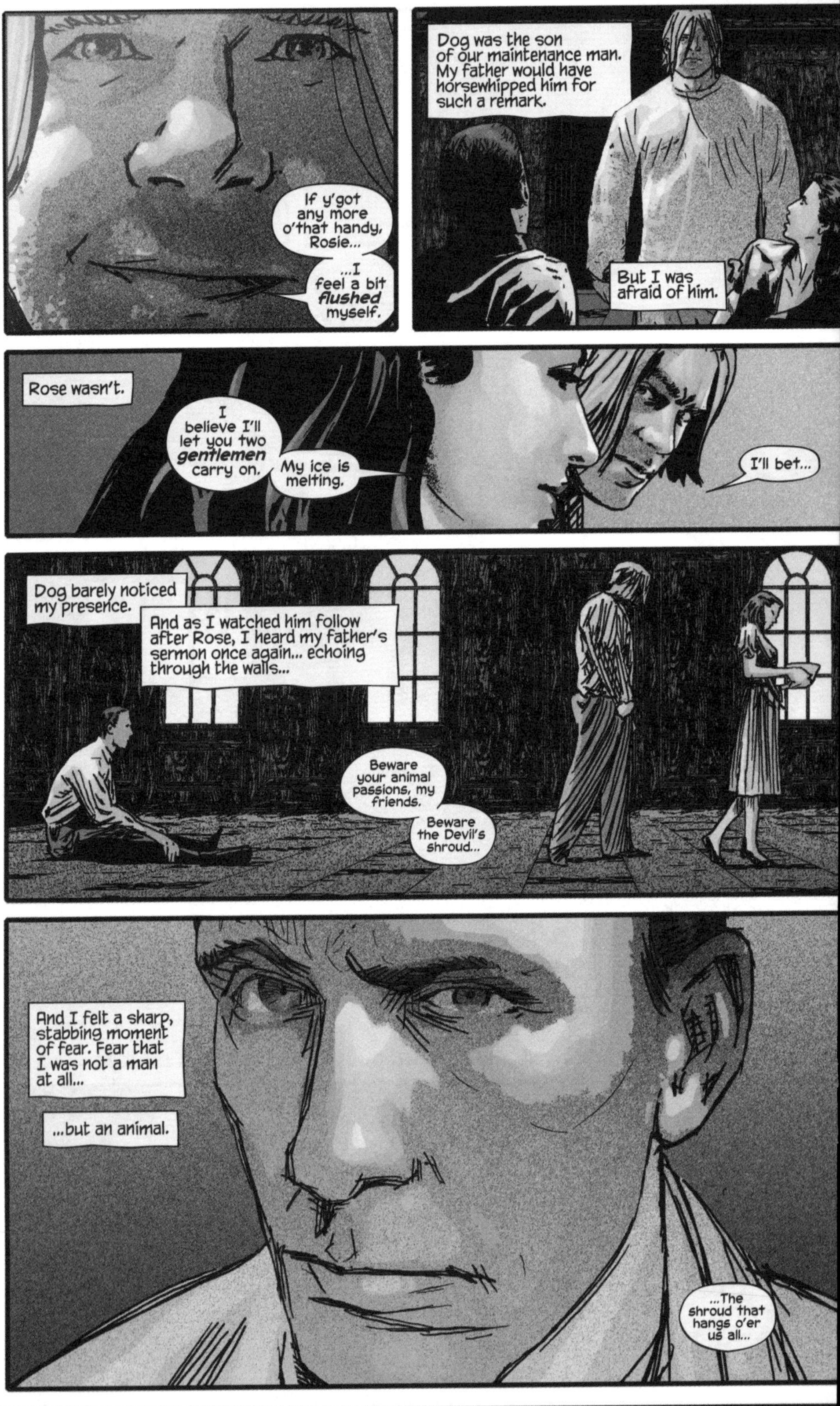
If y'got any more o'that handy, Rosie...
...I feel a bit *flushed* myself.
Dog was the son of our maintenance man. My father would have horsewhipped him for such a remark.
But I was afraid of him.
Rose wasn't.
I believe I'll let you two *gentlemen* carry on.
My ice is melting.
I'll bet...
Dog barely noticed my presence.
And as I watched him follow after Rose, I heard my father's sermon once again... echoing through the walls...
Beware your animal passions, my friends.
Beware the Devil's shroud...
And I felt a sharp, stabbing moment of fear. Fear that I was not a man at all...
...but an animal.
...The shroud that hangs o'er us all...

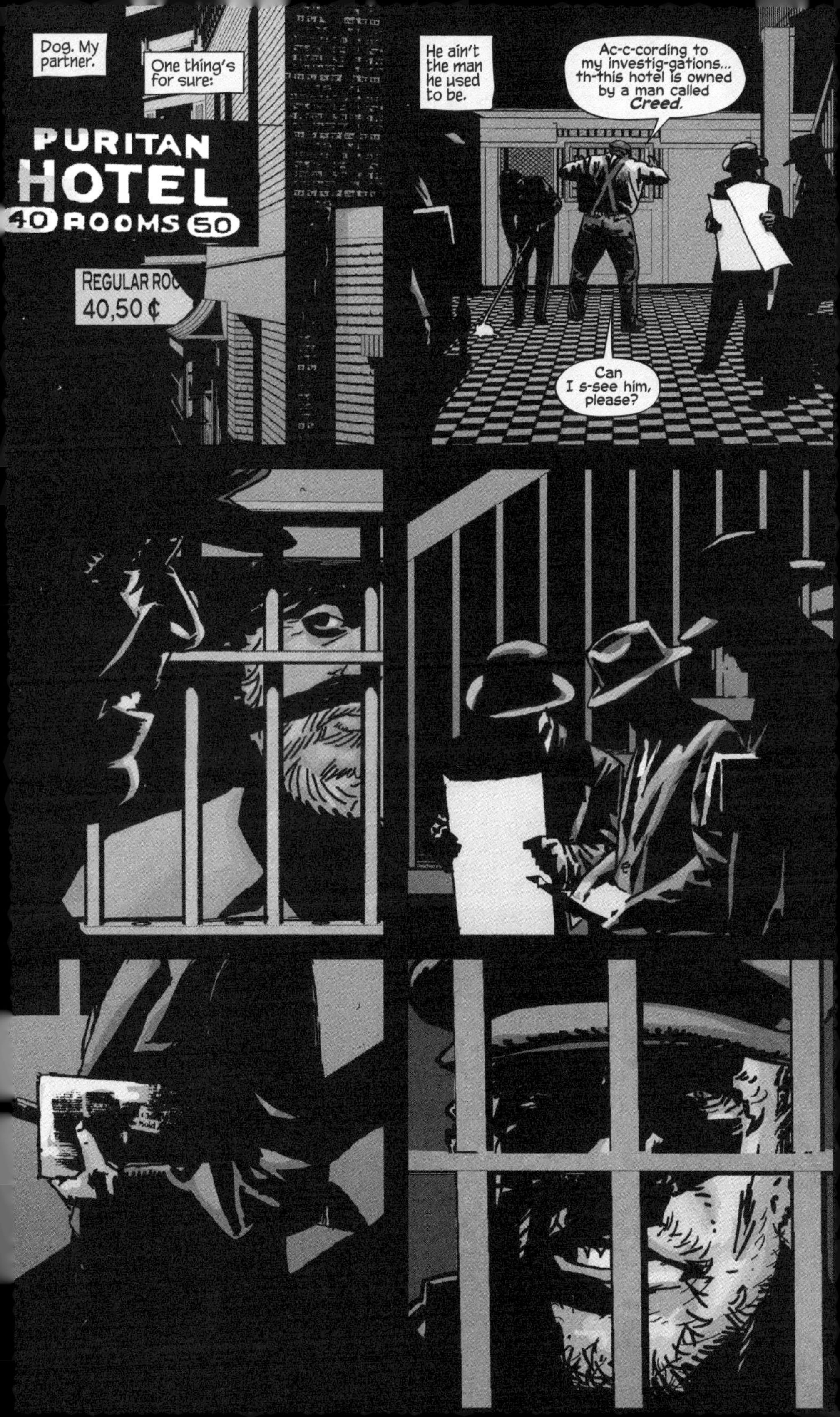
Dog. My partner.
One thing's for sure:
PURITAN HOTEL
40 ROOMS 50
REGULAR RO
40,50 ¢
He ain't the man he used to be.
Ac-c-cording to my investig-gations... th-this hotel is owned by a man called Creed.
Can I s-see him, please?

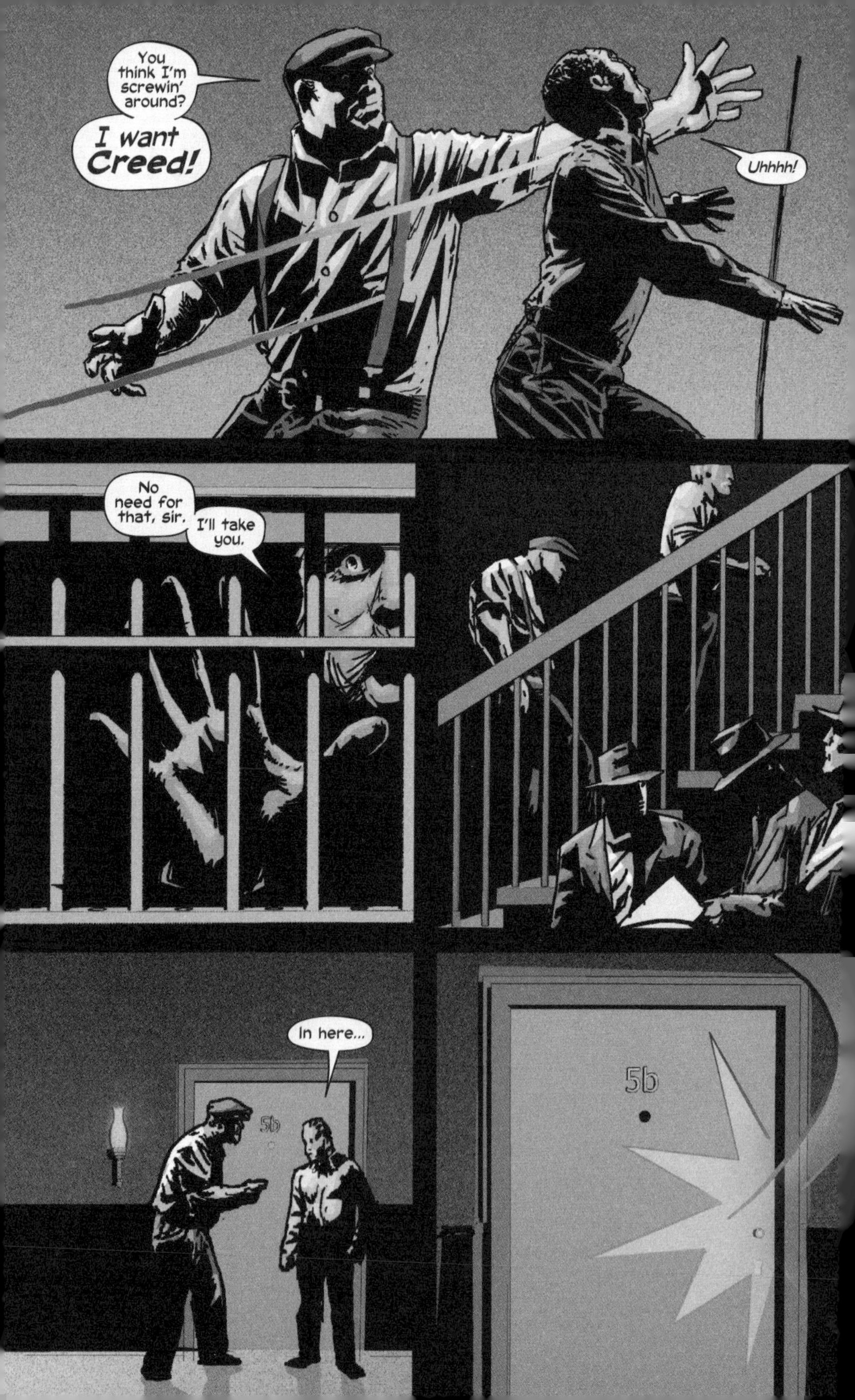
You think I'm screwin' around?
I want Creed!
Uhhhh!
No need for that, sir.
I'll take you.
In here...
5b

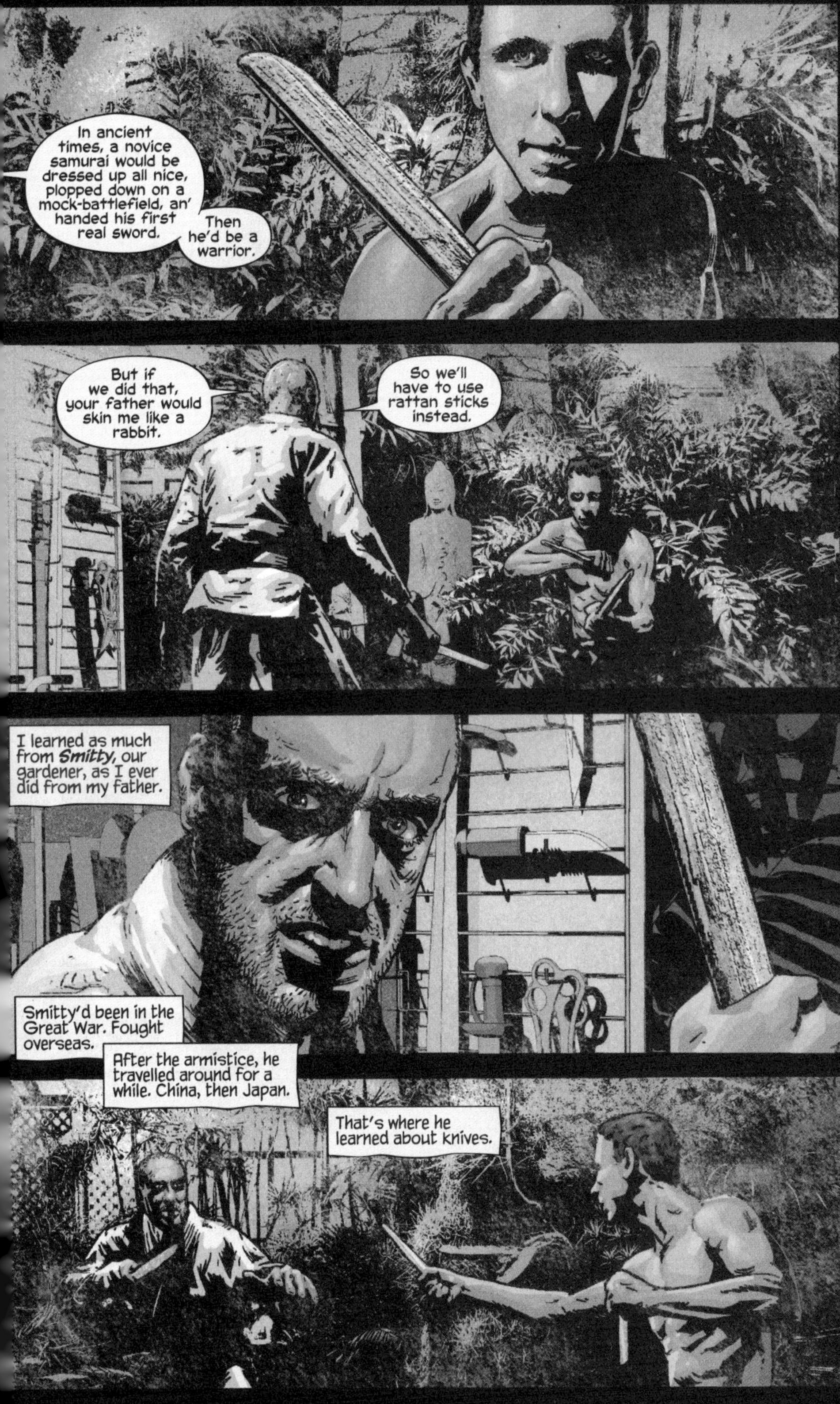

In ancient times, a novice samurai would be dressed up all nice, plopped down on a mock-battlefield, an' handed his first real sword.
Then he'd be a warrior.
But if we did that, your father would skin me like a rabbit.
So we'll have to use rattan sticks instead.
I learned as much from *Smitty*, our gardener, as I ever did from my father.
Smitty'd been in the Great War. Fought overseas.
After the armistice, he travelled around for a while. China, then Japan.
That's where he learned about knives.

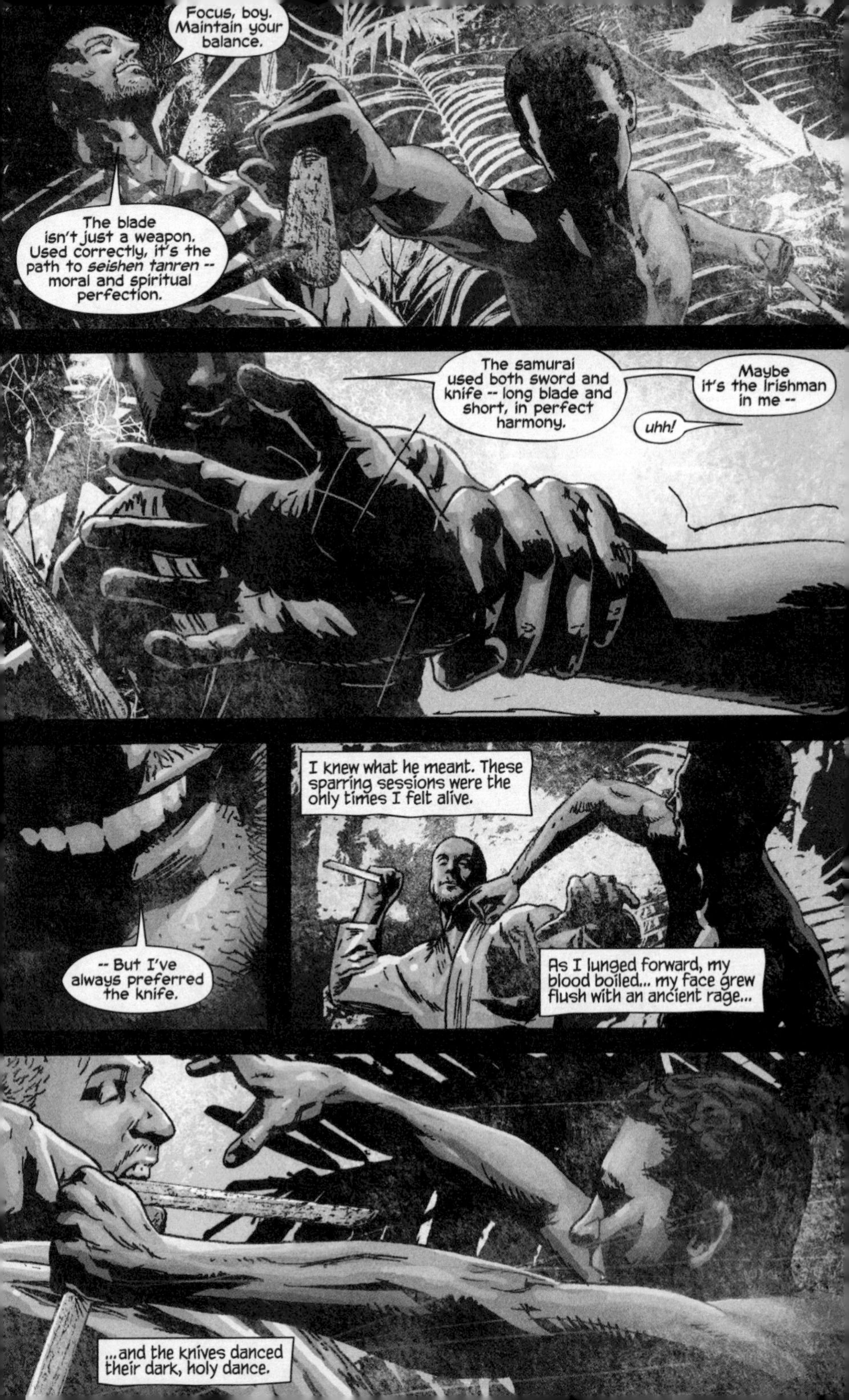
Focus, boy. Maintain your balance.
The blade isn't just a weapon. Used correctly, it's the path to *seishen tanren* -- moral and spiritual perfection.
The samurai used both sword and knife -- long blade and short, in perfect harmony.
Maybe it's the Irishman in me --
uhh!
-- But I've always preferred the knife.
I knew what he meant. These sparring sessions were the only times I felt alive.
As I lunged forward, my blood boiled... my face grew flush with an ancient rage...
...and the knives danced their dark, holy dance.

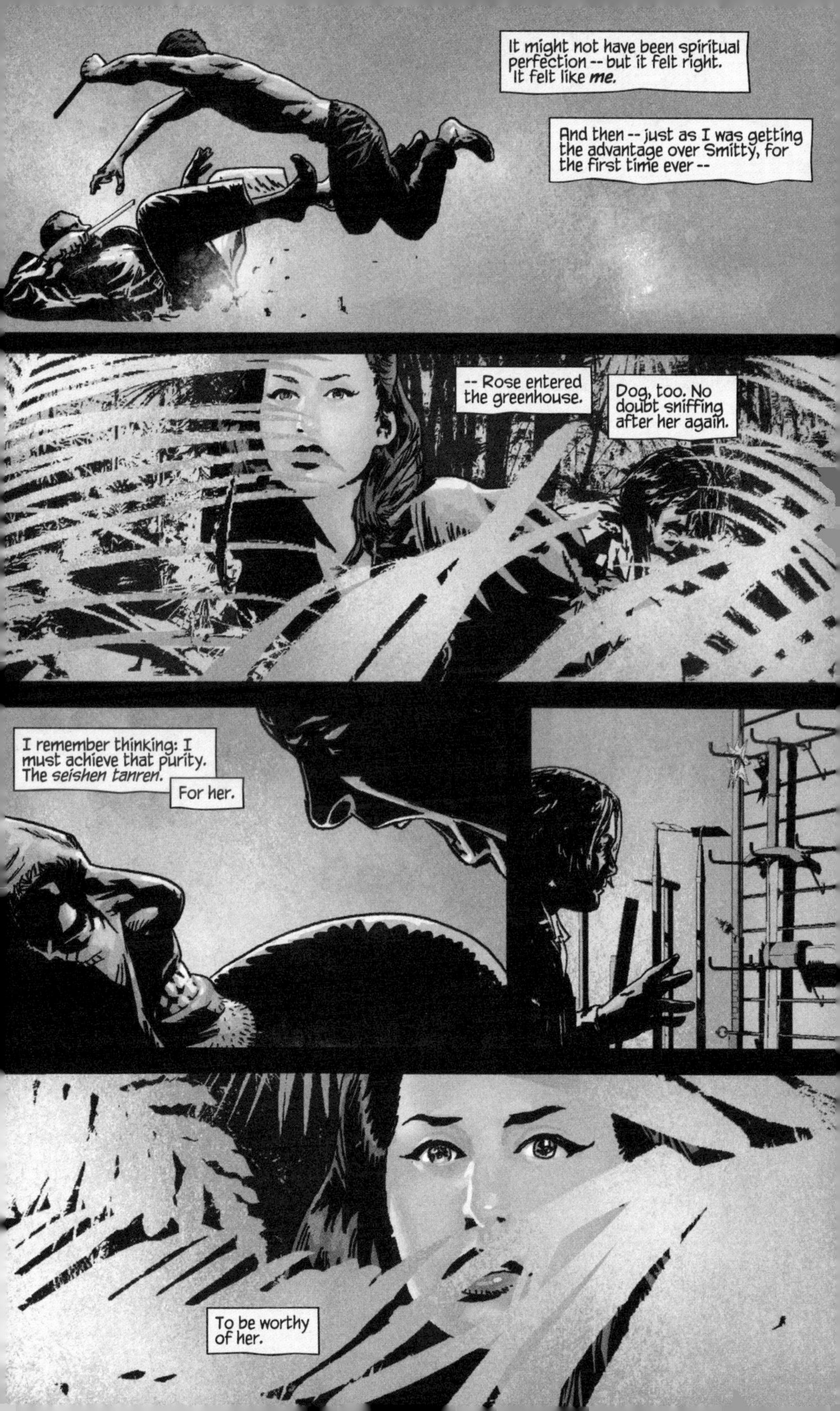
It might not have been spiritual perfection -- but it felt right. It felt like *me.*
And then -- just as I was getting the advantage over Smitty, for the first time ever --
-- Rose entered the greenhouse.
Dog, too. No doubt sniffing after her again.
I remember thinking: I must achieve that purity. The *seishen tanren.*
For her.
To be worthy of her.

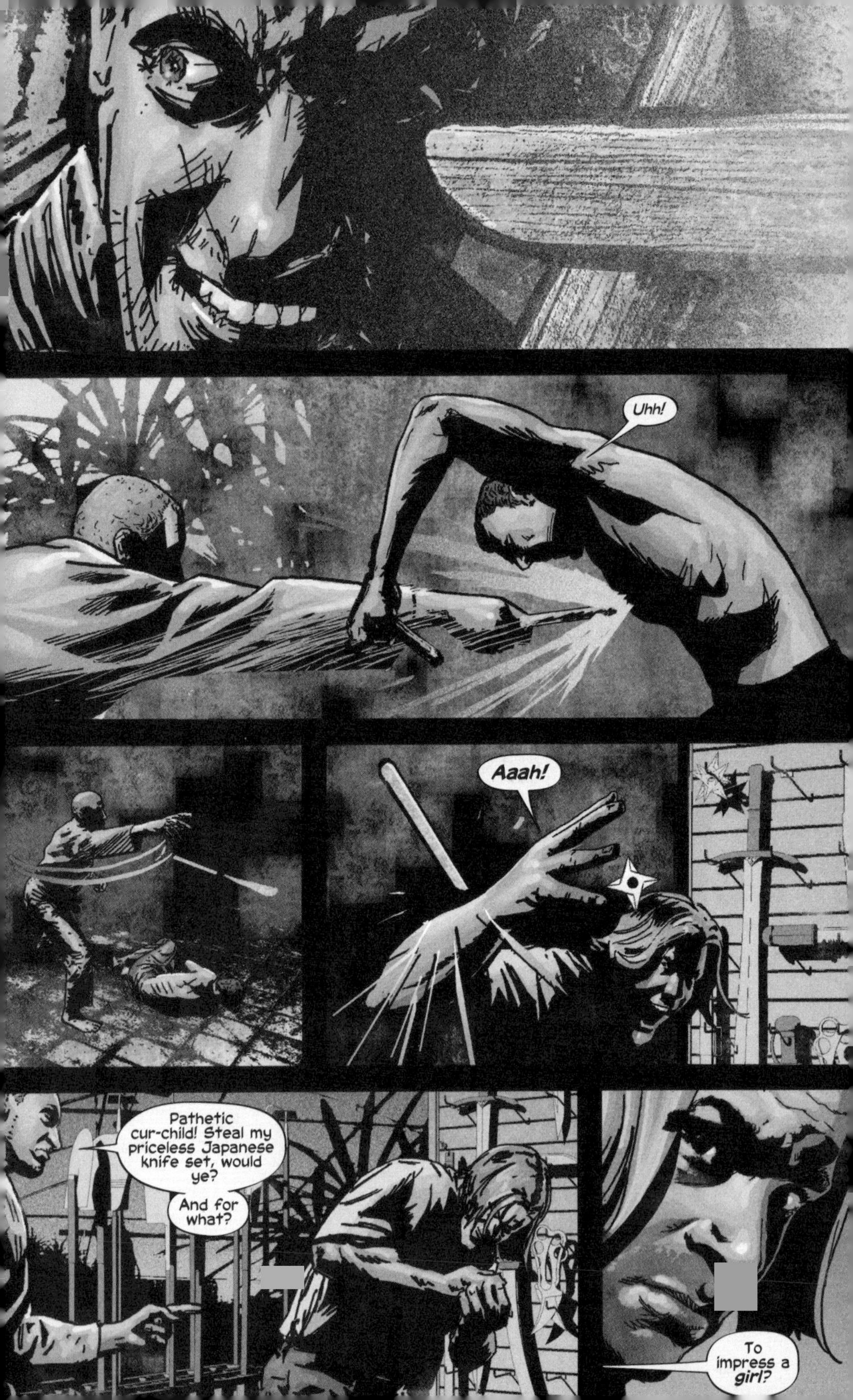
Uhh!
Aaah!
Pathetic cur-child! Steal my priceless Japanese knife set, would ye?
And for what?
To impress a girl?

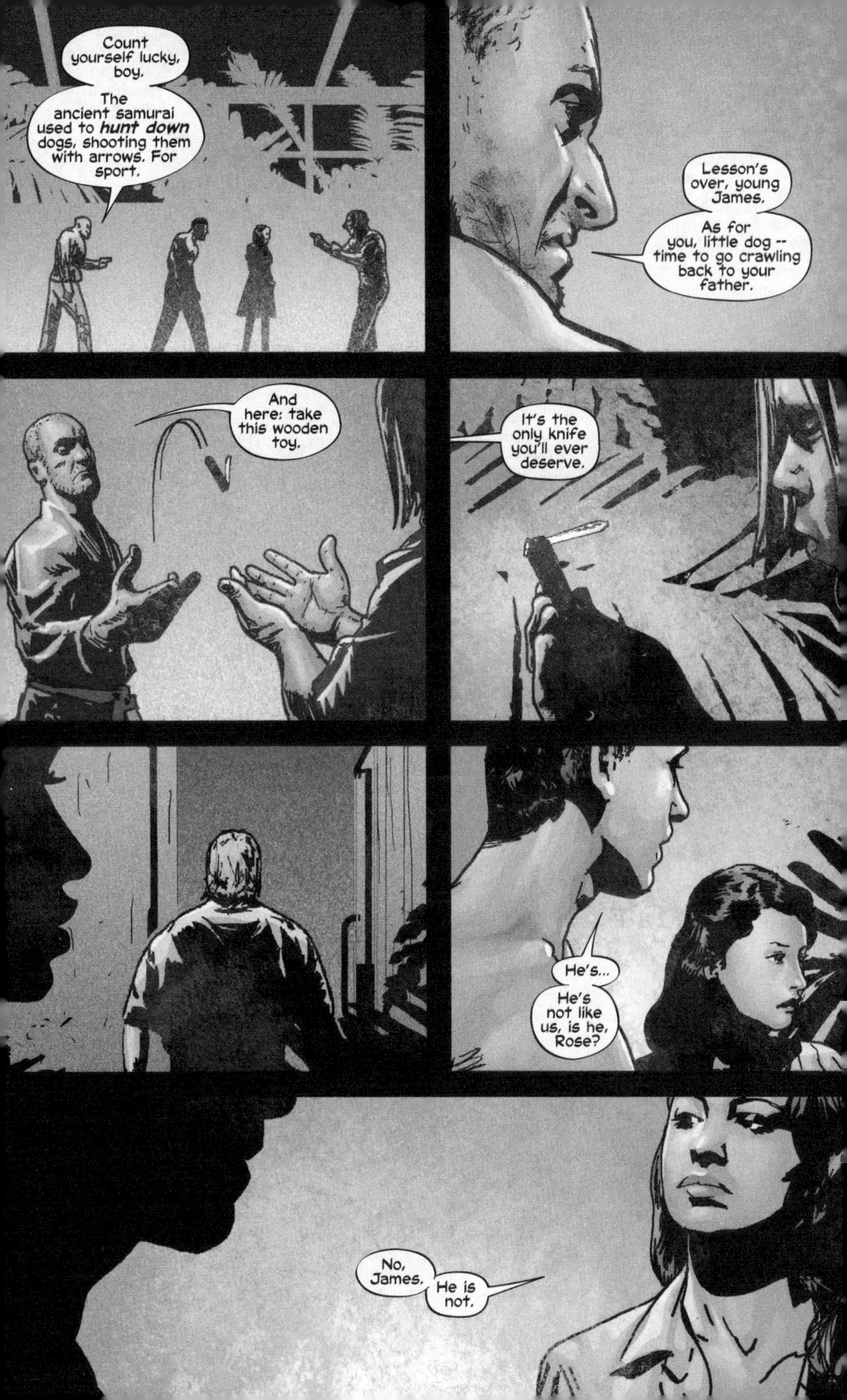
Count yourself lucky, boy.
The ancient samurai used to ***hunt down*** dogs, shooting them with arrows. For sport.
Lesson's over, young James.
As for you, little dog -- time to go crawling back to your father.
And here: take this wooden toy.
It's the only knife you'll ever deserve.
He's...
He's not like us, is he, Rose?
No, James.
He is not.

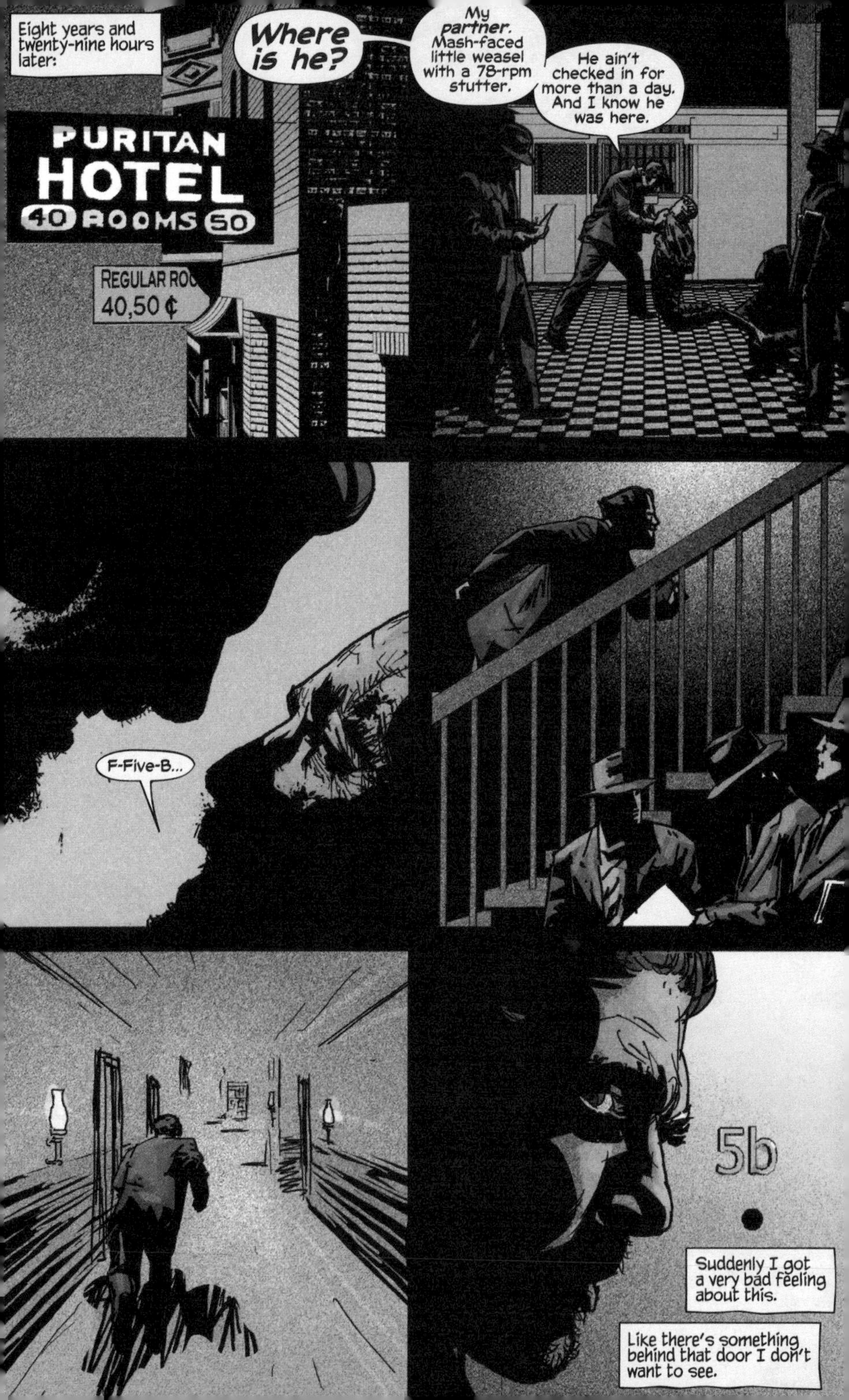
Eight years and twenty-nine hours later:
PURITAN HOTEL
40 ROOMS 50
REGULAR RO
40,50 ¢
Where is he?
My partner. Mash-faced little weasel with a 78-rpm stutter.
He ain't checked in for more than a day. And I know he was here.
F-Five-B...
5b
Suddenly I got a very bad feeling about this.
Like there's something behind that door I don't want to see.

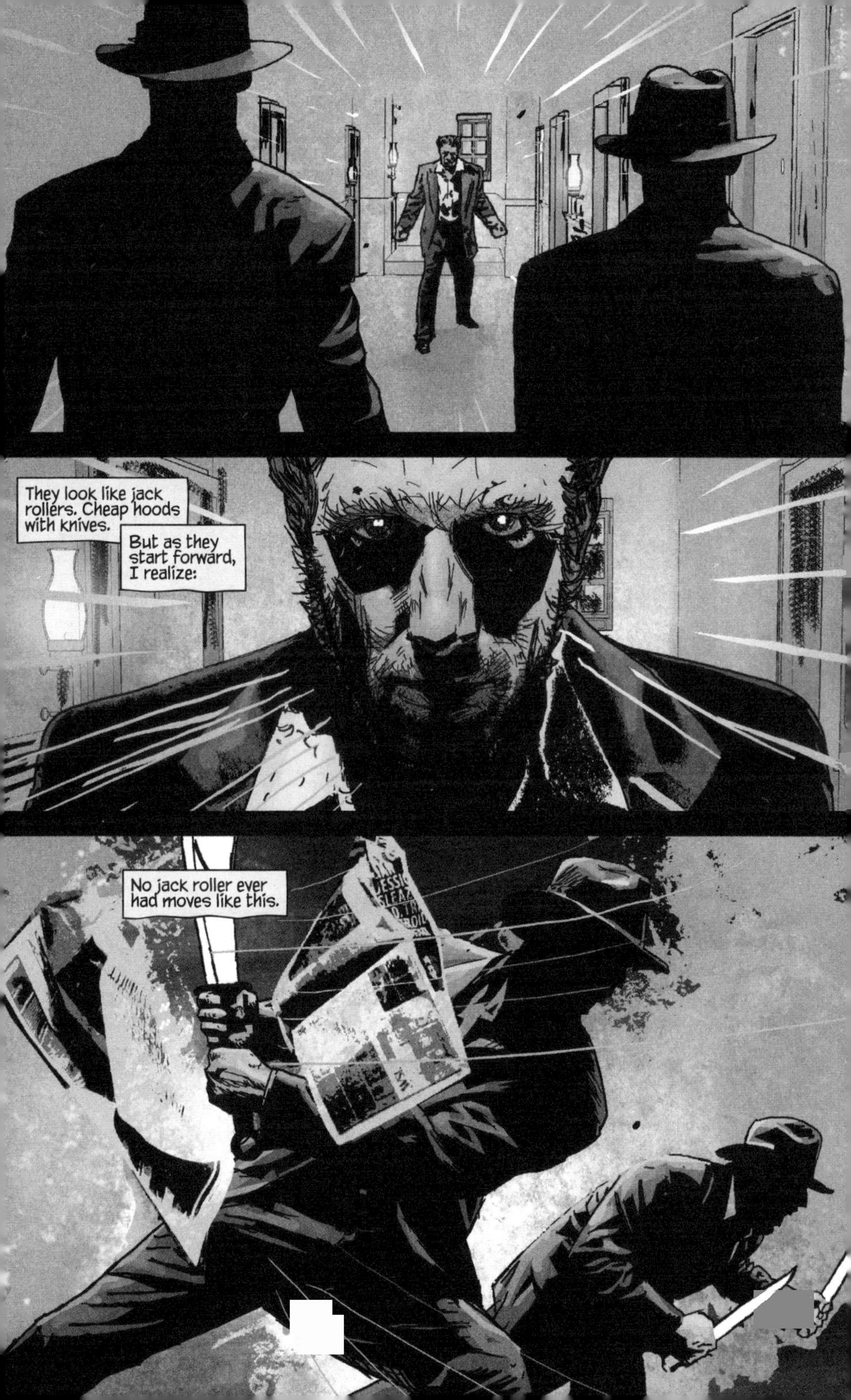
They look like jack rollers. Cheap hoods with knives.
But as they start forward, I realize:
No jack roller ever had moves like this.

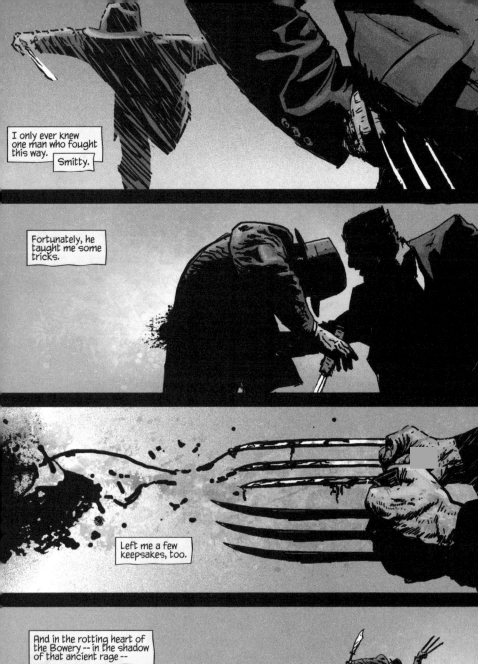

I only ever knew one man who fought this way. Smitty.

Fortunately, he taught me some tricks.

Left me a few keepsakes, too.

And in the rotting heart of the Bowery -- in the shadow of that ancient rage --

-- the knives dance again.

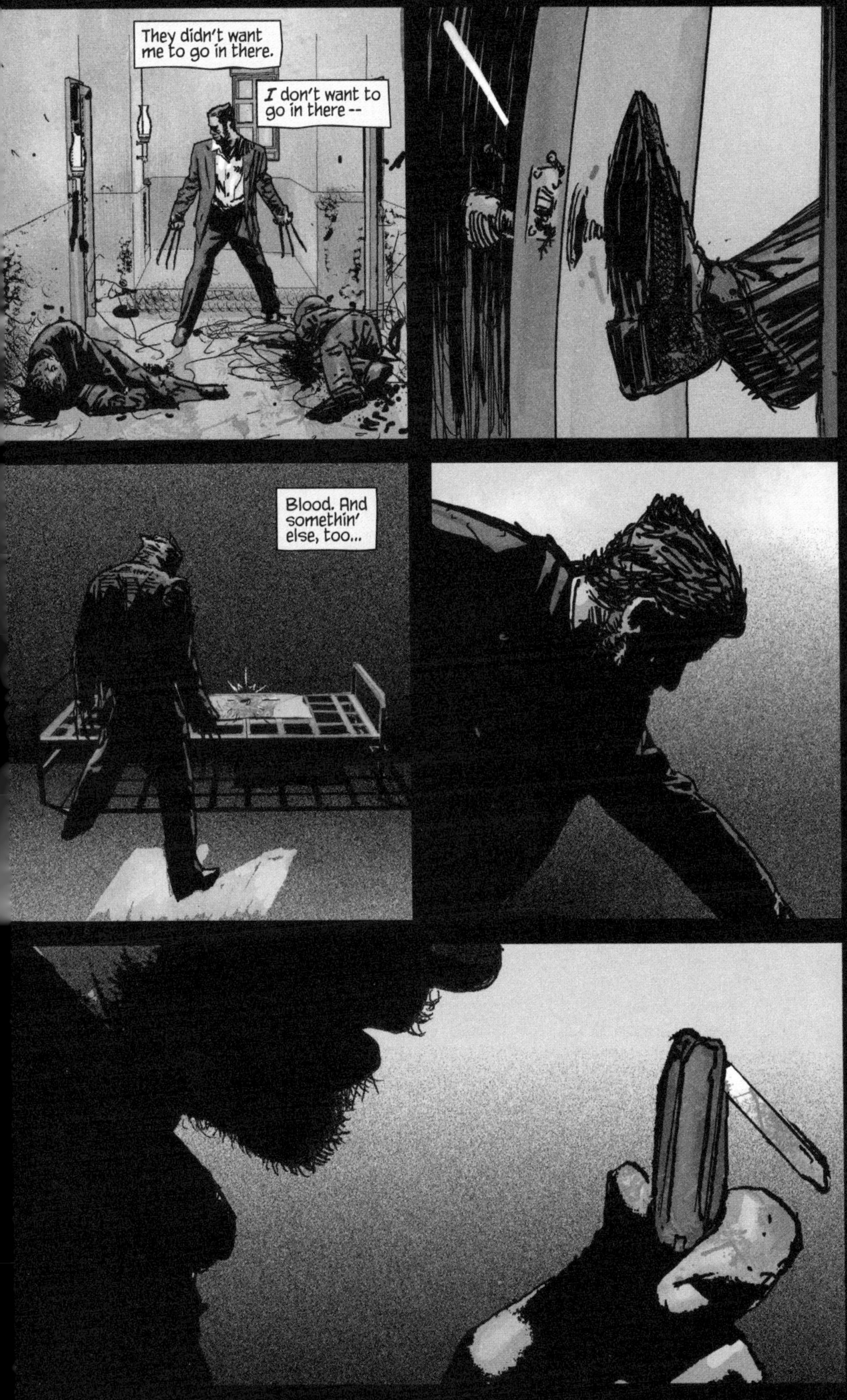
They didn't want me to go in there.
I don't want to go in there --
Blood. And somethin' else, too...

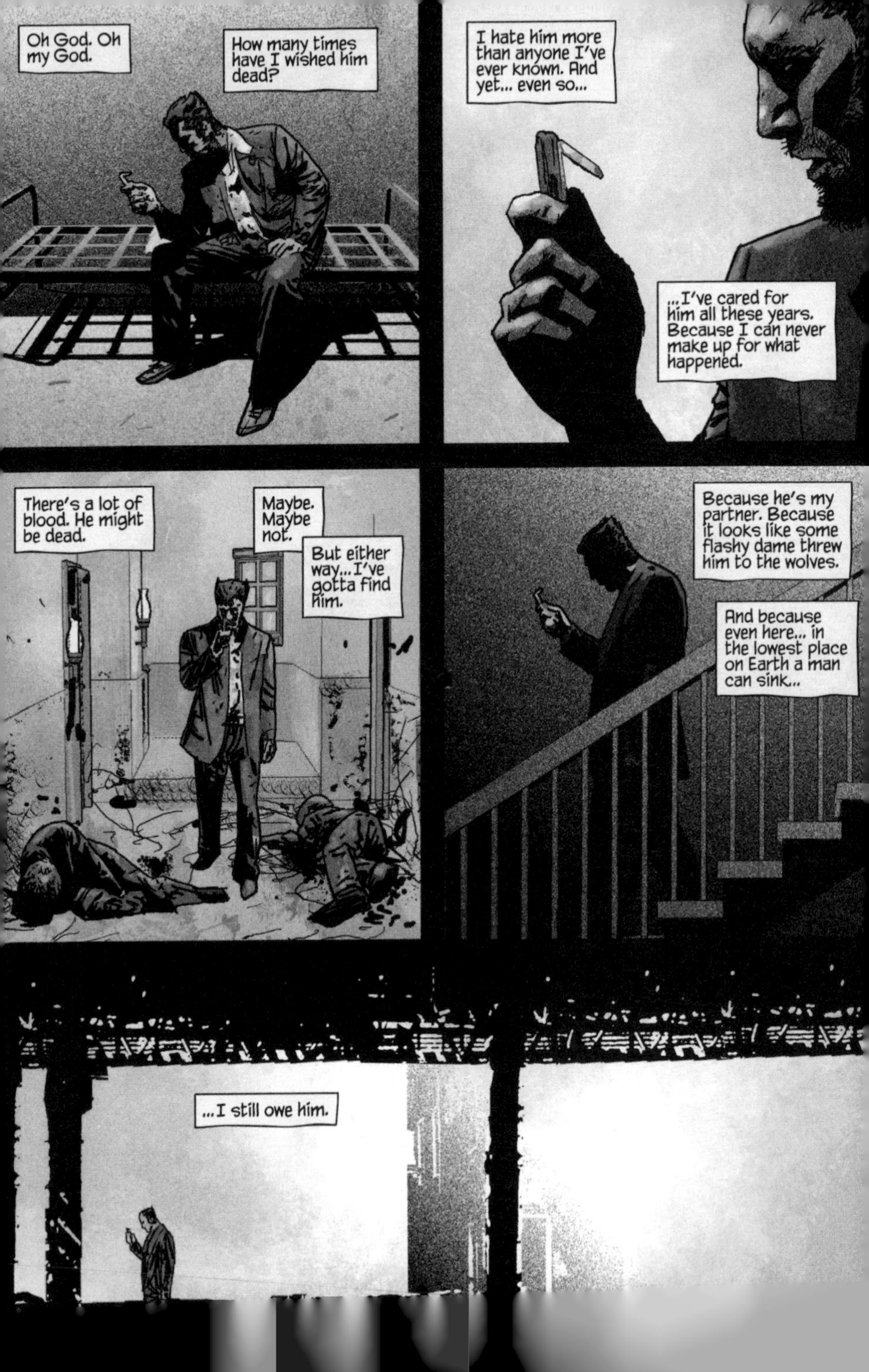
Oh God. Oh my God.
How many times have I wished him dead?
I hate him more than anyone I've ever known. And yet... even so...
...I've cared for him all these years. Because I can never make up for what happened.
There's a lot of blood. He might be dead.
Maybe. Maybe not.
But either way... I've gotta find him.
Because he's my partner. Because it looks like some flashy dame threw him to the wolves.
And because even here... in the lowest place on Earth a man can sink...
...I still owe him.

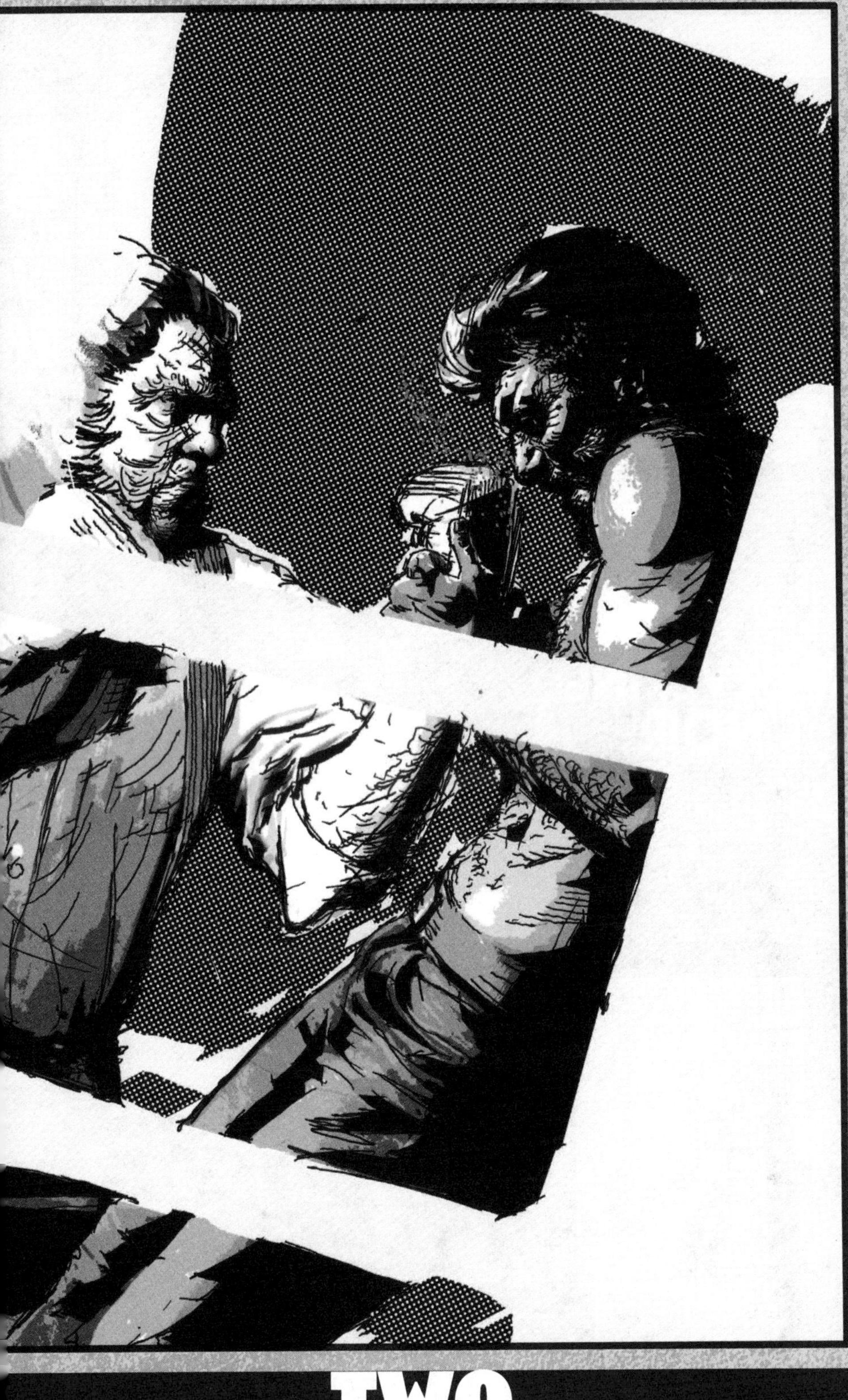

TWO

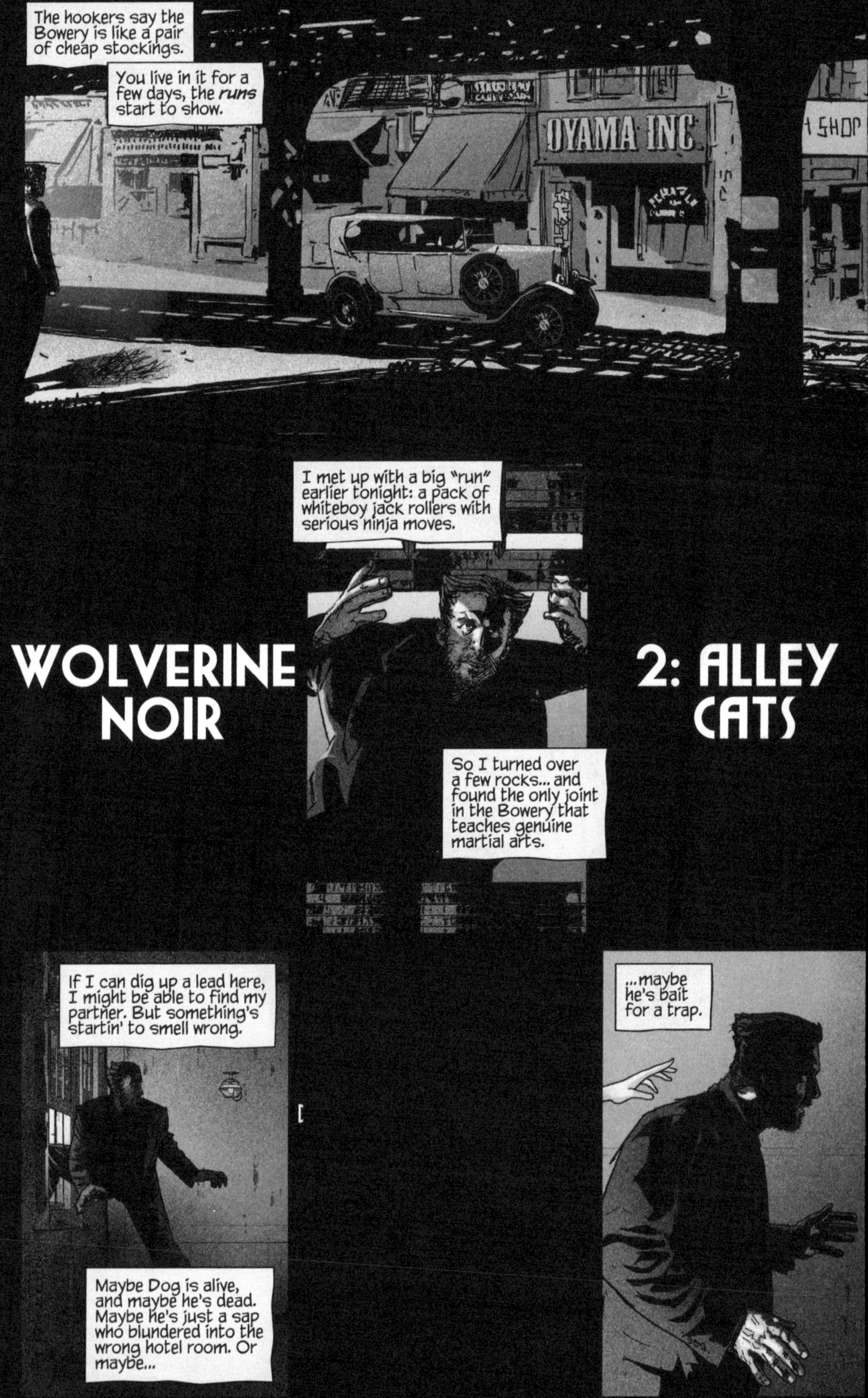
The hookers say the Bowery is like a pair of cheap stockings.
You live in it for a few days, the *runs* start to show.
OYAMA INC
SHOP
I met up with a big "run" earlier tonight: a pack of whiteboy jack rollers with serious ninja moves.
WOLVERINE NOIR
2: ALLEY CATS
So I turned over a few rocks... and found the only joint in the Bowery that teaches genuine martial arts.
If I can dig up a lead here, I might be able to find my partner. But something's startin' to smell wrong.
Maybe Dog is alive, and maybe he's dead. Maybe he's just a sap who blundered into the wrong hotel room. Or maybe...
...maybe he's bait for a trap.

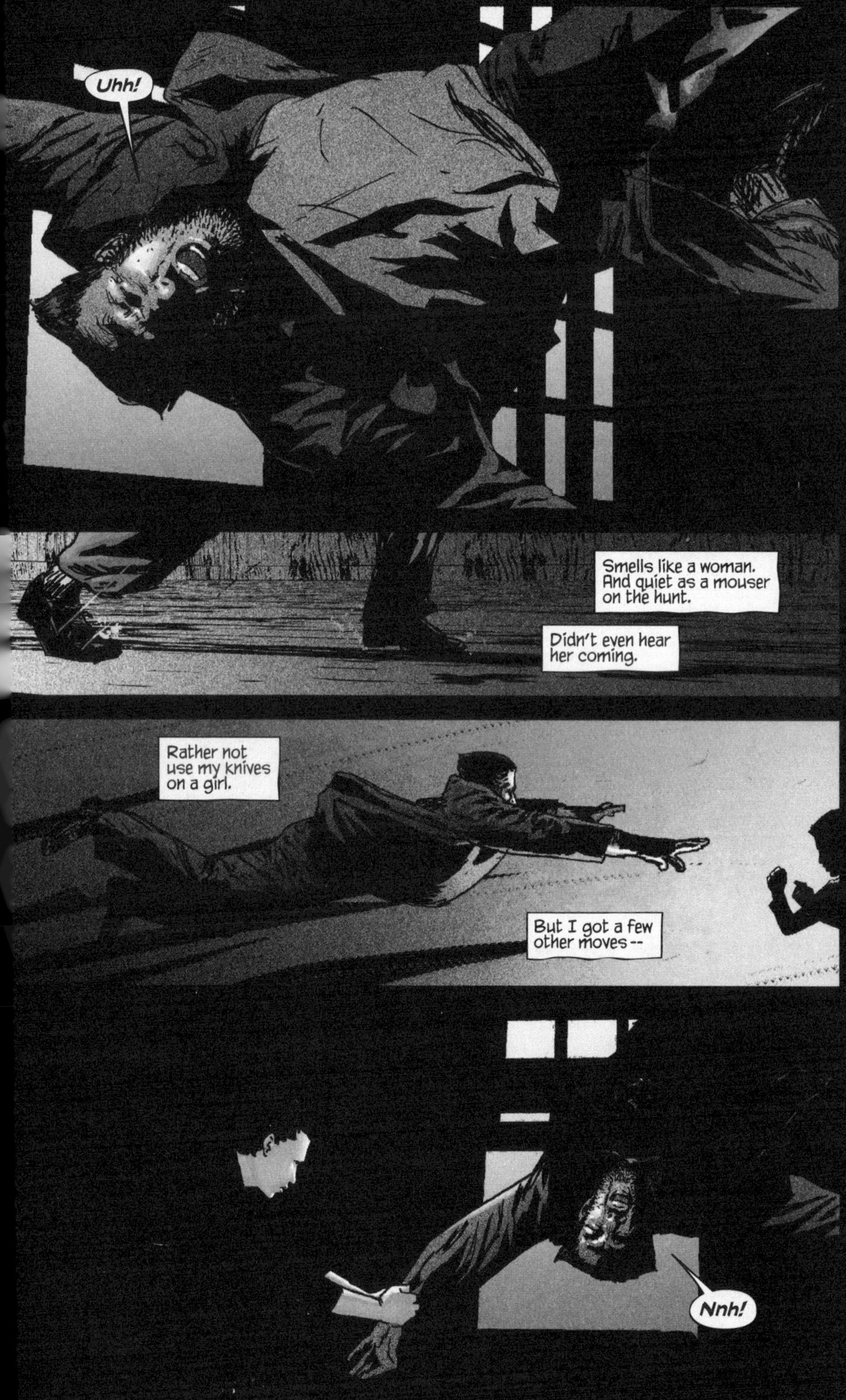
Uhh!
Smells like a woman. And quiet as a mouser on the hunt.
Didn't even hear her coming.
Rather not use my knives on a girl.
But I got a few other moves --
Nnh!

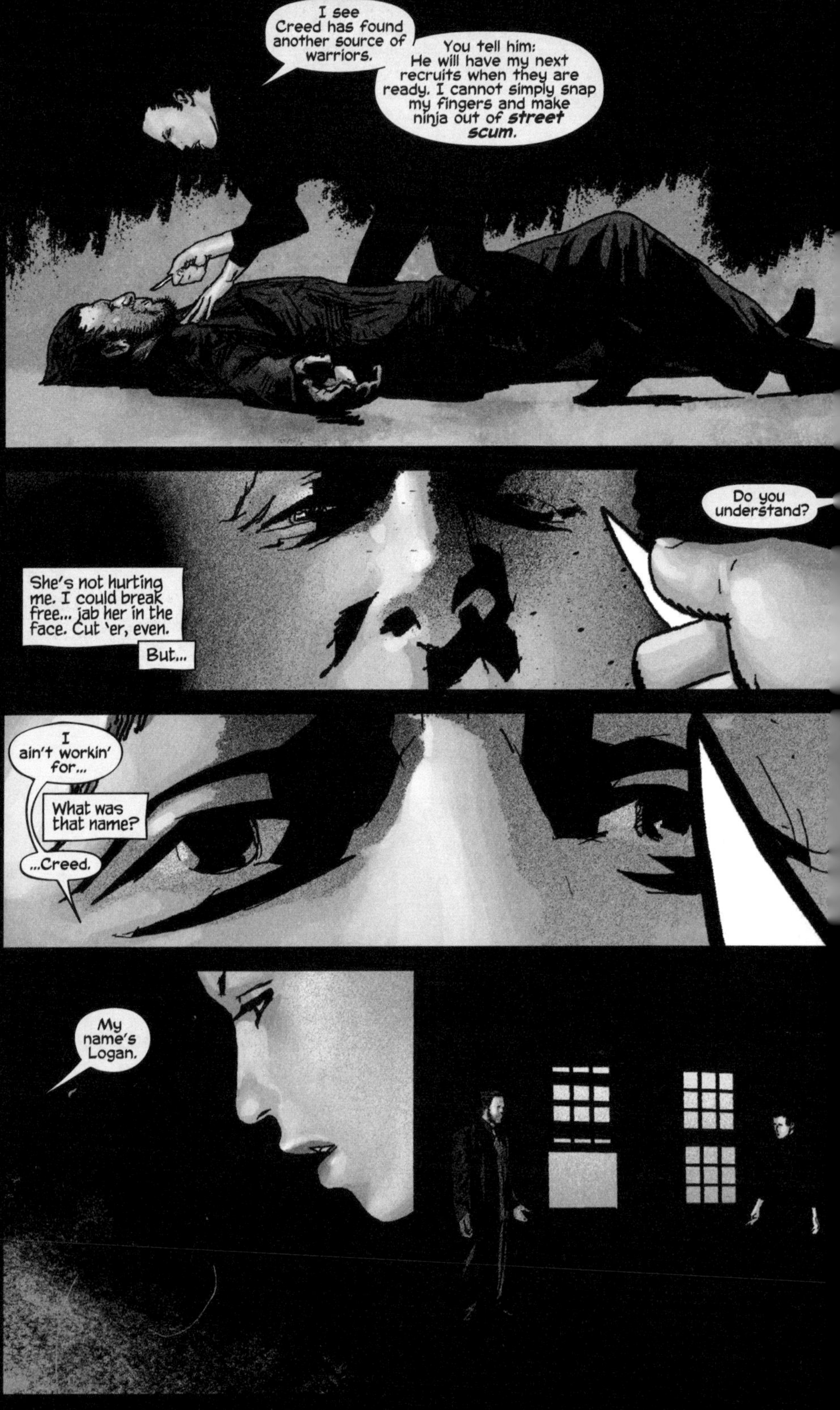
I see Creed has found another source of warriors.
You tell him: He will have my next recruits when they are ready. I cannot simply snap my fingers and make ninja out of *street scum*.
Do you understand?
She's not hurting me. I could break free... jab her in the face. Cut 'er, even.
But...
I ain't workin' for...
What was that name?
...Creed.
My name's Logan.

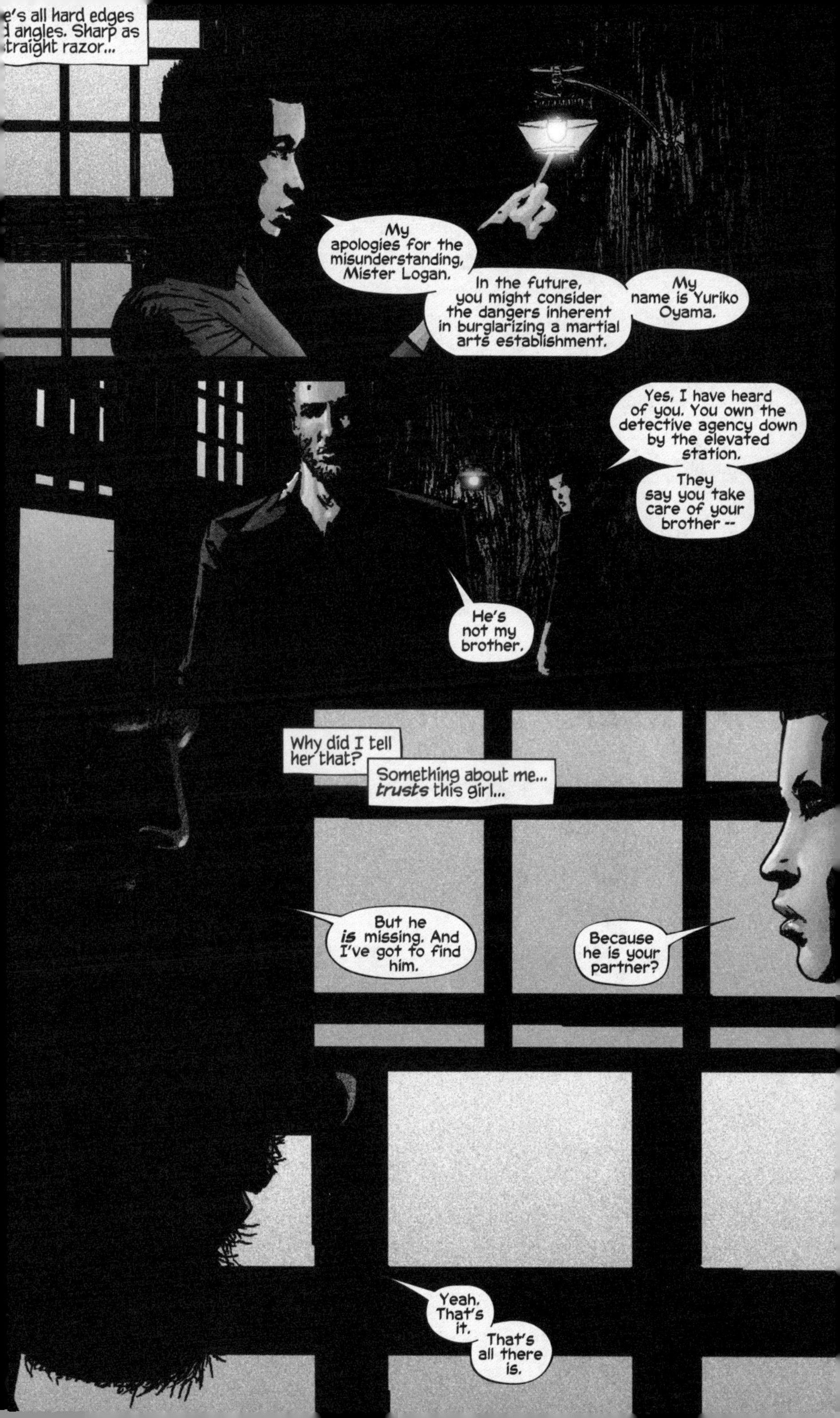
e's all hard edges
d angles. Sharp as
traight razor...
My apologies for the misunderstanding, Mister Logan.
In the future, you might consider the dangers inherent in burglarizing a martial arts establishment.
My name is Yuriko Oyama.
Yes, I have heard of you. You own the detective agency down by the elevated station.
They say you take care of your brother --
He's not my brother.
Why did I tell her that?
Something about me... *trusts* this girl...
But he *is* missing. And I've got to find him.
Because he is your partner?
Yeah. That's it.
That's all there is.

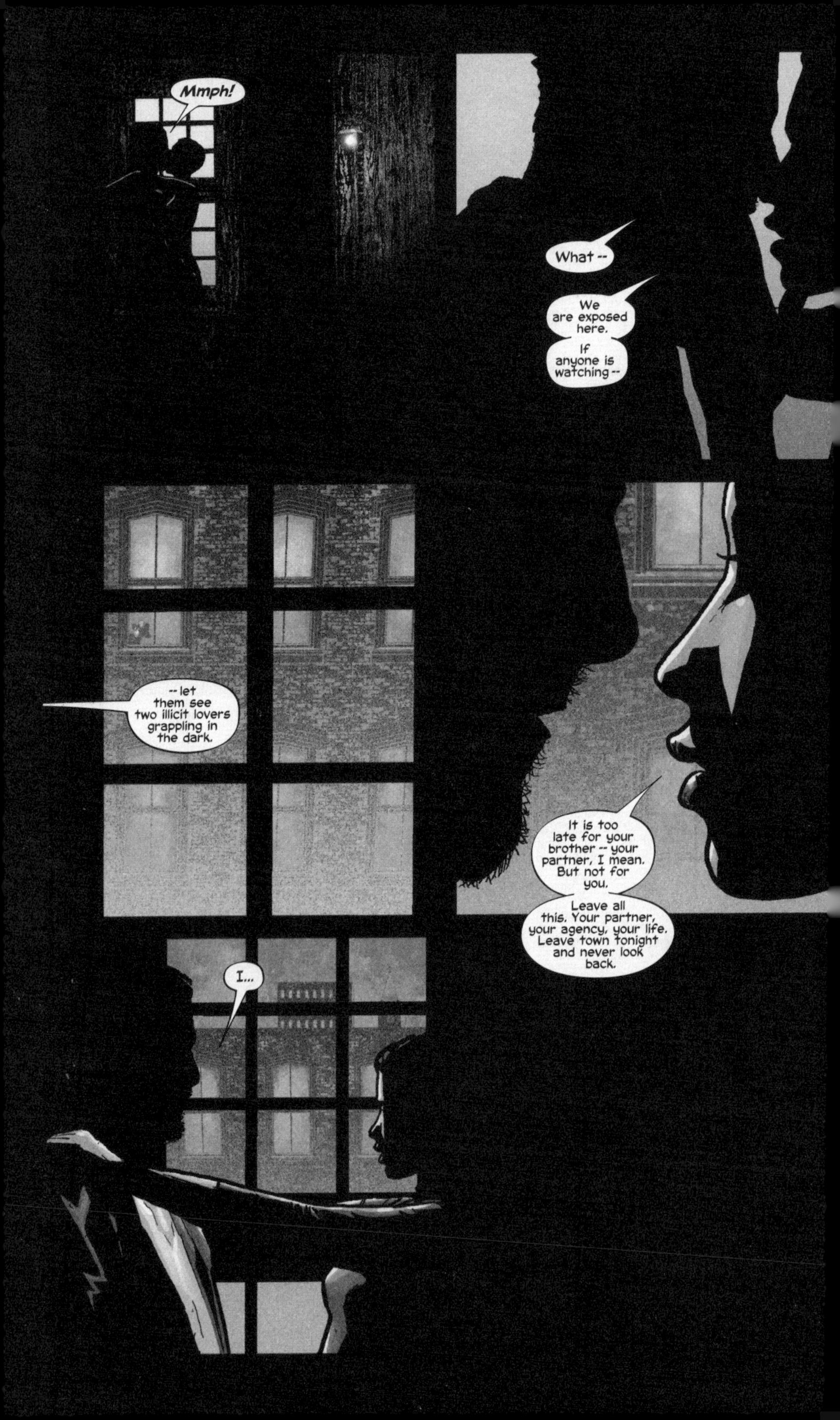
Mmph!
What --
We are exposed here.
If anyone is watching --
-- let them see two illicit lovers grappling in the dark.
It is too late for your brother -- your partner, I mean. But not for you.
Leave all this. Your partner, your agency, your life. Leave town tonight and never look back.
I...

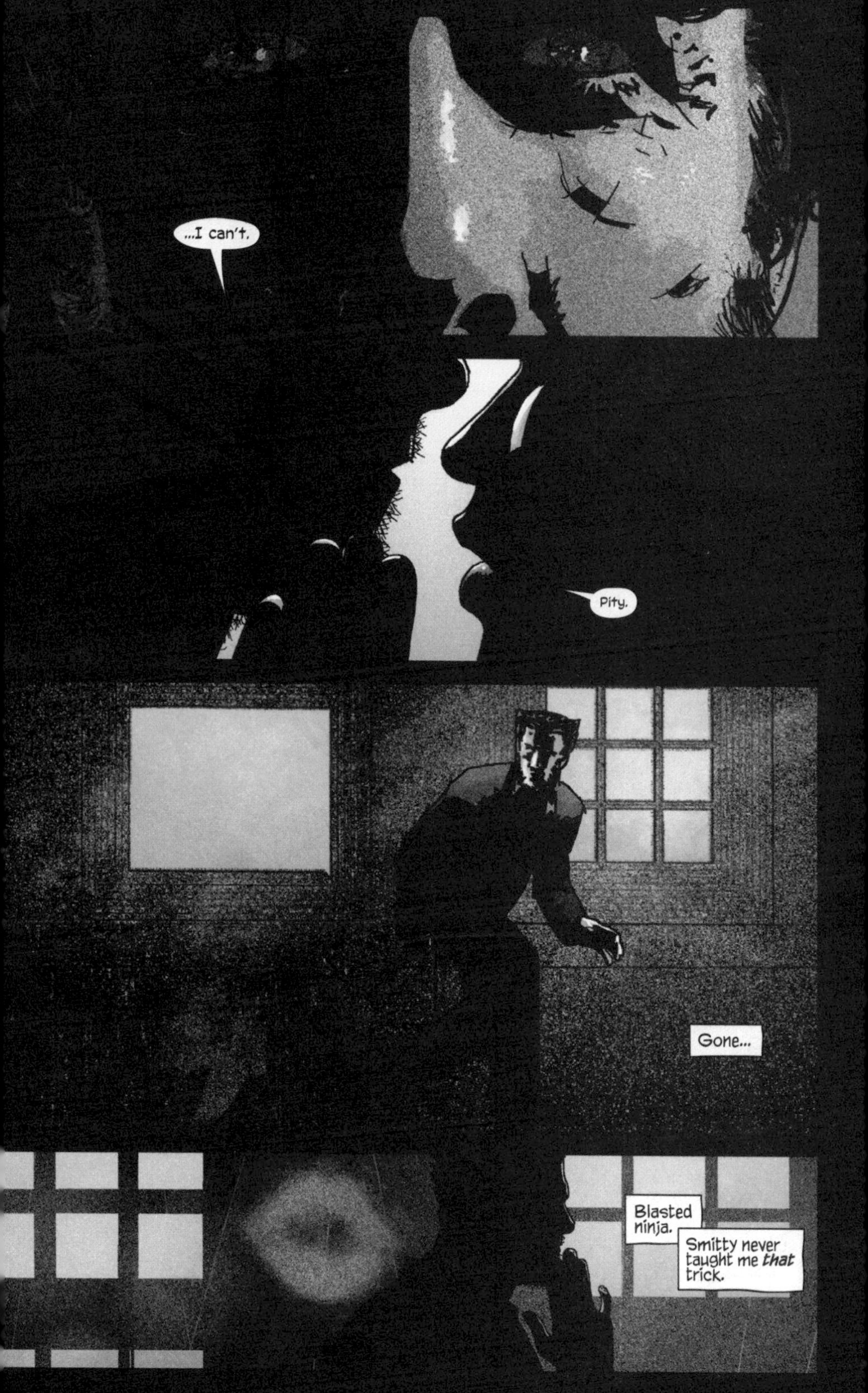
...I can't.
Pity.
Gone...
Blasted ninja.
Smitty never taught me *that* trick.

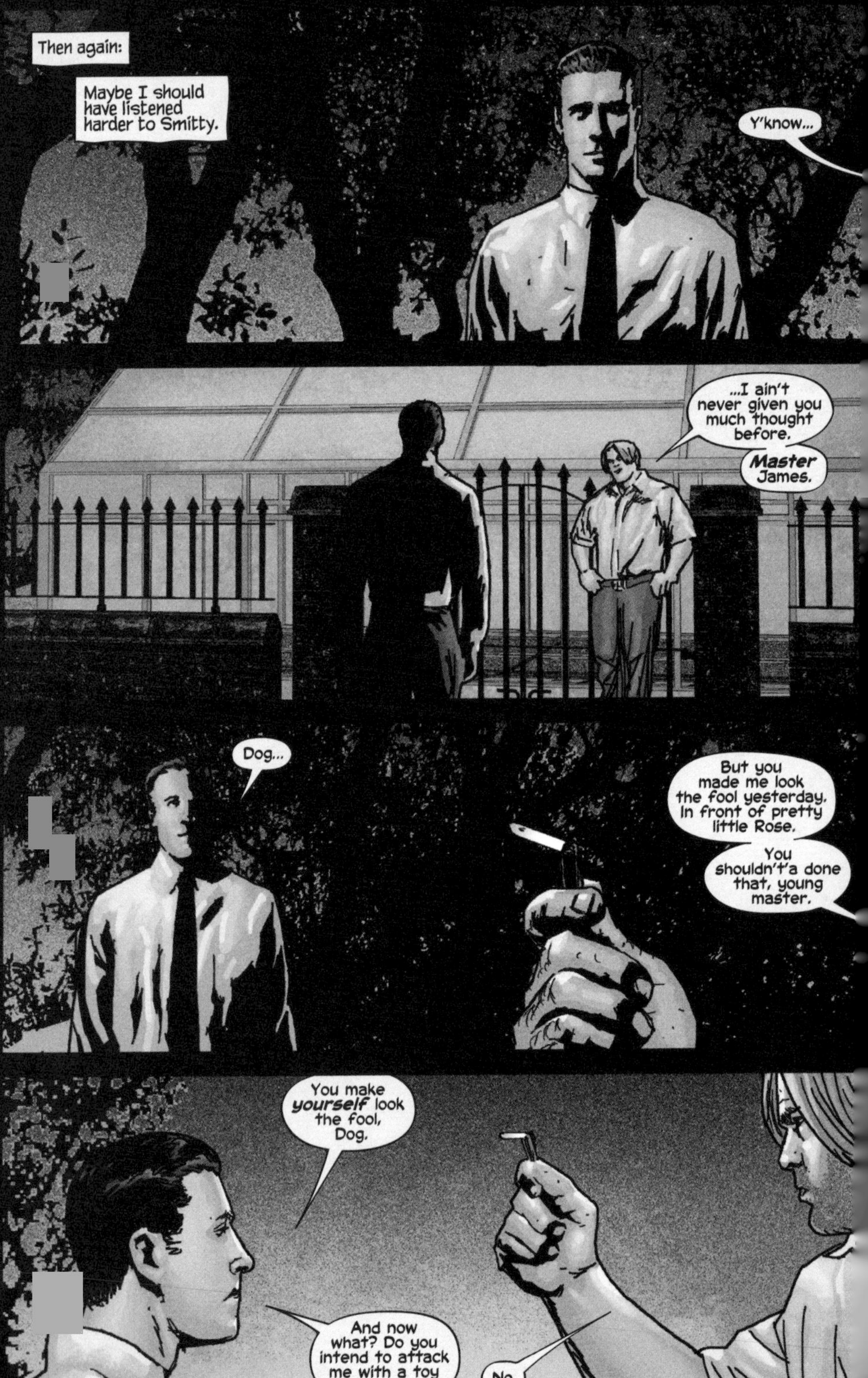
Then again:
Maybe I should have listened harder to Smitty.
Y'know...
...I ain't never given you much thought before.
Master James.
Dog...
But you made me look the fool yesterday. In front of pretty little Rose.
You shouldn't'a done that, young master.
You make yourself look the fool, Dog.
And now what? Do you intend to attack me with a toy knife?
No.

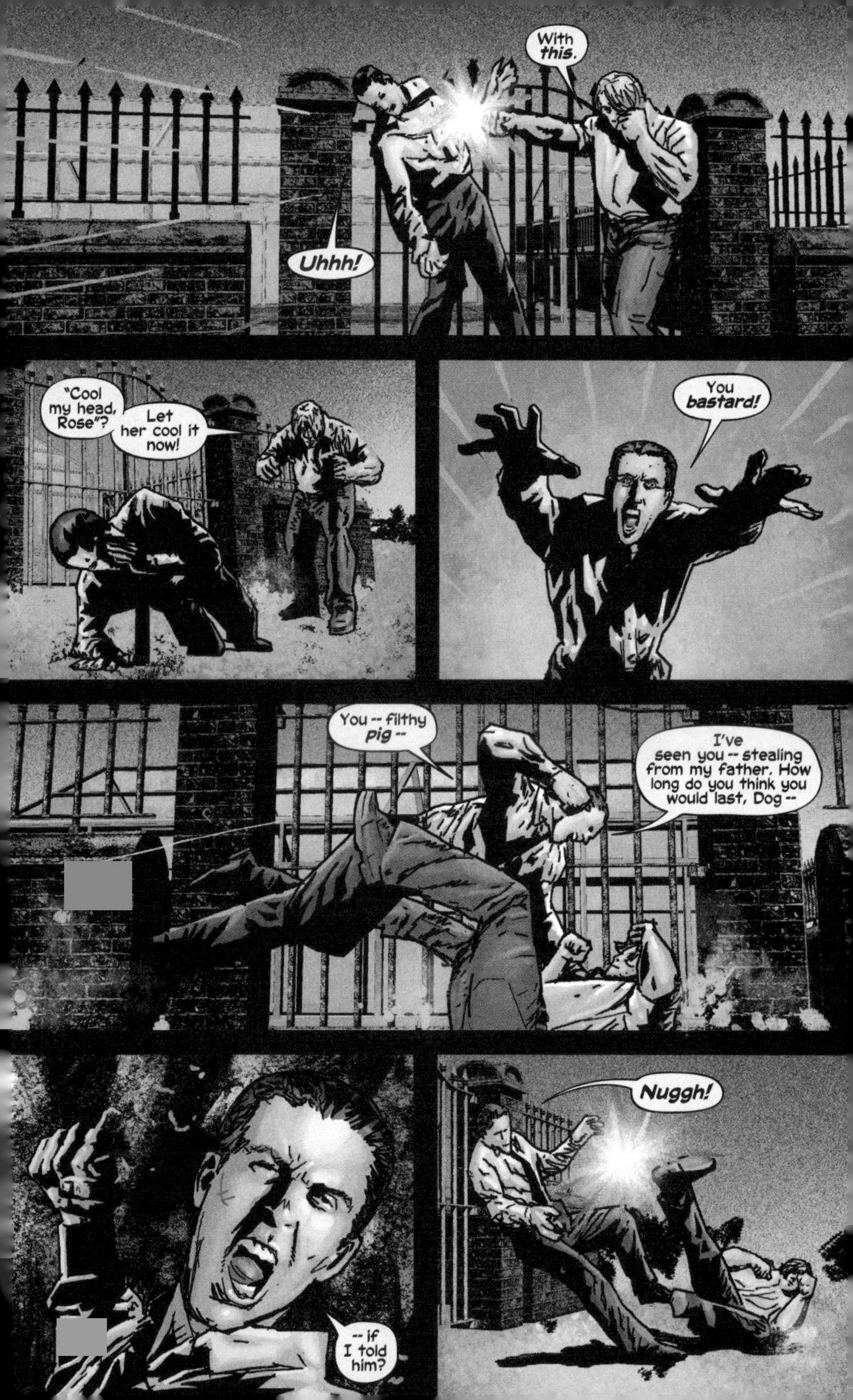
With this.
Uhhh!
"Cool my head, Rose"?
Let her cool it now!
You bastard!
You -- filthy pig --
I've seen you -- stealing from my father. How long do you think you would last, Dog --
-- if I told him?
Nuggh!

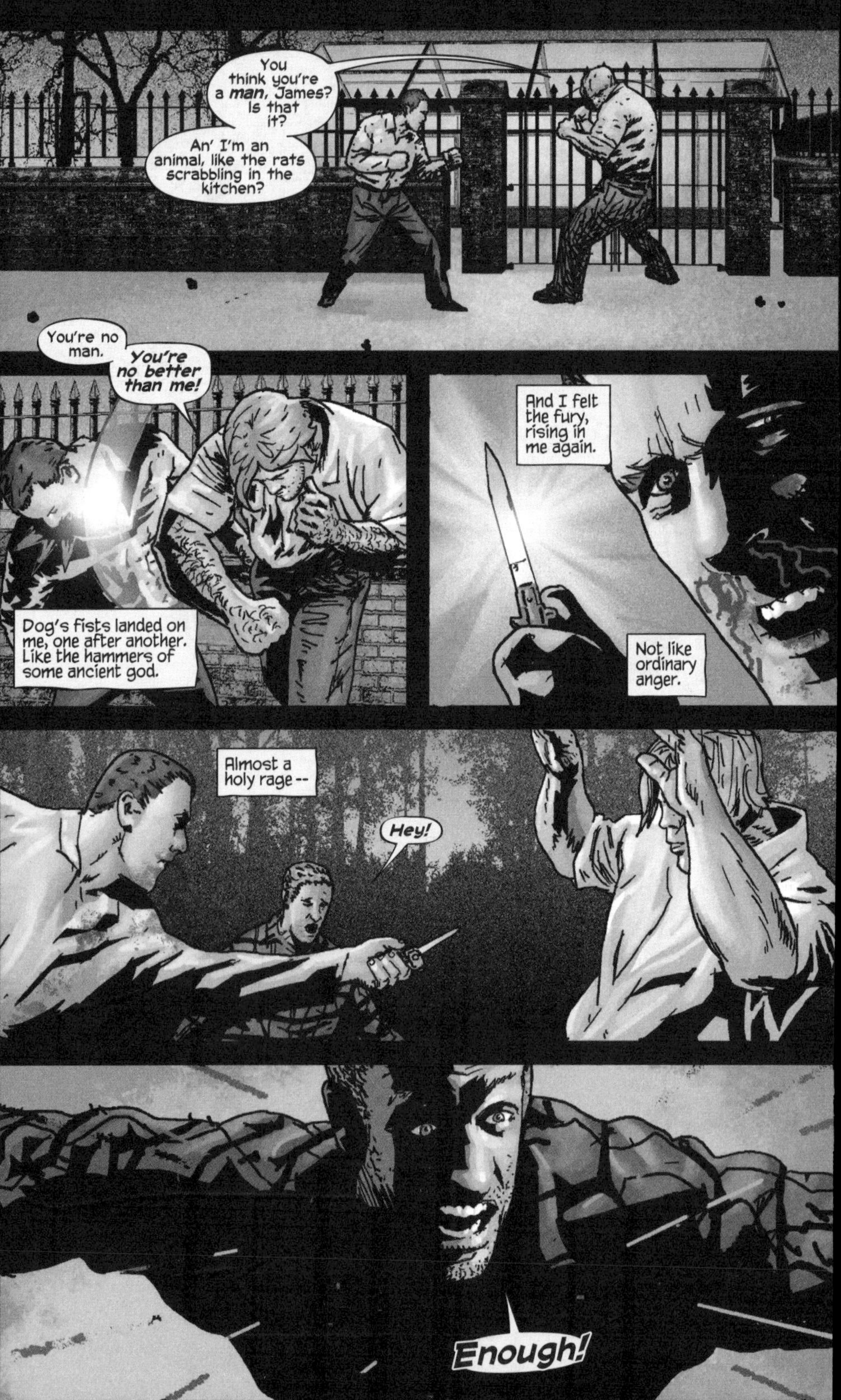
You think you're a *man*, James? Is that it?
An' I'm an animal, like the rats scrabbling in the kitchen?
You're no man.
You're no better than me!
Dog's fists landed on me, one after another. Like the hammers of some ancient god.
And I felt the fury, rising in me again.
Not like ordinary anger.
Almost a holy rage --
Hey!
Enough!

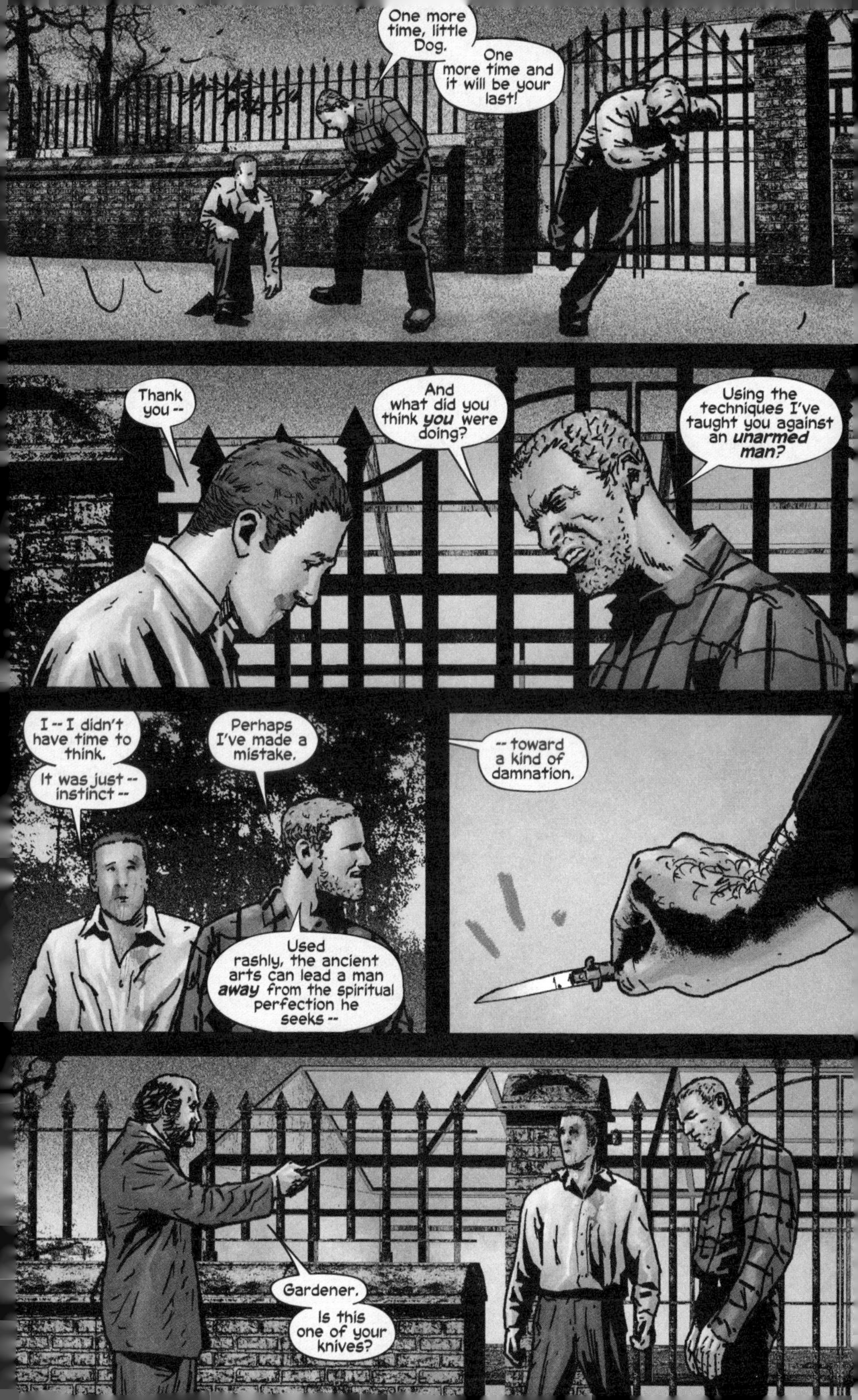

One more time, little Dog.
One more time and it will be your last!
Thank you --
And what did you think *you* were doing?
Using the techniques I've taught you against an *unarmed man?*
I -- I didn't have time to think.
It was just -- instinct --
Perhaps I've made a mistake.
Used rashly, the ancient arts can lead a man *away* from the spiritual perfection he seeks --
-- toward a kind of damnation.
Gardener.
Is this one of your knives?

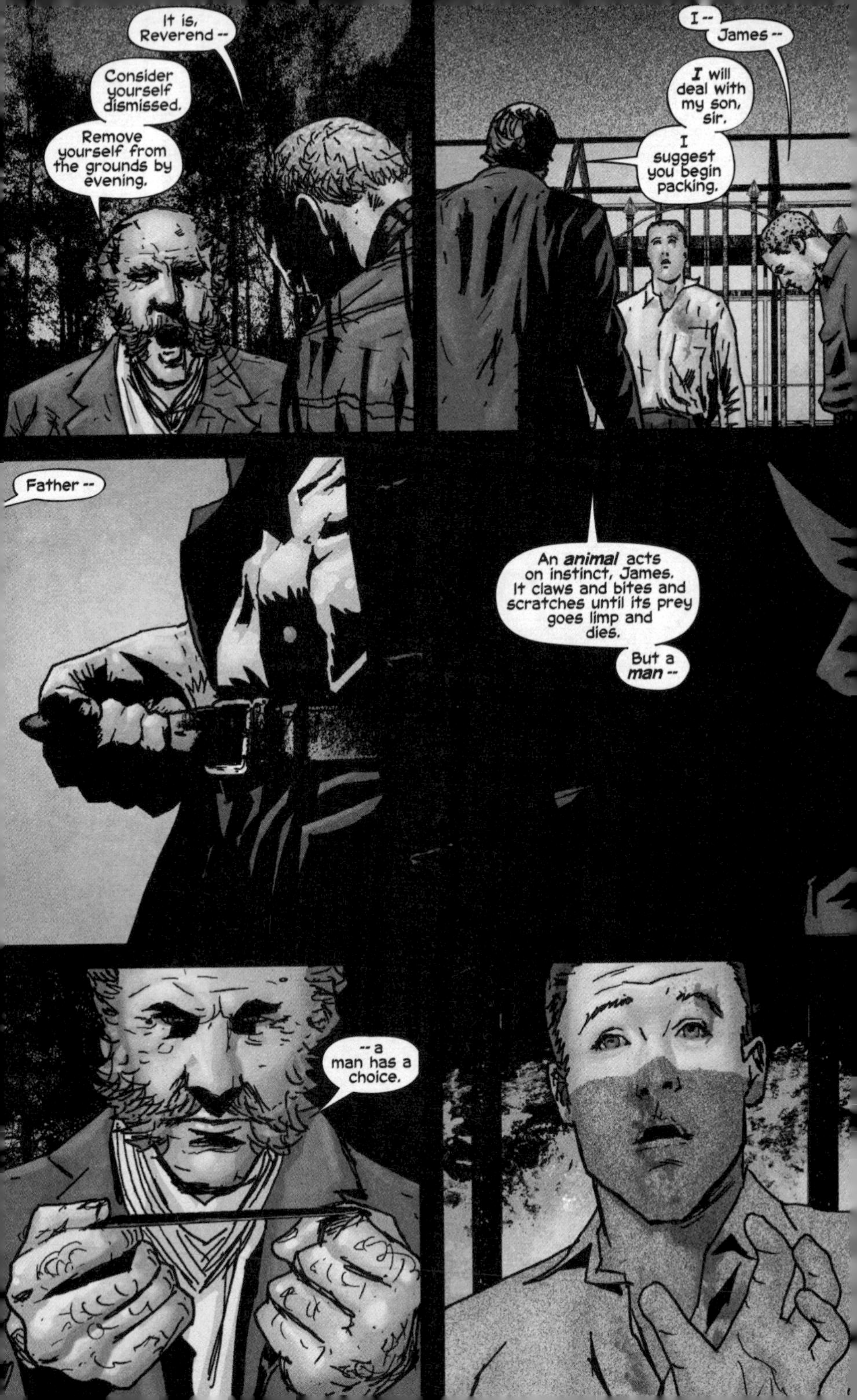
It is, Reverend --
Consider yourself dismissed.
Remove yourself from the grounds by evening.
I -- James --
I will deal with my son, sir.
I suggest you begin packing.
Father --
An animal acts on instinct, James. It claws and bites and scratches until its prey goes limp and dies.
But a man --
-- a man has a choice.

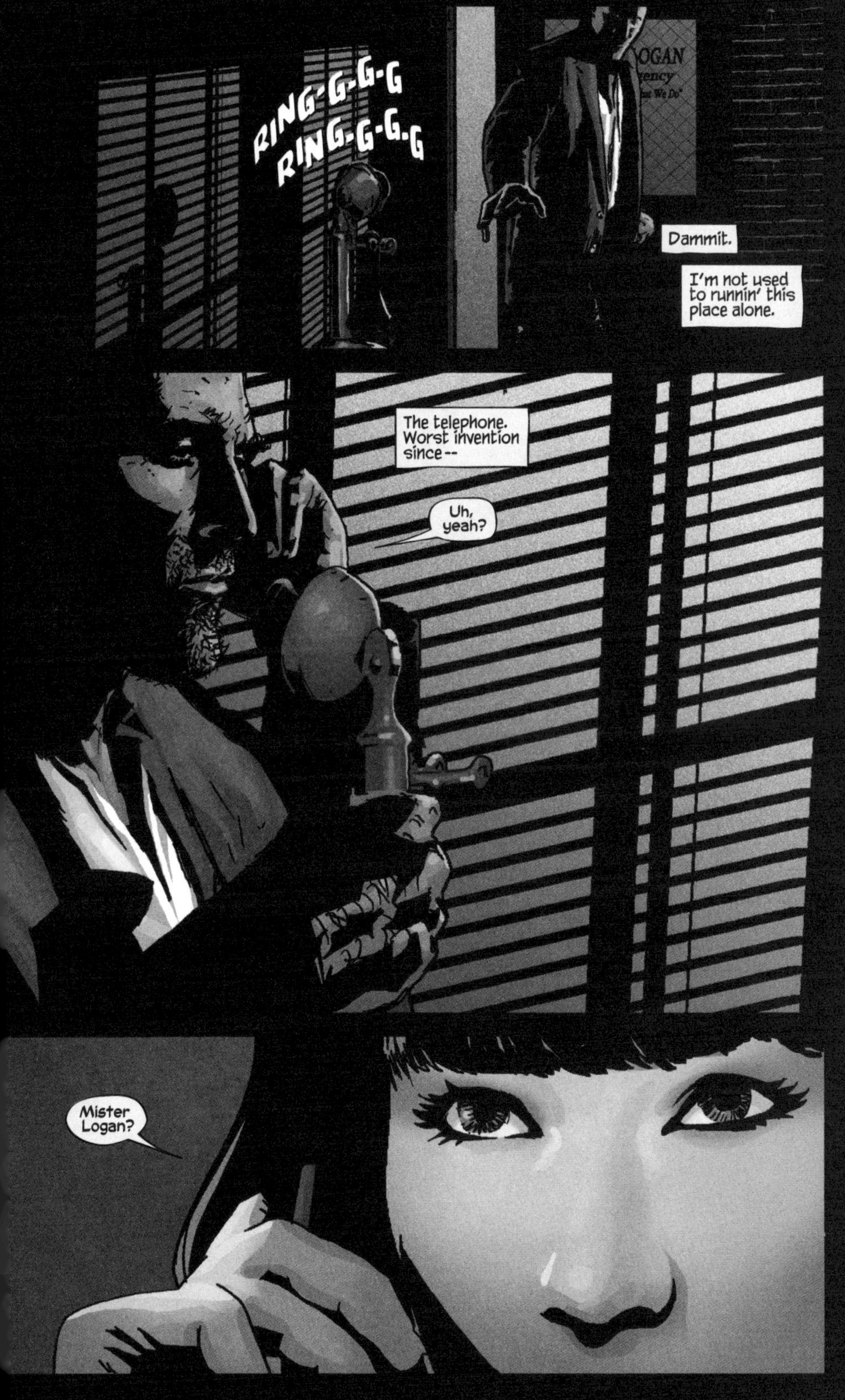
RING-G-G-G
RING-G-G-G
Dammit.
I'm not used to runnin' this place alone.
The telephone. Worst invention since--
Uh, yeah?
Mister Logan?

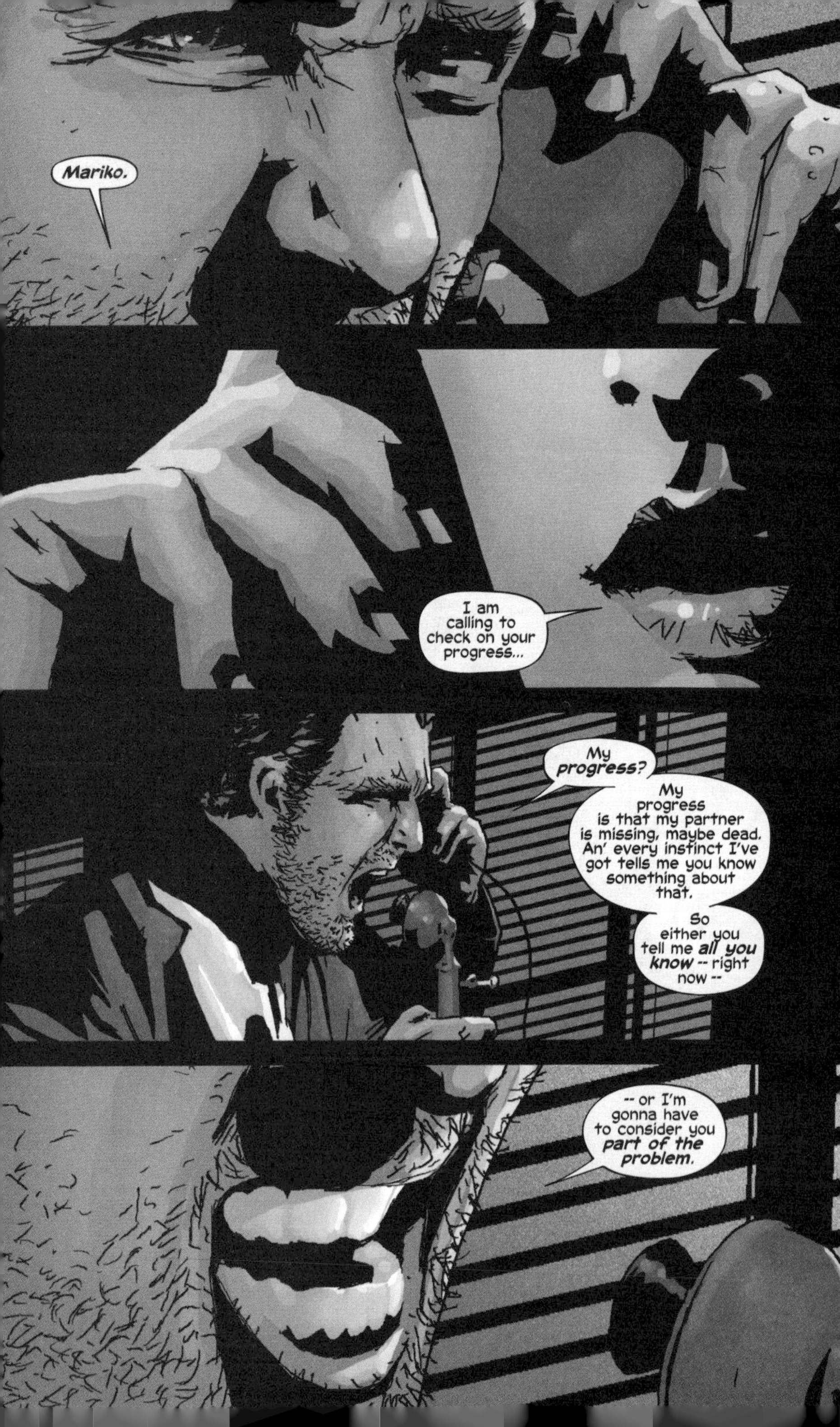
Mariko.
I am calling to check on your progress...
My *progress?*
My progress is that my partner is missing, maybe dead. An' every instinct I've got tells me you know something about that.
So either you tell me *all you know* -- right now --
-- or I'm gonna have to consider you *part of the problem.*

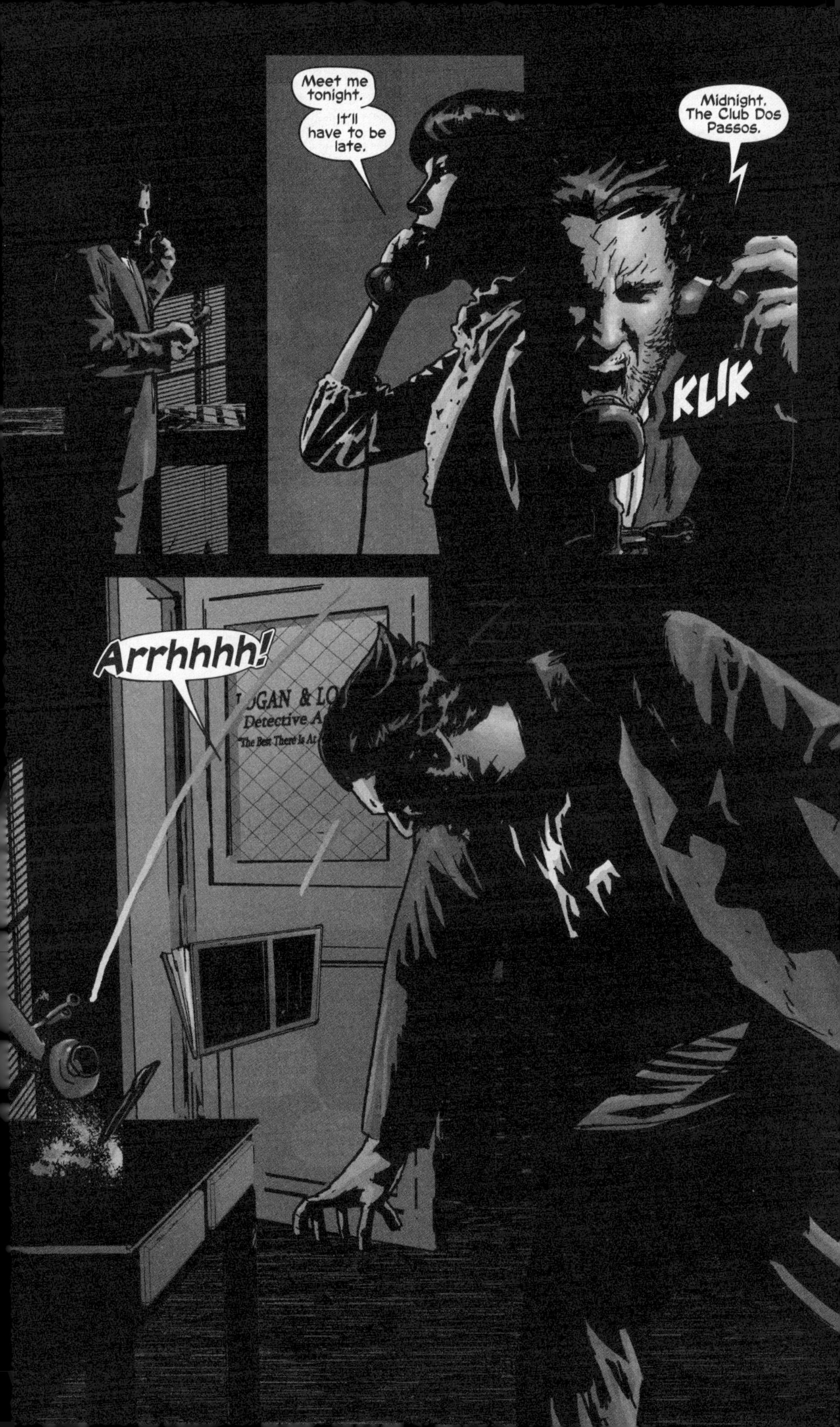
Meet me tonight.
It'll have to be late.
Midnight. The Club Dos Passos.
KLIK
Arrhhhh!

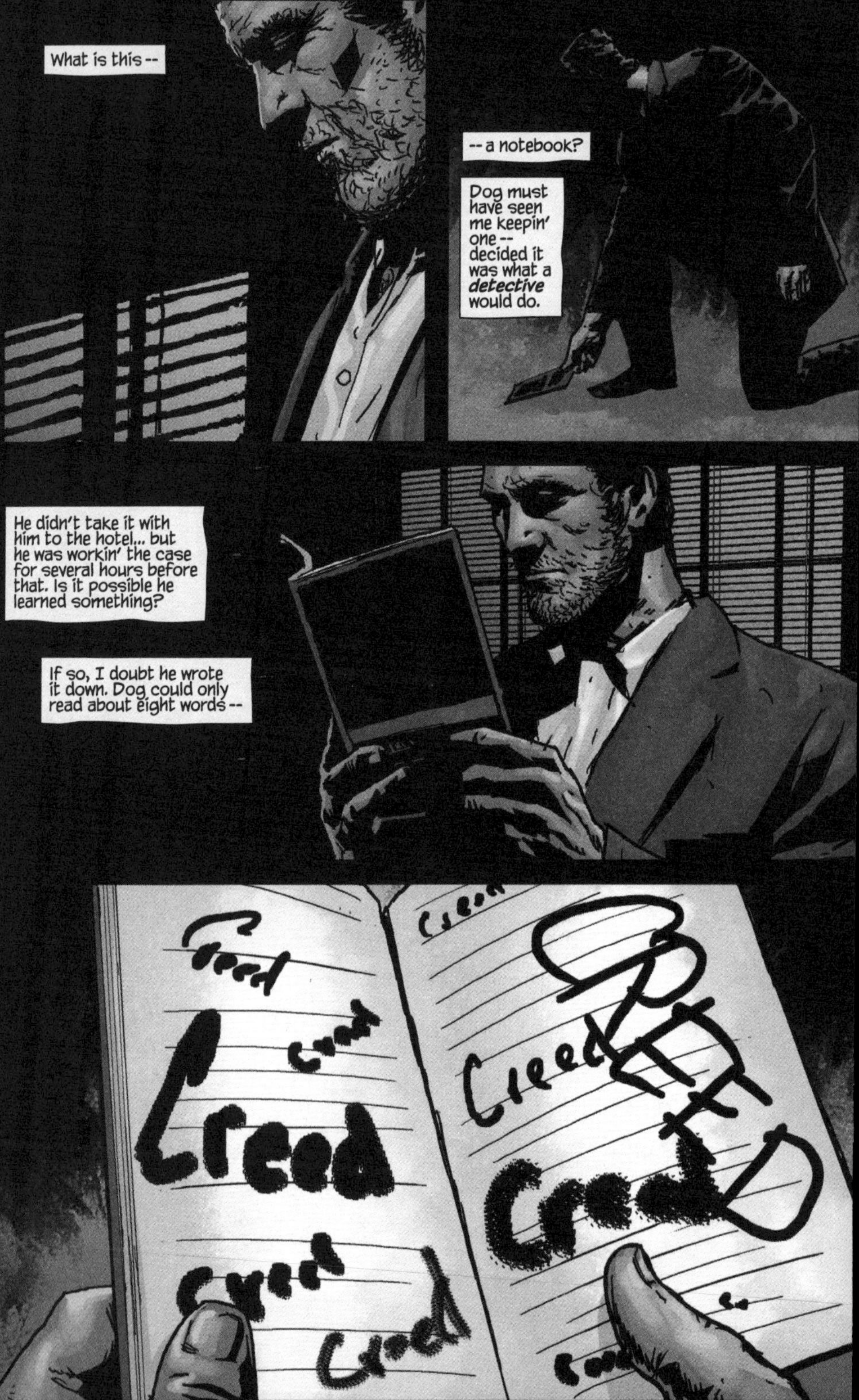
What is this --
-- a notebook?
Dog must have seen me keepin' one -- decided it was what a ***detective*** would do.
He didn't take it with him to the hotel... but he was workin' the case for several hours before that. Is it possible he learned something?
If so, I doubt he wrote it down. Dog could only read about eight words --
Creed
Creed
CREED

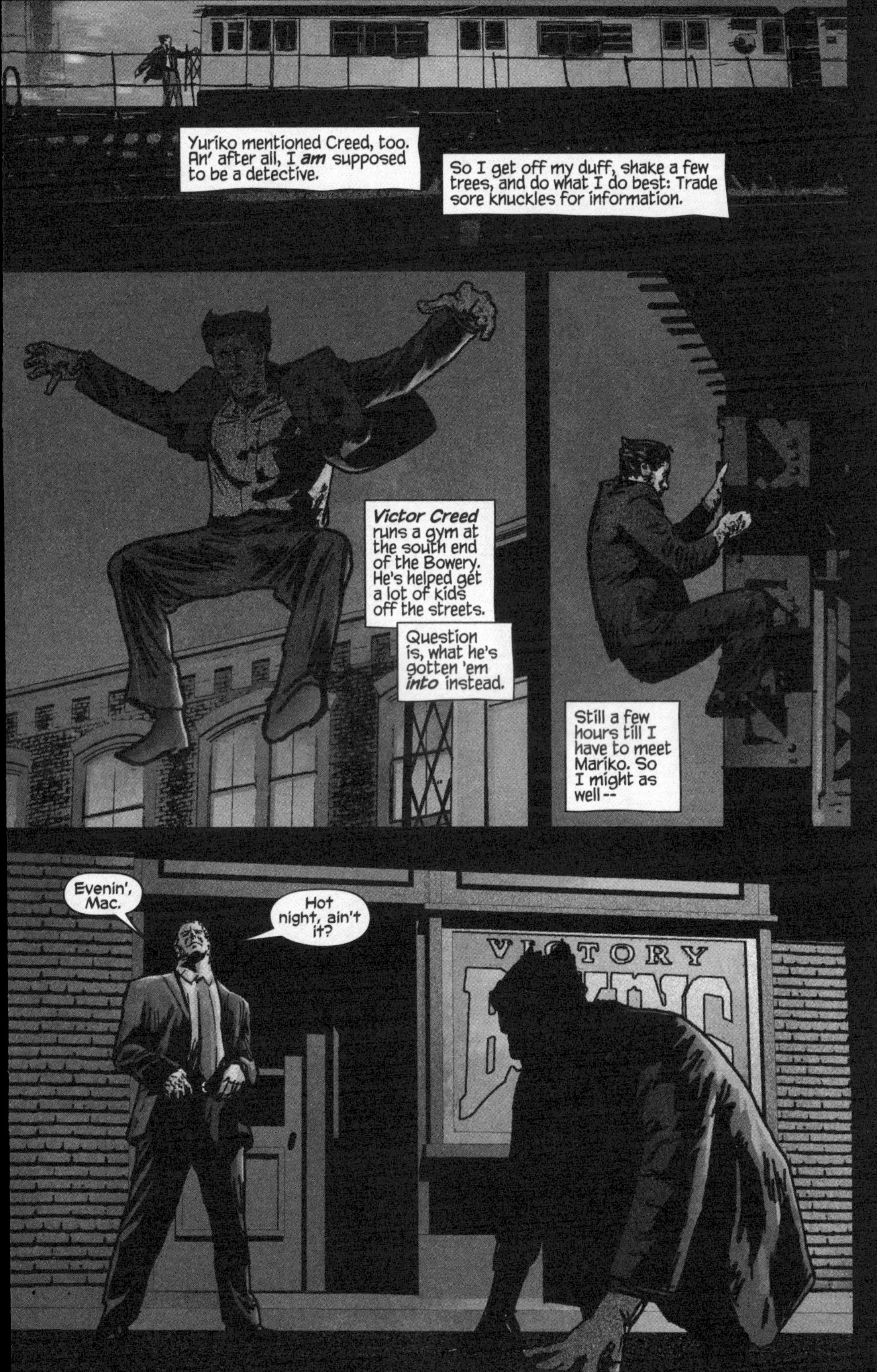
Yuriko mentioned Creed, too. An' after all, I *am* supposed to be a detective.
So I get off my duff, shake a few trees, and do what I do best: Trade sore knuckles for information.
Victor Creed runs a gym at the south end of the Bowery. He's helped get a lot of kids off the streets.
Question is, what he's gotten 'em *into* instead.
Still a few hours till I have to meet Mariko. So I might as well --
Evenin', Mac.
Hot night, ain't it?
VICTORY

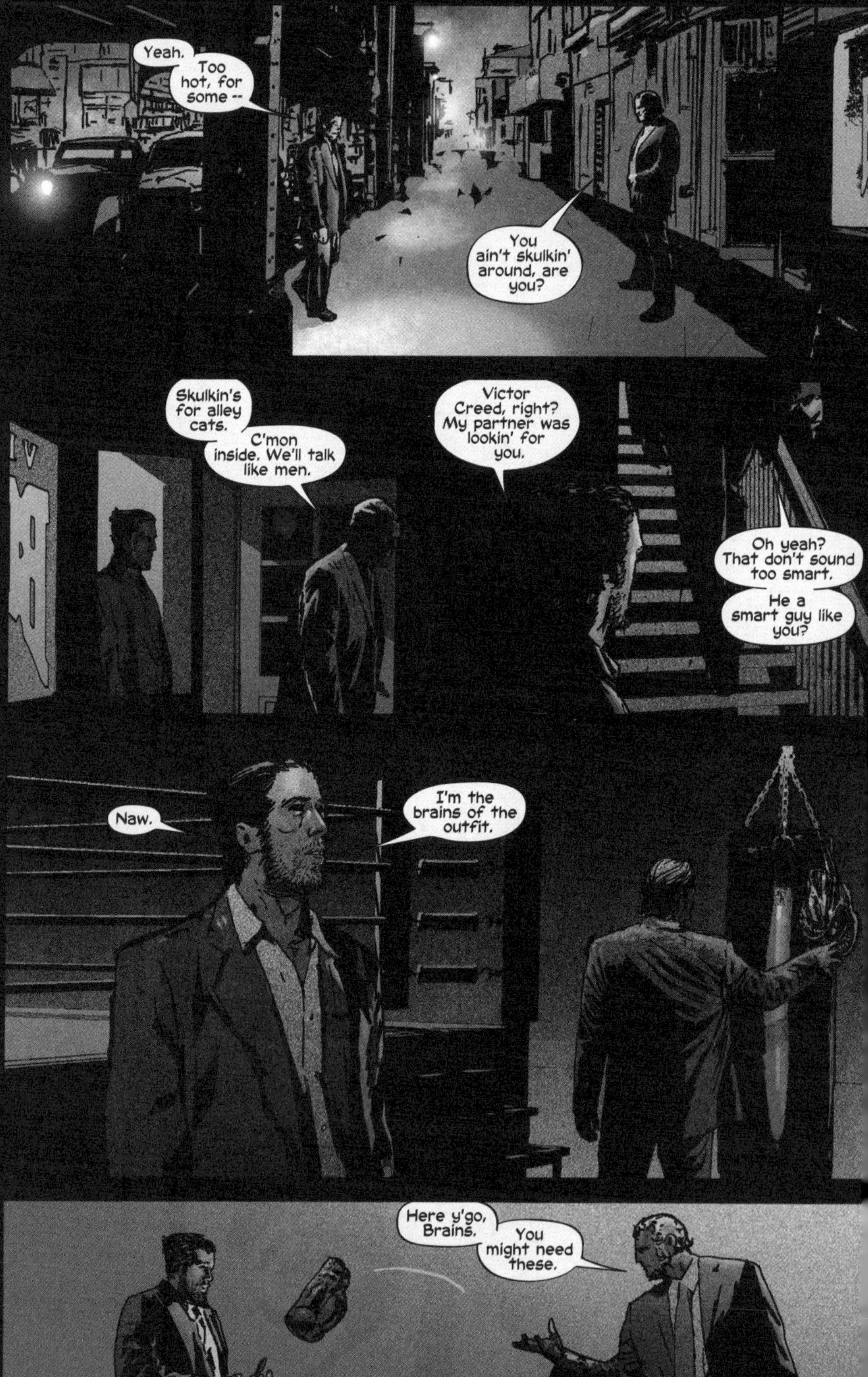

Yeah.
Too hot, for some --
You ain't skulkin' around, are you?
Skulkin's for alley cats.
C'mon inside. We'll talk like men.
Victor Creed, right? My partner was lookin' for you.
Oh yeah? That don't sound too smart.
He a smart guy like you?
Naw.
I'm the brains of the outfit.
Here y'go, Brains.
You might need these.

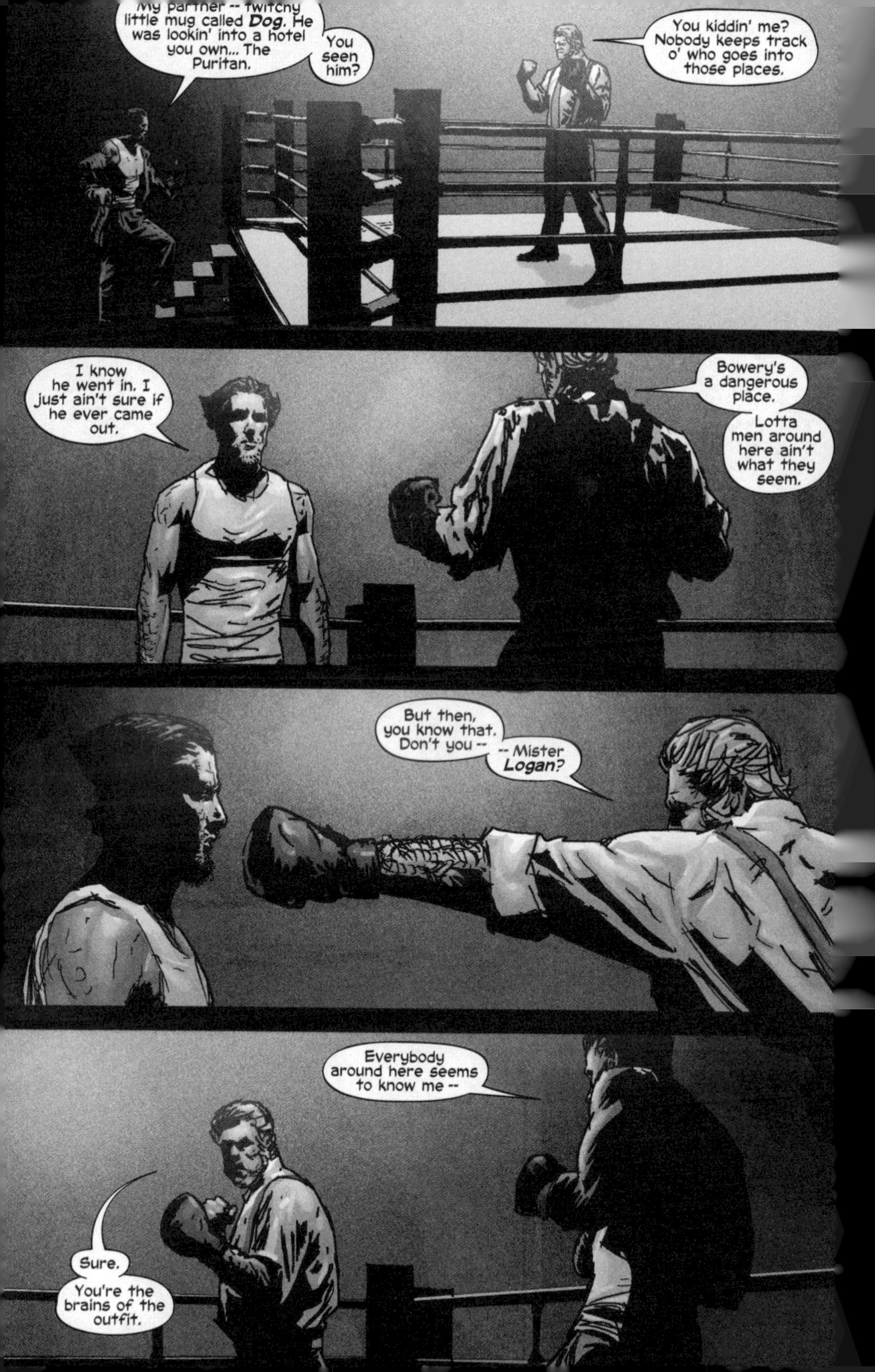
My partner -- twitchy little mug called Dog. He was lookin' into a hotel you own... The Puritan.
You seen him?
You kiddin' me? Nobody keeps track o' who goes into those places.
I know he went in. I just ain't sure if he ever came out.
Bowery's a dangerous place.
Lotta men around here ain't what they seem.
But then, you know that. Don't you --
-- Mister Logan?
Everybody around here seems to know me --
Sure.
You're the brains of the outfit.

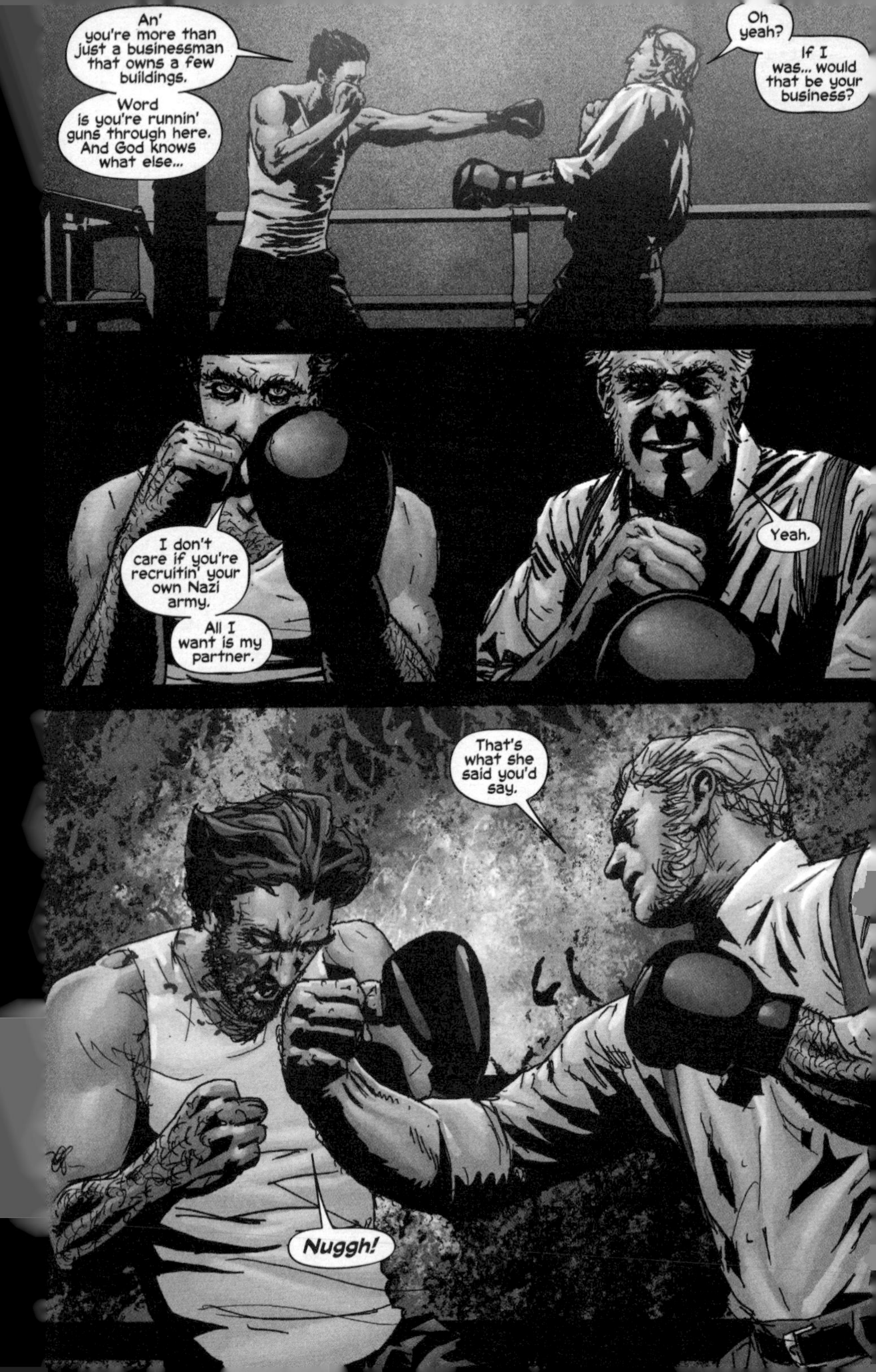
An' you're more than just a businessman that owns a few buildings.
Word is you're runnin' guns through here. And God knows what else...
Oh yeah?
If I was... would that be your business?
I don't care if you're recruitin' your own Nazi army.
All I want is my partner.
Yeah.
That's what she said you'd say.
Nuggh!

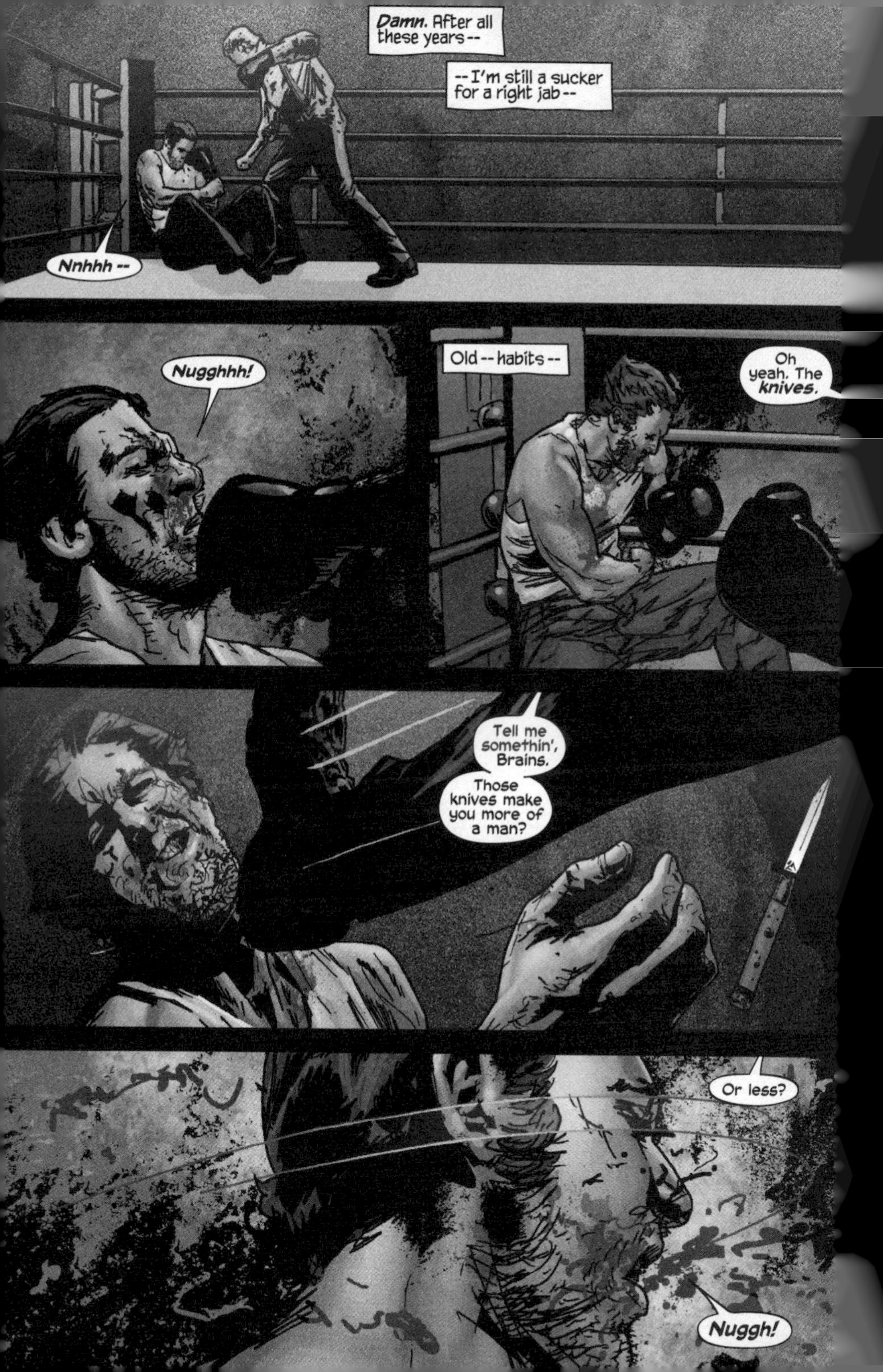

Damn. After all these years --
-- I'm still a sucker for a right jab --
Nnhhh --
Nugghhh!
Old -- habits --
Oh yeah. The knives.
Tell me somethin', Brains.
Those knives make you more of a man?
Or less?
Nuggh!

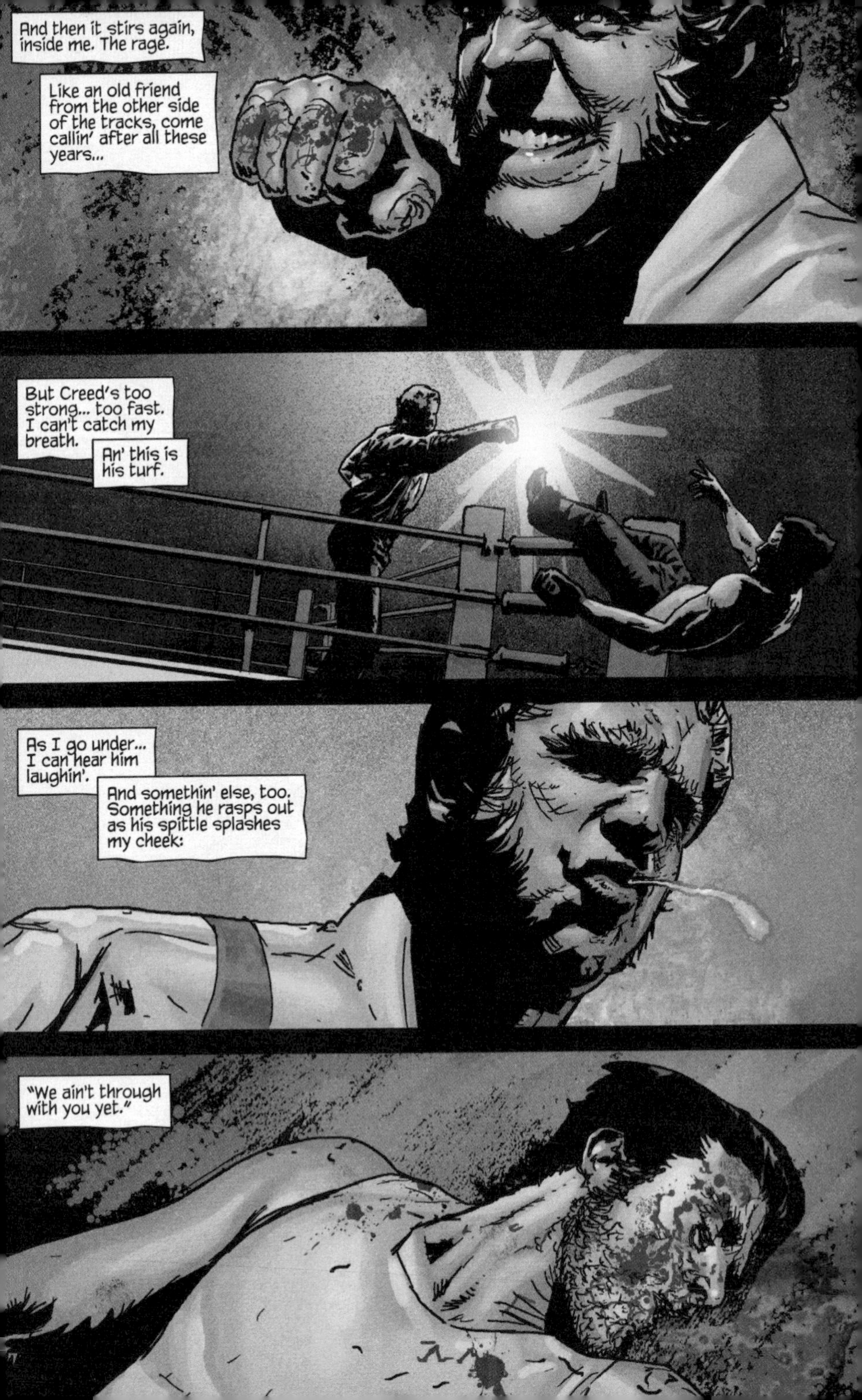
And then it stirs again, inside me. The rage.
Like an old friend from the other side of the tracks, come callin' after all these years...
But Creed's too strong... too fast. I can't catch my breath.
An' this is his turf.
As I go under... I can hear him laughin'.
And somethin' else, too. Something he rasps out as his spittle splashes my cheek:
"We ain't through with you yet."

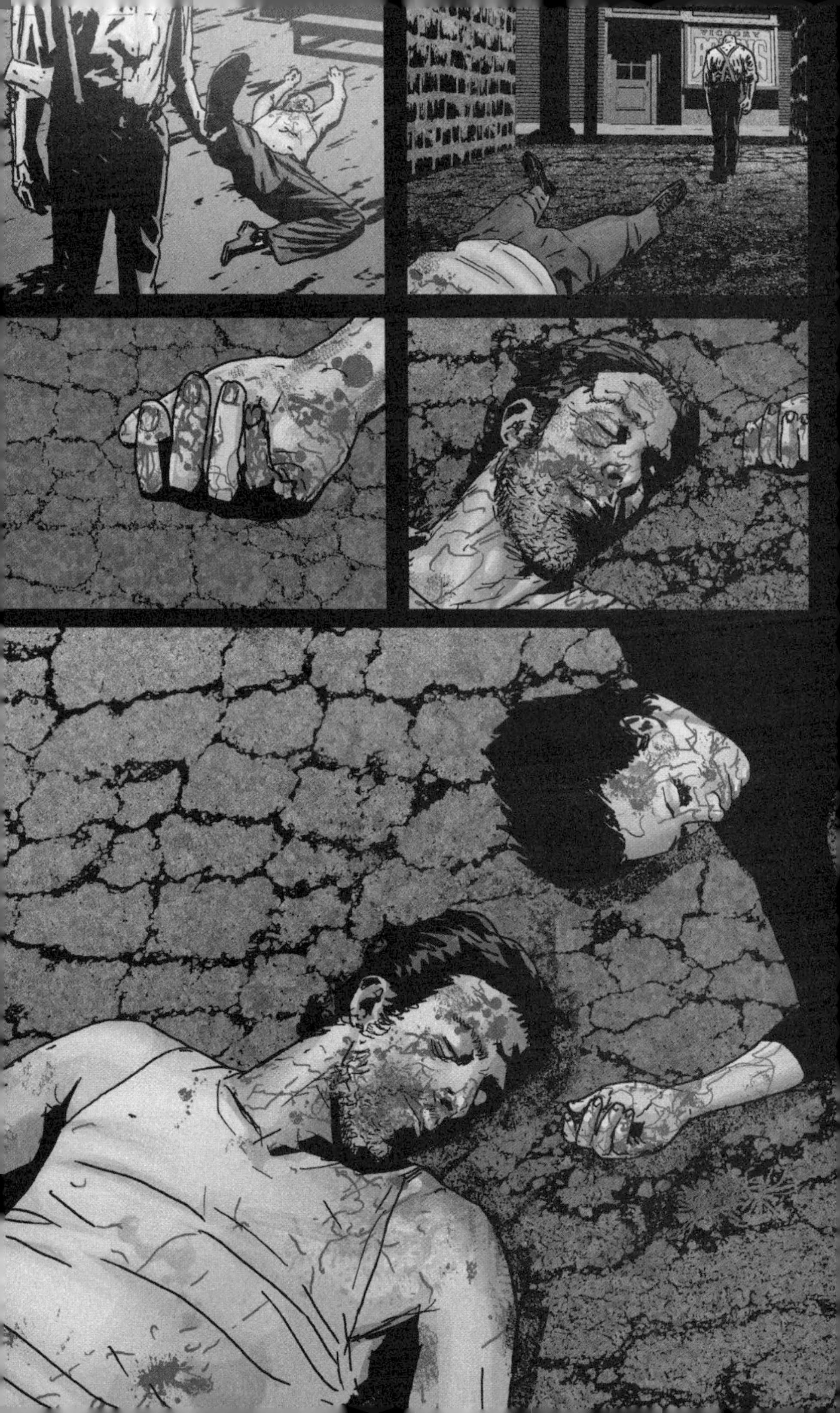
VICTORY

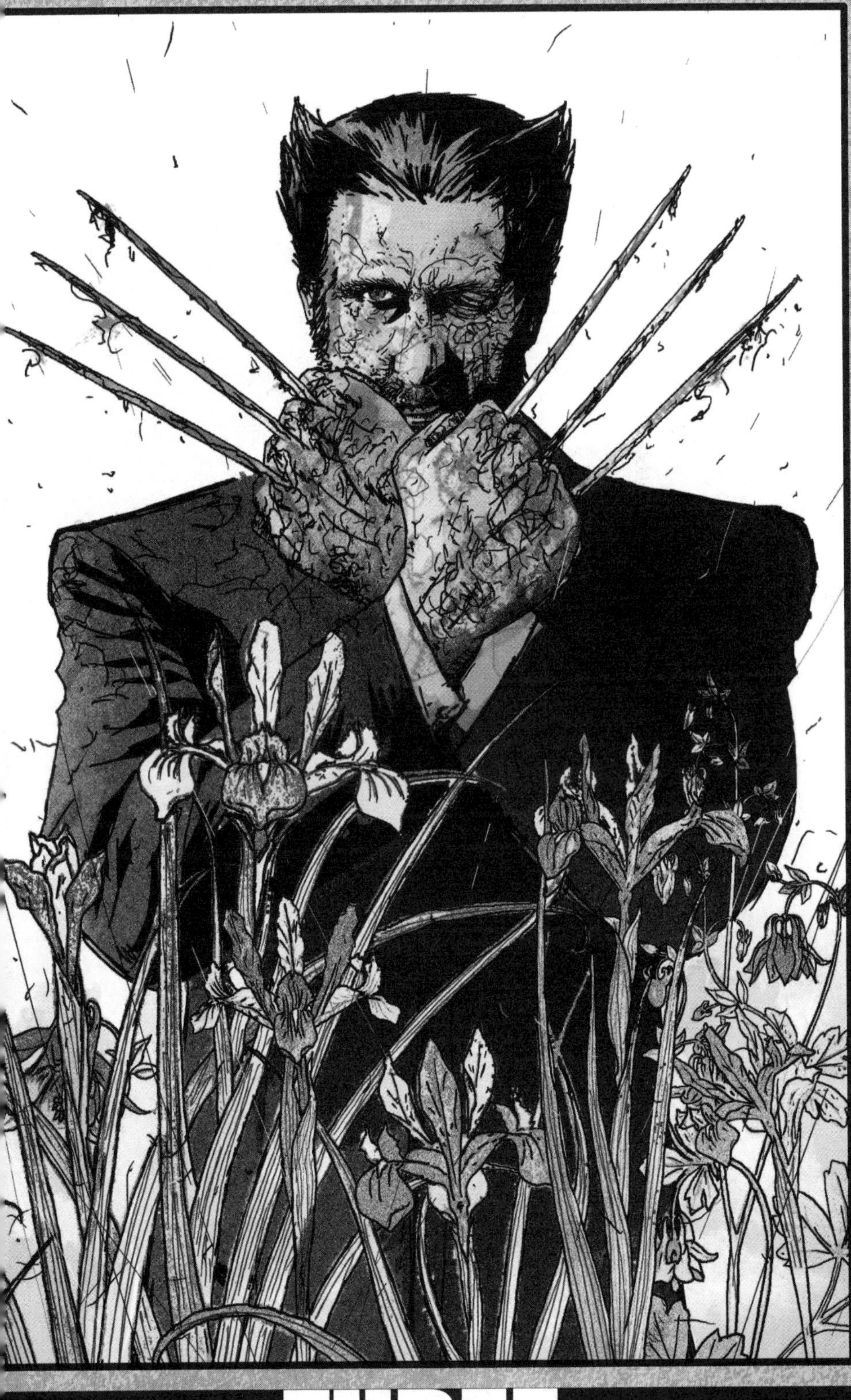

THREE

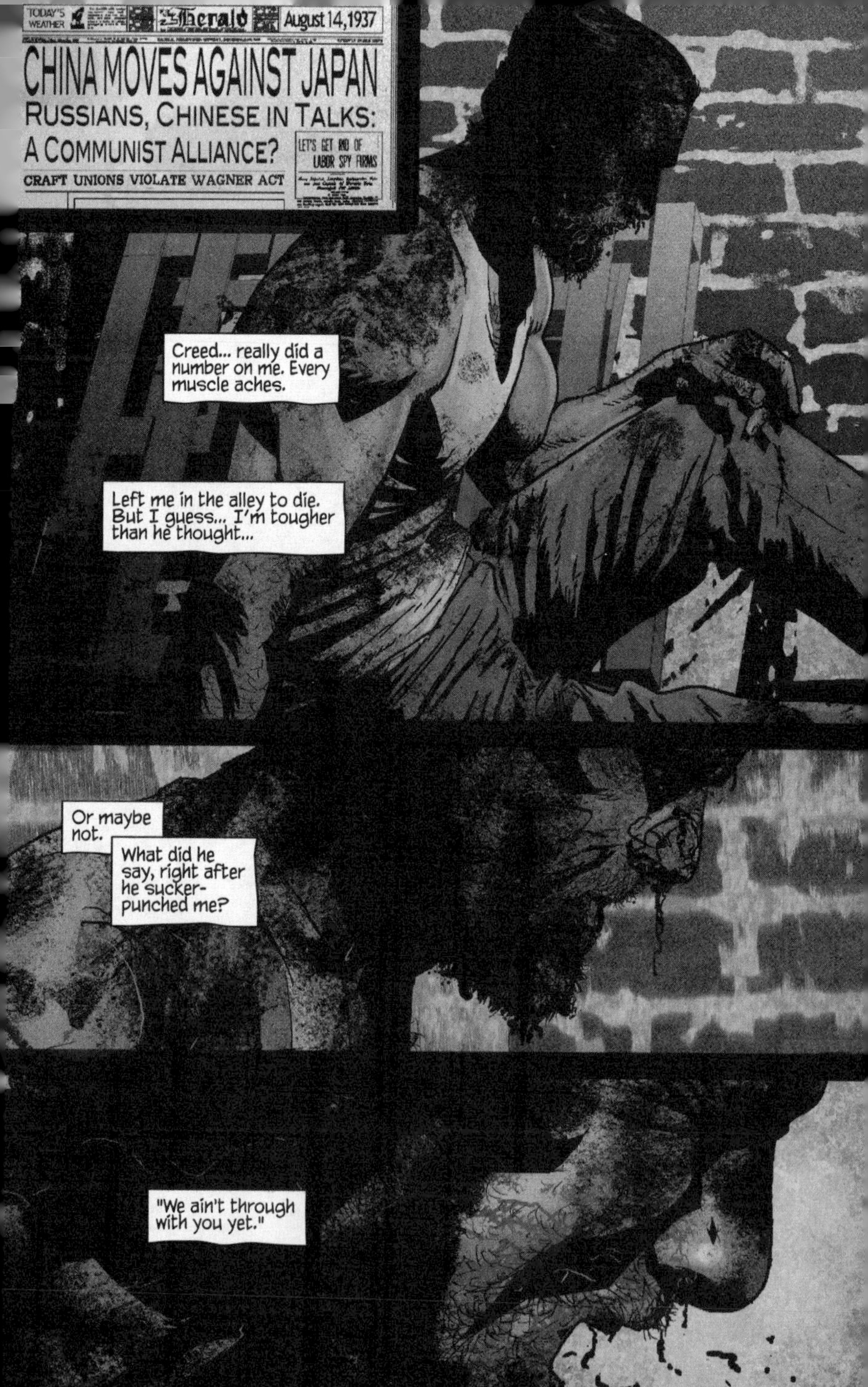
TODAY'S WEATHER
Herald
August 14,1937
CHINA MOVES AGAINST JAPAN
RUSSIANS, CHINESE IN TALKS:
A COMMUNIST ALLIANCE?
LET'S GET RID OF LABOR SPY FIRMS
CRAFT UNIONS VIOLATE WAGNER ACT
Creed... really did a number on me. Every muscle aches.
Left me in the alley to die. But I guess... I'm tougher than he thought...
Or maybe not.
What did he say, right after he sucker-punched me?
"We ain't through with you yet."

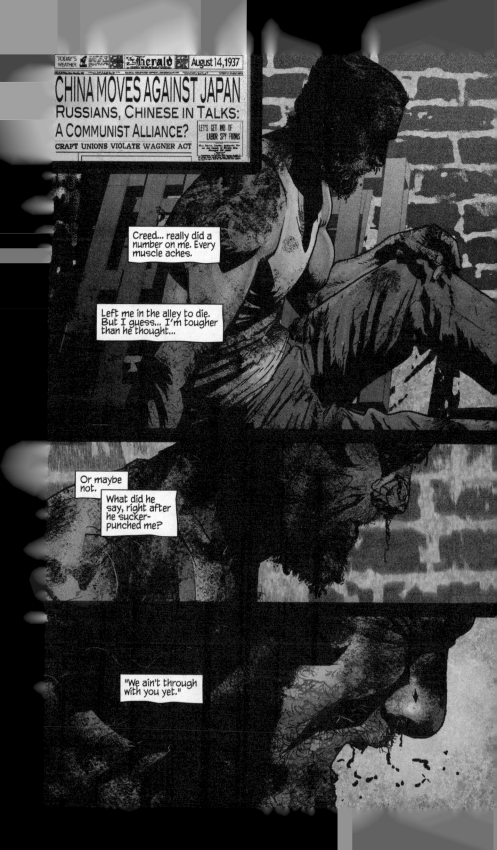

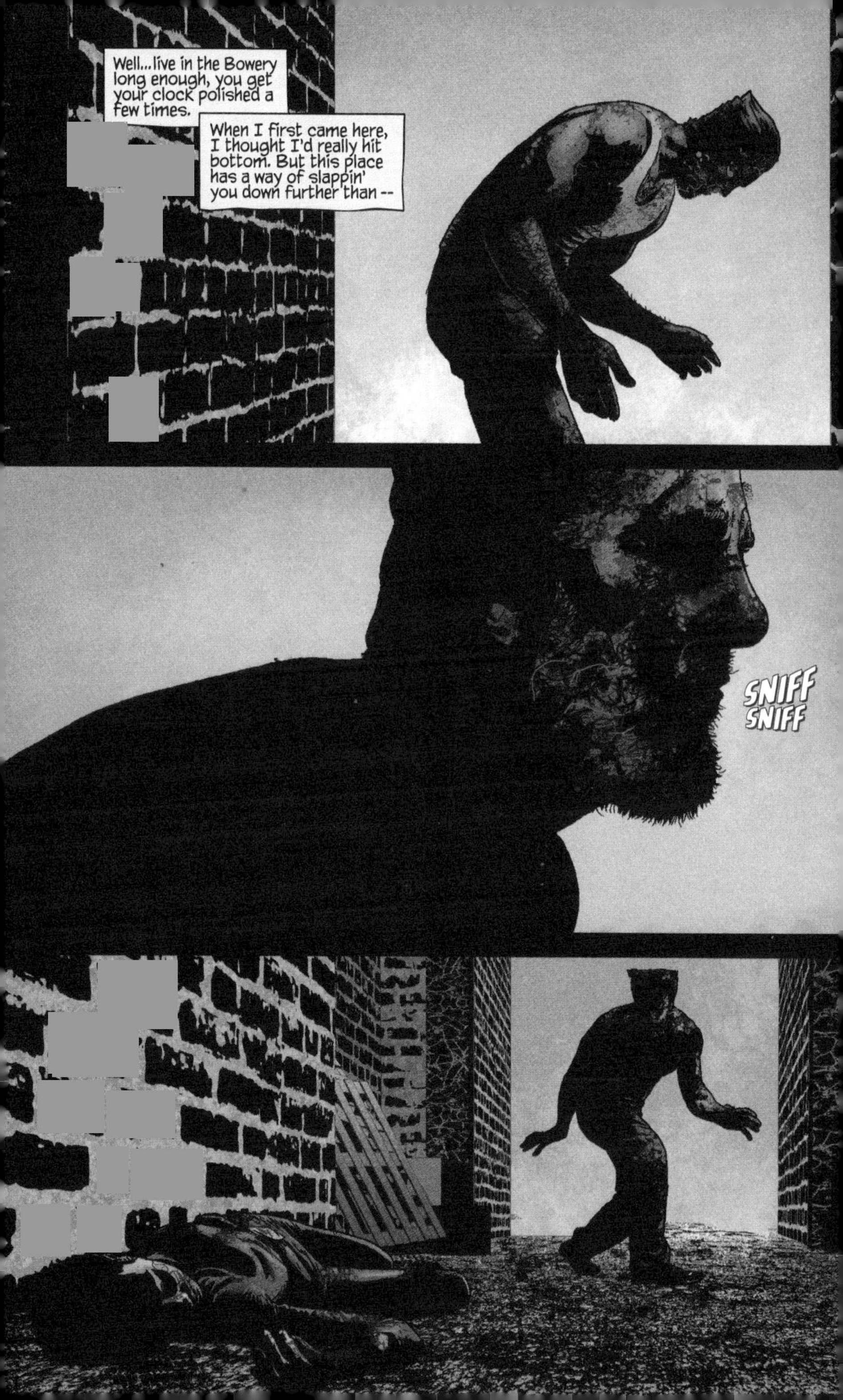

Well...live in the Bowery long enough, you get your clock polished a few times.
When I first came here, I thought I'd really hit bottom. But this place has a way of slappin' you down further than --
SNIFF SNIFF

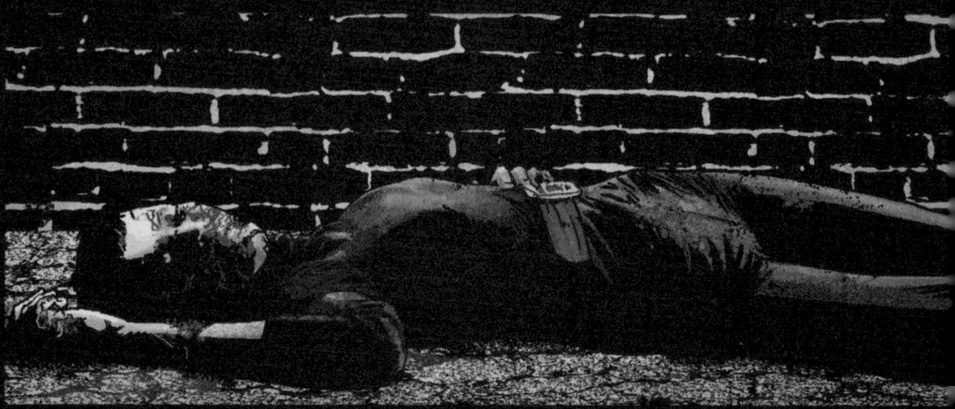

WOLVERINE NOIR

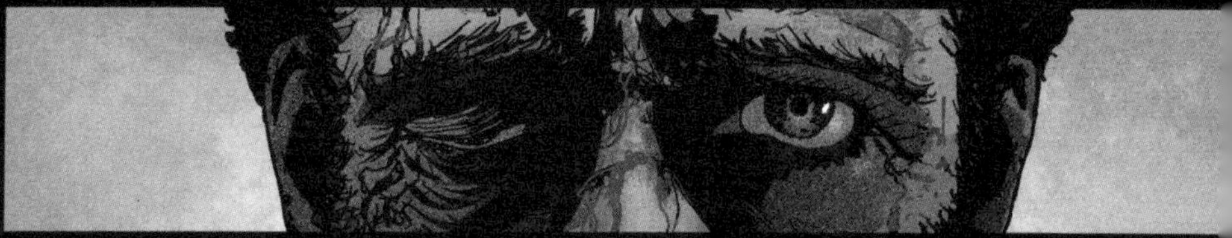

3: ORIGINAL SIN

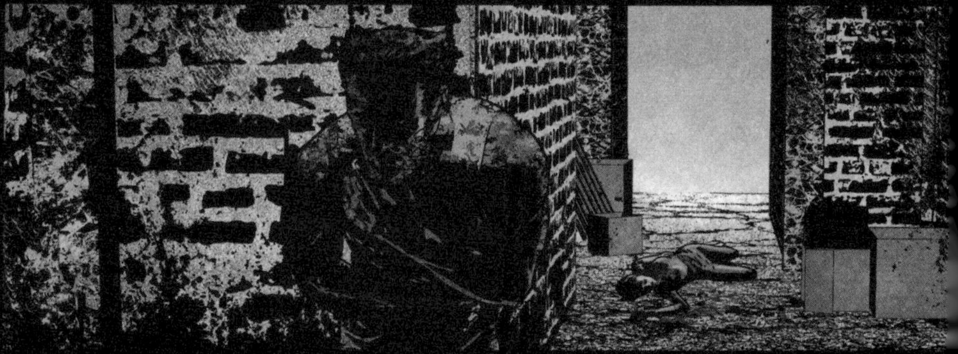

Seven years, five months, and a lifetime ago:

A Christian is a fully developed man.

A superior being...

...with a body, intellect, and soul.

Since his dismissal from my father's service, Smitty -- my knife teacher -- had descended into disease and alcohol abuse.

Despite my father's stern warnings, I had kept in touch with Smitty... sneaking out to spar with him when I could.

MASTER SCHMI...
...D TO REST
...NG HE...
...REST

That morning, Smitty died of consumption.

And as I sat in my father's church that day, listening to his hollow words...

A Christian is *not* an animal. Unless he chooses to be.

Unless he *falls*.

...I felt Smitty's hidden legacy, cold and solid in my hand.

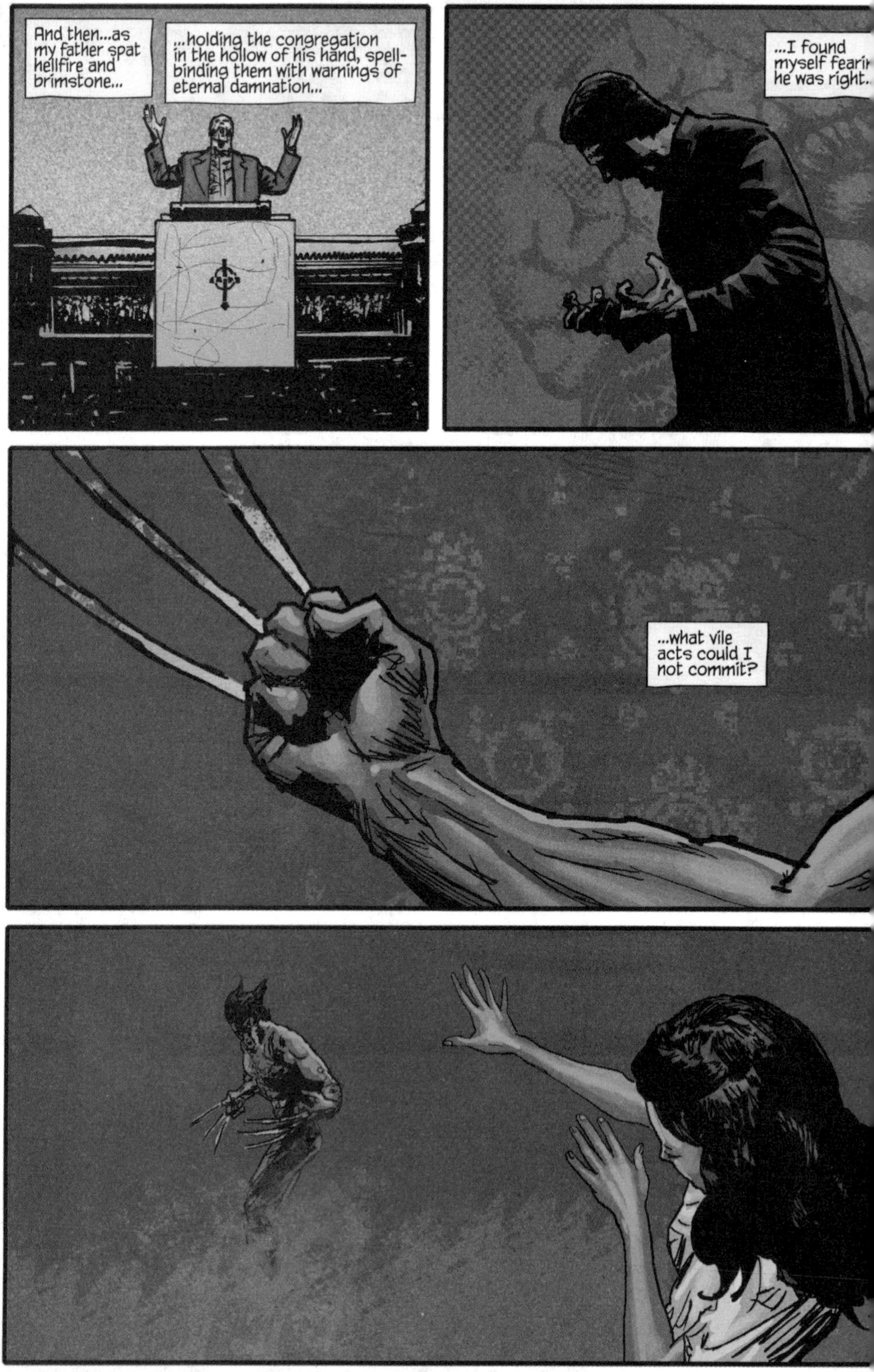
And then...as my father spat hellfire and brimstone...
...holding the congregation in the hollow of his hand, spell-binding them with warnings of eternal damnation...
...I found myself fearir
he was right..
...what vile acts could I not commit?

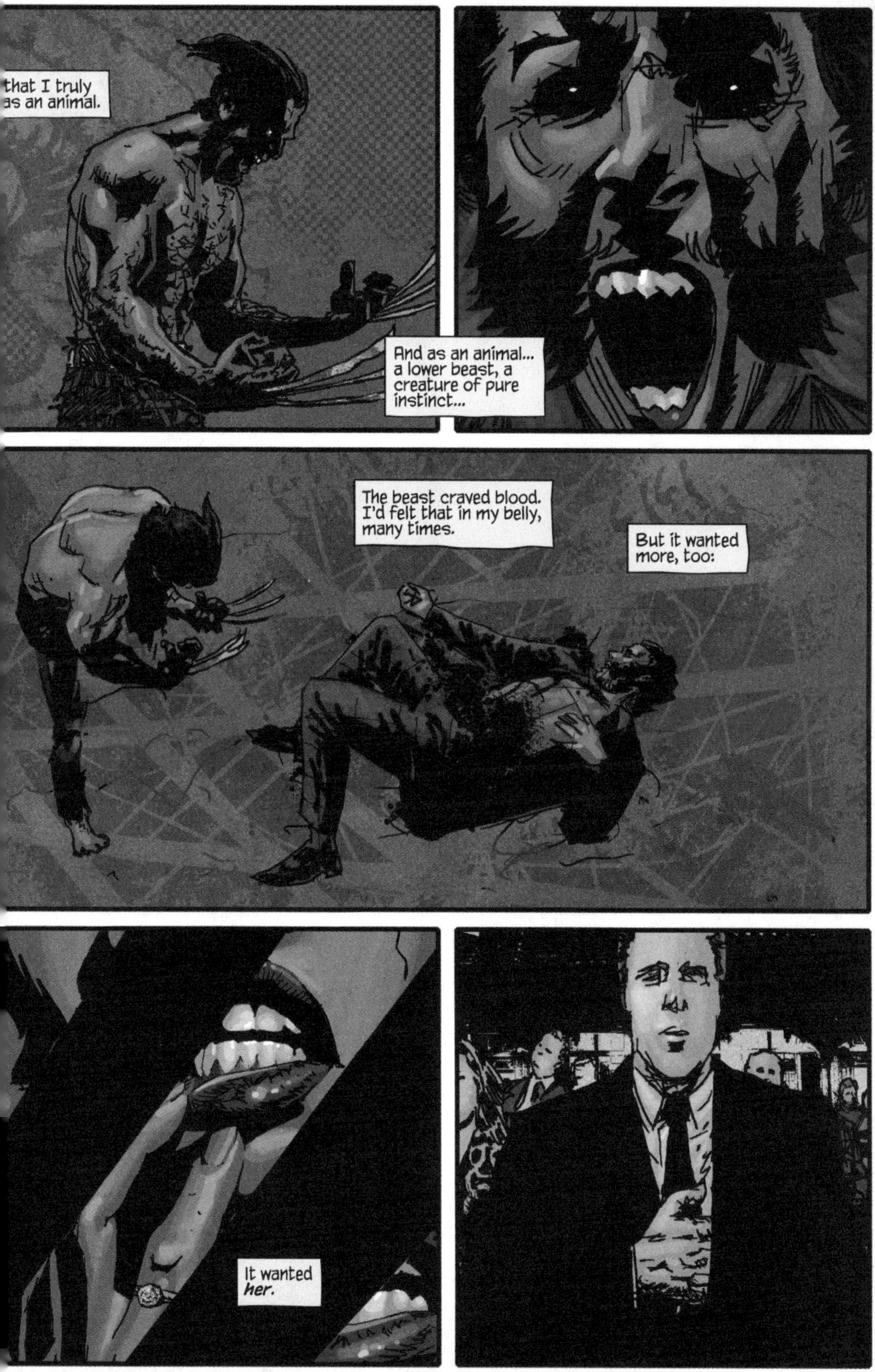
that I truly
as an animal.
And as an animal... a lower beast, a creature of pure instinct...
The beast craved blood. I'd felt that in my belly, many times.
But it wanted more, too:
It wanted ***her.***

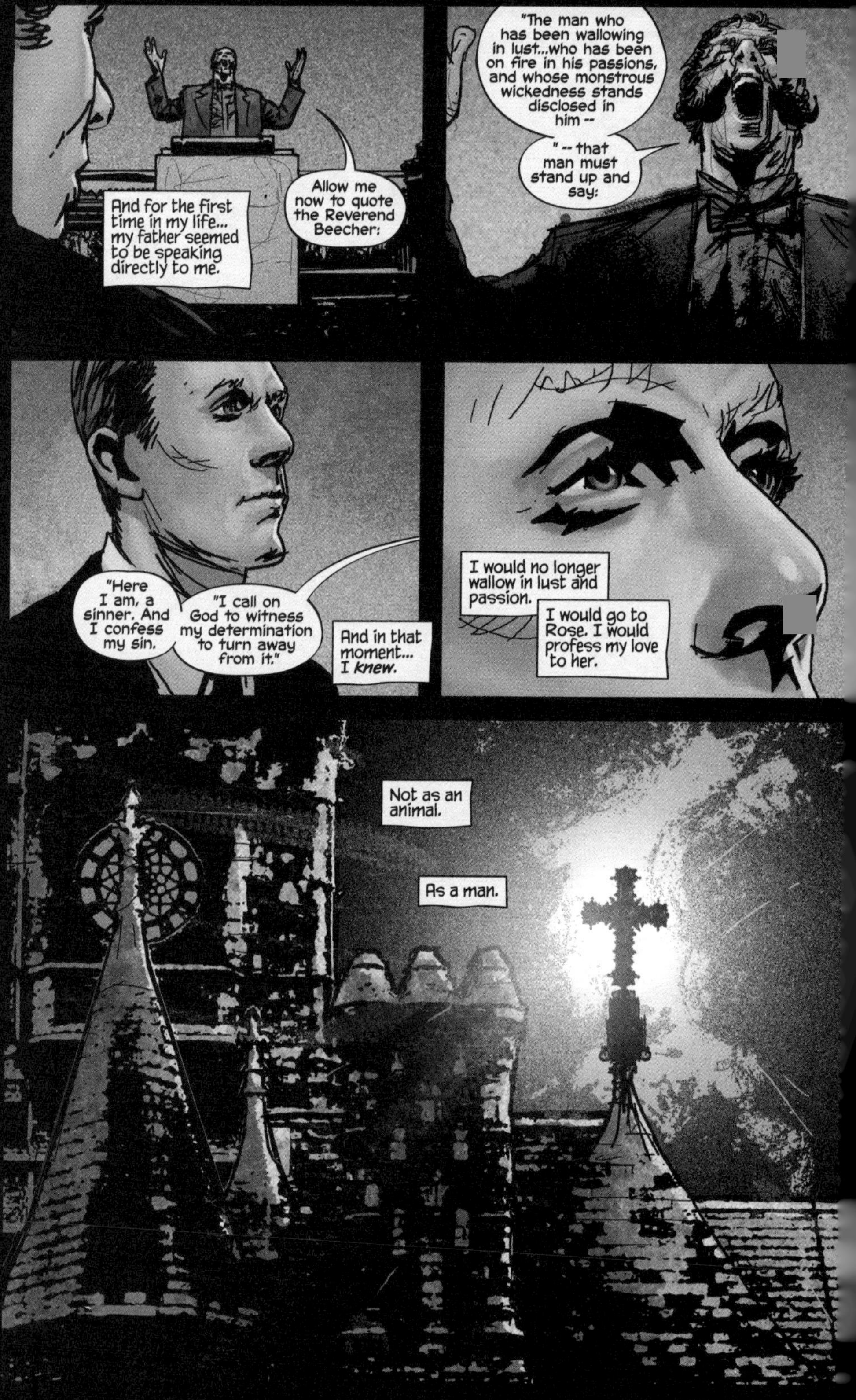
And for the first time in my life... my father seemed to be speaking directly to me.
Allow me now to quote the Reverend Beecher:
"The man who has been wallowing in lust...who has been on fire in his passions, and whose monstrous wickedness stands disclosed in him --
" -- that man must stand up and say:
"Here I am, a sinner. And I confess my sin.
"I call on God to witness my determination to turn away from it."
And in that moment... I *knew*.
I would no longer wallow in lust and passion.
I would go to Rose. I would profess my love to her.
Not as an animal.
As a man.

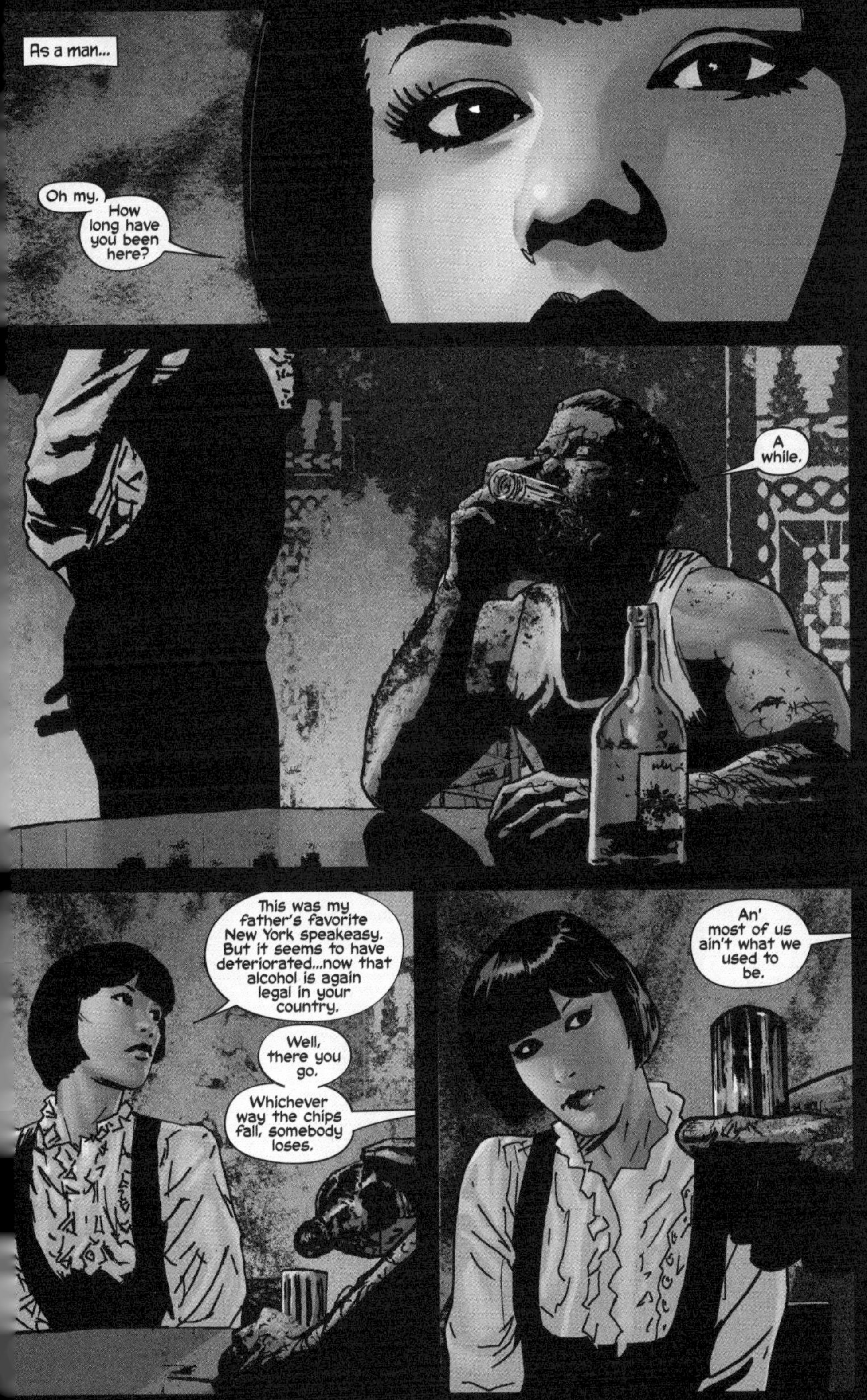
As a man...
Oh my. How long have you been here?
A while.
This was my father's favorite New York speakeasy. But it seems to have deteriorated...now that alcohol is again legal in your country.
Well, there you go.
Whichever way the chips fall, somebody loses.
An' most of us ain't what we used to be.

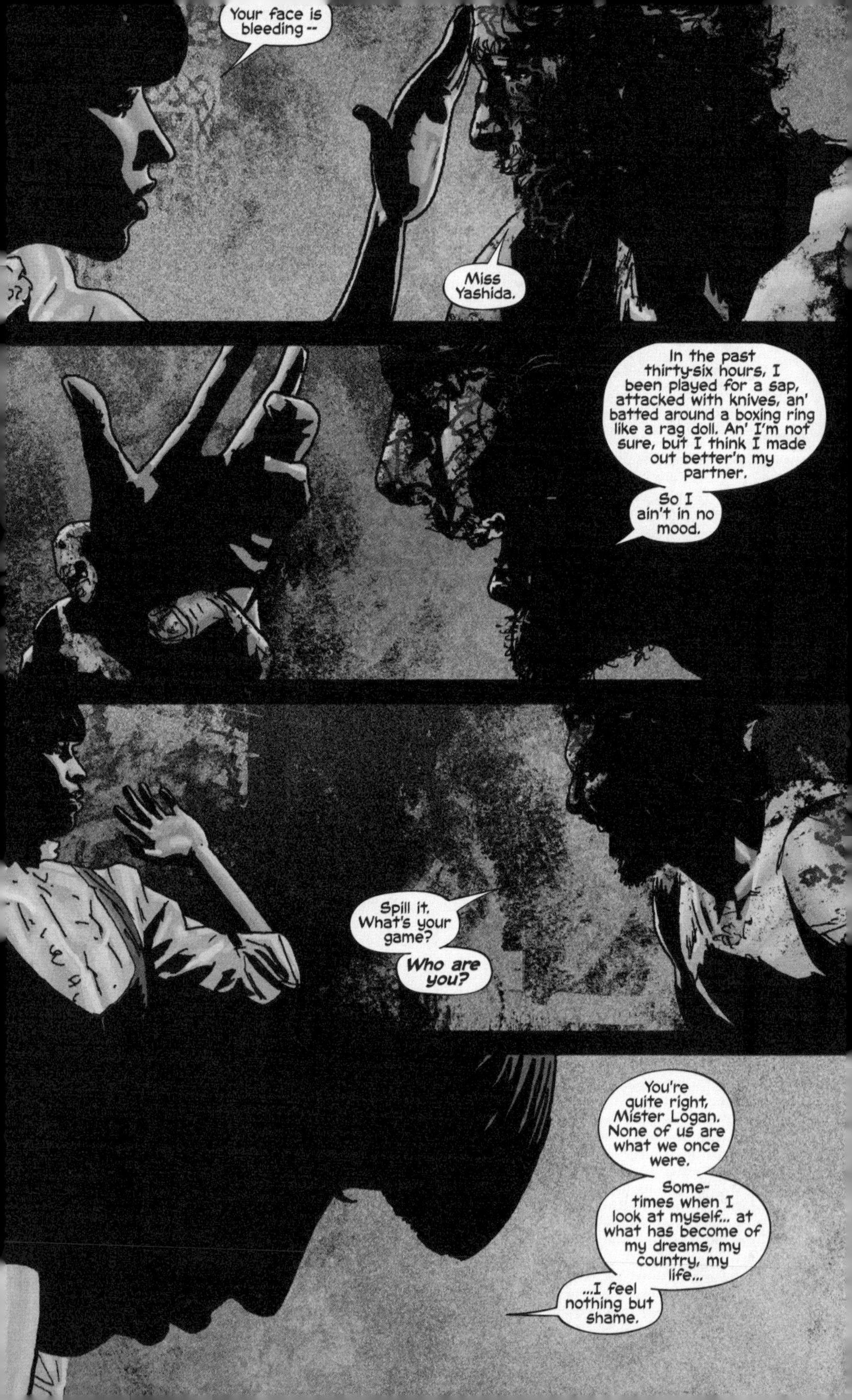
Your face is bleeding --
Miss Yashida.
In the past thirty-six hours, I been played for a sap, attacked with knives, an' batted around a boxing ring like a rag doll. An' I'm not sure, but I think I made out better'n my partner.
So I ain't in no mood.
Spill it. What's your game?
Who are you?
You're quite right, Mister Logan. None of us are what we once were.
Some-times when I look at myself... at what has become of my dreams, my country, my life...
...I feel nothing but shame.

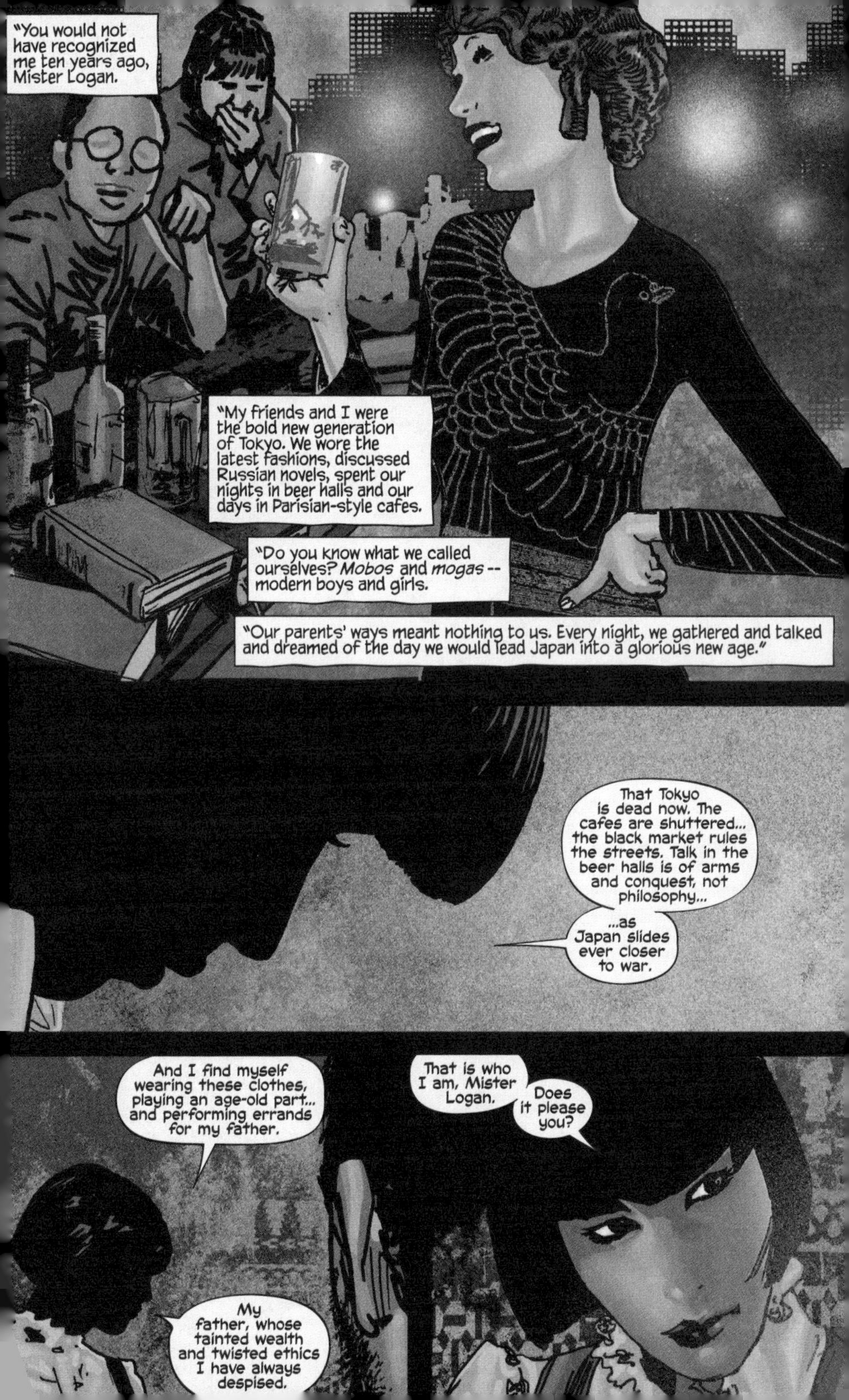
"You would not have recognized me ten years ago, Mister Logan.
"My friends and I were the bold new generation of Tokyo. We wore the latest fashions, discussed Russian novels, spent our nights in beer halls and our days in Parisian-style cafes.
"Do you know what we called ourselves? *Mobos* and *mogas* -- modern boys and girls.
"Our parents' ways meant nothing to us. Every night, we gathered and talked and dreamed of the day we would lead Japan into a glorious new age."
That Tokyo is dead now. The cafes are shuttered... the black market rules the streets. Talk in the beer halls is of arms and conquest, not philosophy...
...as Japan slides ever closer to war.
And I find myself wearing these clothes, playing an age-old part... and performing errands for my father.
My father, whose tainted wealth and twisted ethics I have always despised.
That is who I am, Mister Logan.
Does it please you?

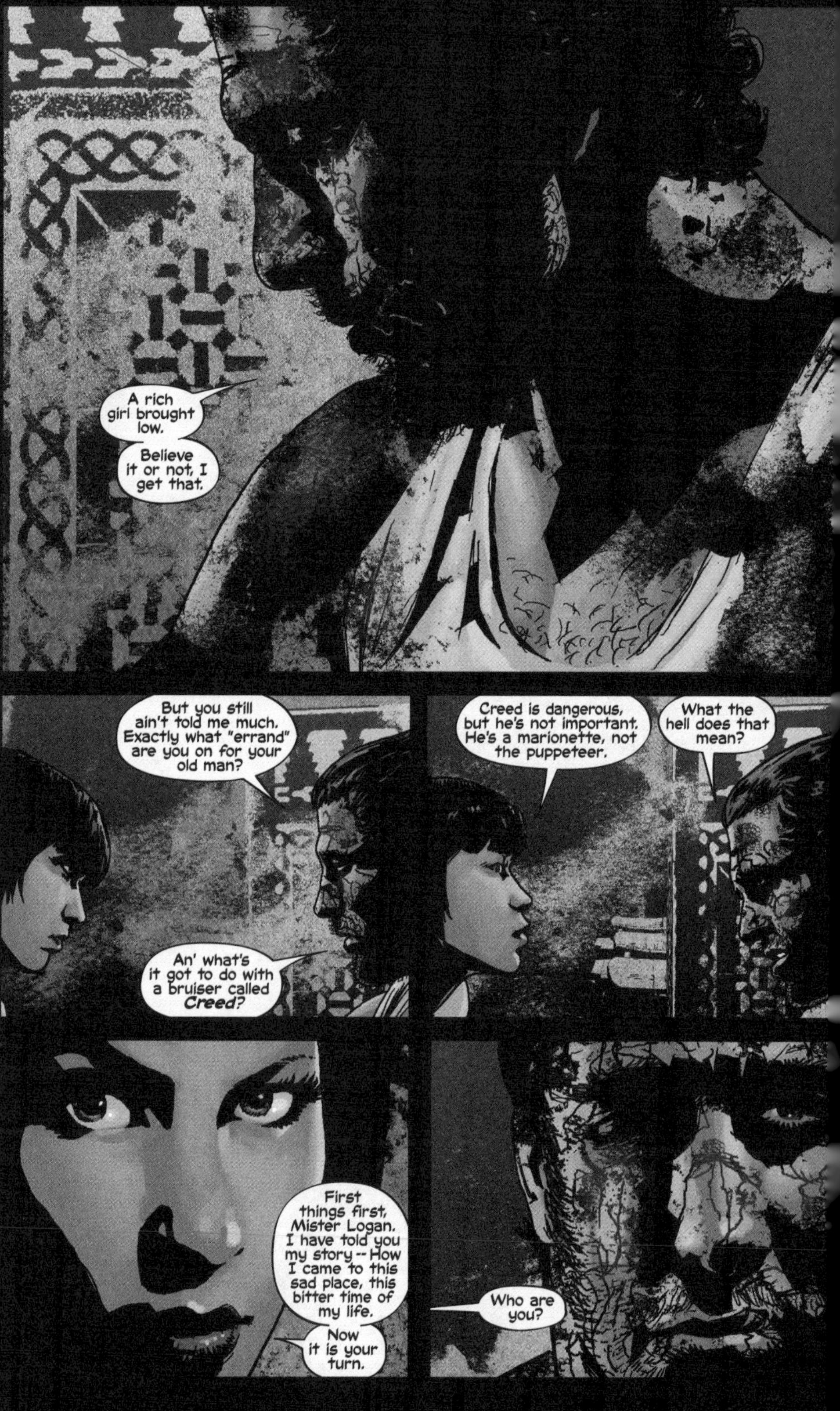
A rich girl brought low.
Believe it or not, I get that.
But you still ain't told me much. Exactly what "errand" are you on for your old man?
An' what's it got to do with a bruiser called *Creed*?
Creed is dangerous, but he's not important. He's a marionette, not the puppeteer.
What the hell does that mean?
First things first, Mister Logan. I have told you my story -- How I came to this sad place, this bitter time of my life.
Now it is your turn.
Who are you?

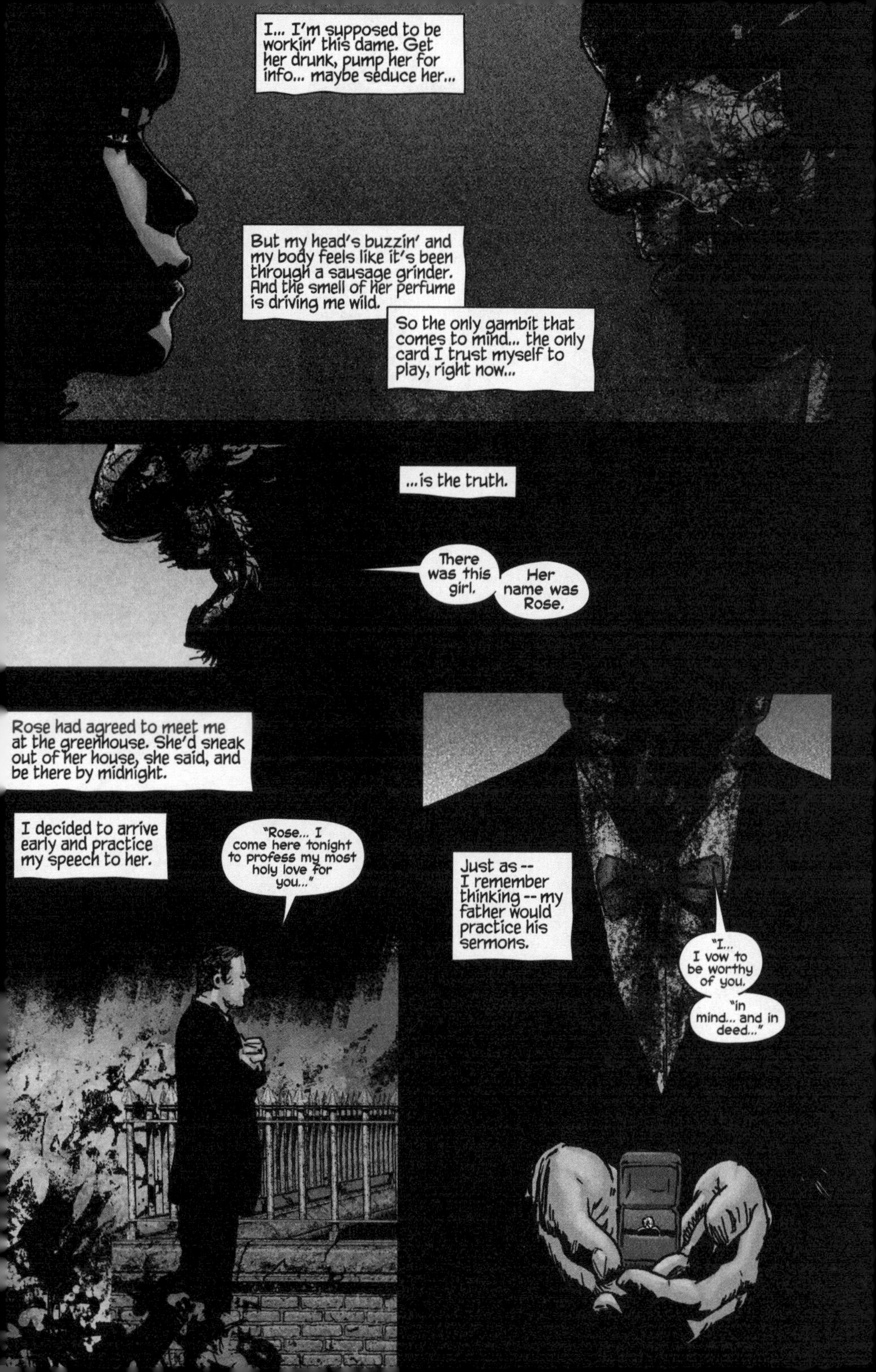
I... I'm supposed to be workin' this dame. Get her drunk, pump her for info... maybe seduce her...
But my head's buzzin' and my body feels like it's been through a sausage grinder. And the smell of her perfume is driving me wild.
So the only gambit that comes to mind... the only card I trust myself to play, right now...
...is the truth.
There was this girl.
Her name was Rose.
Rose had agreed to meet me at the greenhouse. She'd sneak out of her house, she said, and be there by midnight.
I decided to arrive early and practice my speech to her.
"Rose... I come here tonight to profess my most holy love for you..."
Just as -- I remember thinking -- my father would practice his sermons.
"I... I vow to be worthy of you.
"in mind... and in deed..."

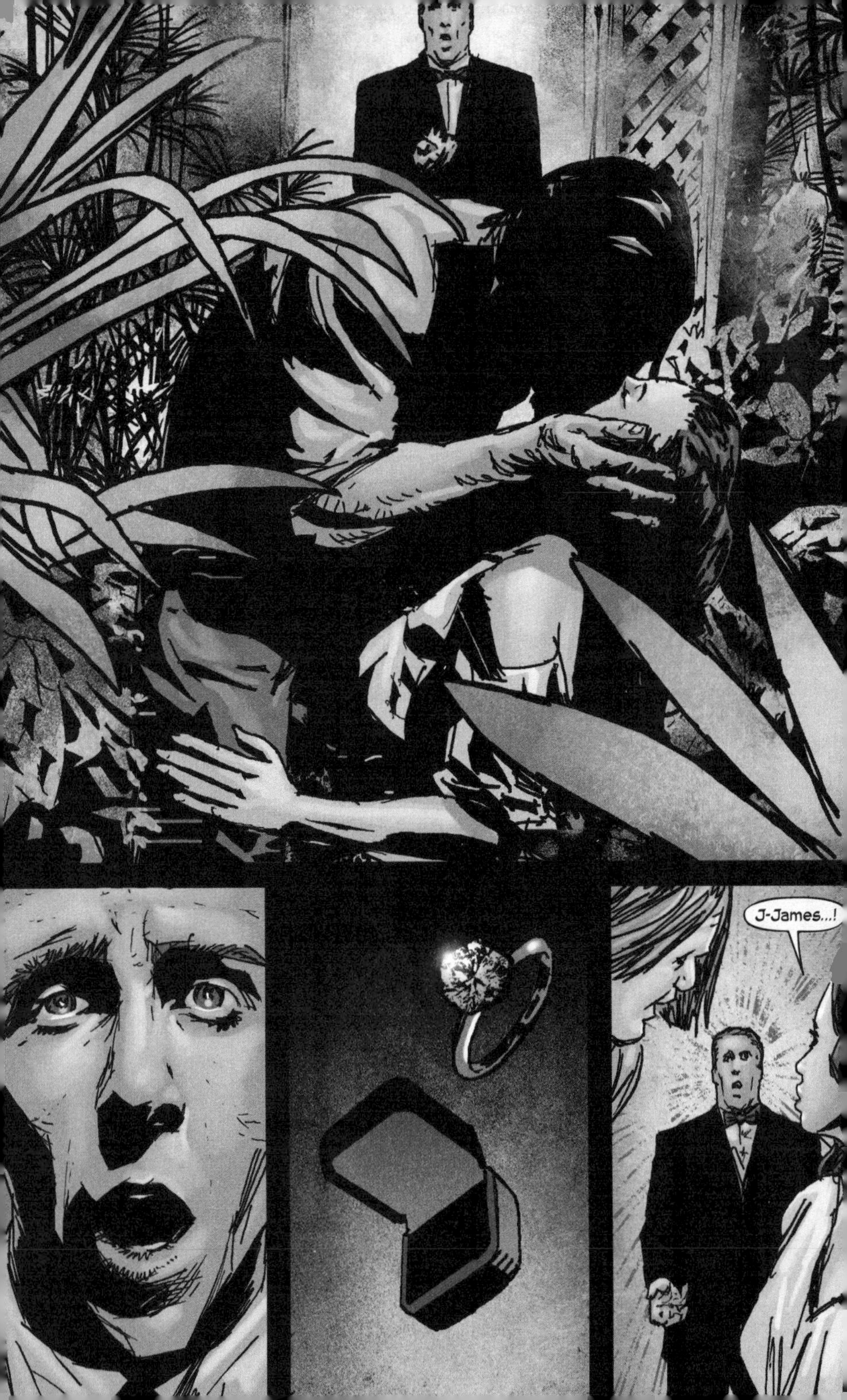
J-James...!

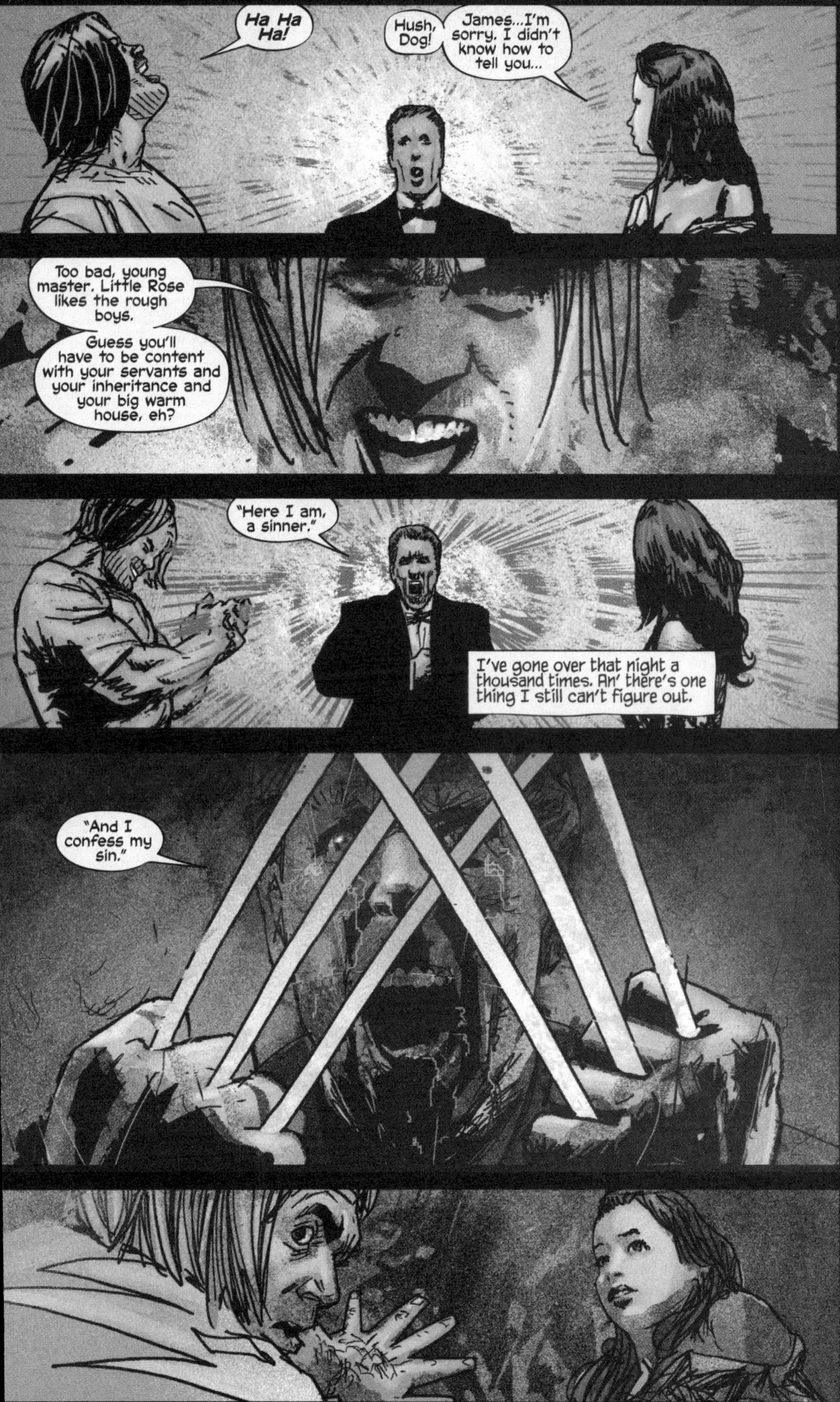
Ha Ha Ha!
Hush, Dog!
James...I'm sorry. I didn't know how to tell you...
Too bad, young master. Little Rose likes the rough boys.
Guess you'll have to be content with your servants and your inheritance and your big warm house, eh?
"Here I am, a sinner."
I've gone over that night a thousand times. An' there's one thing I still can't figure out.
"And I confess my sin."

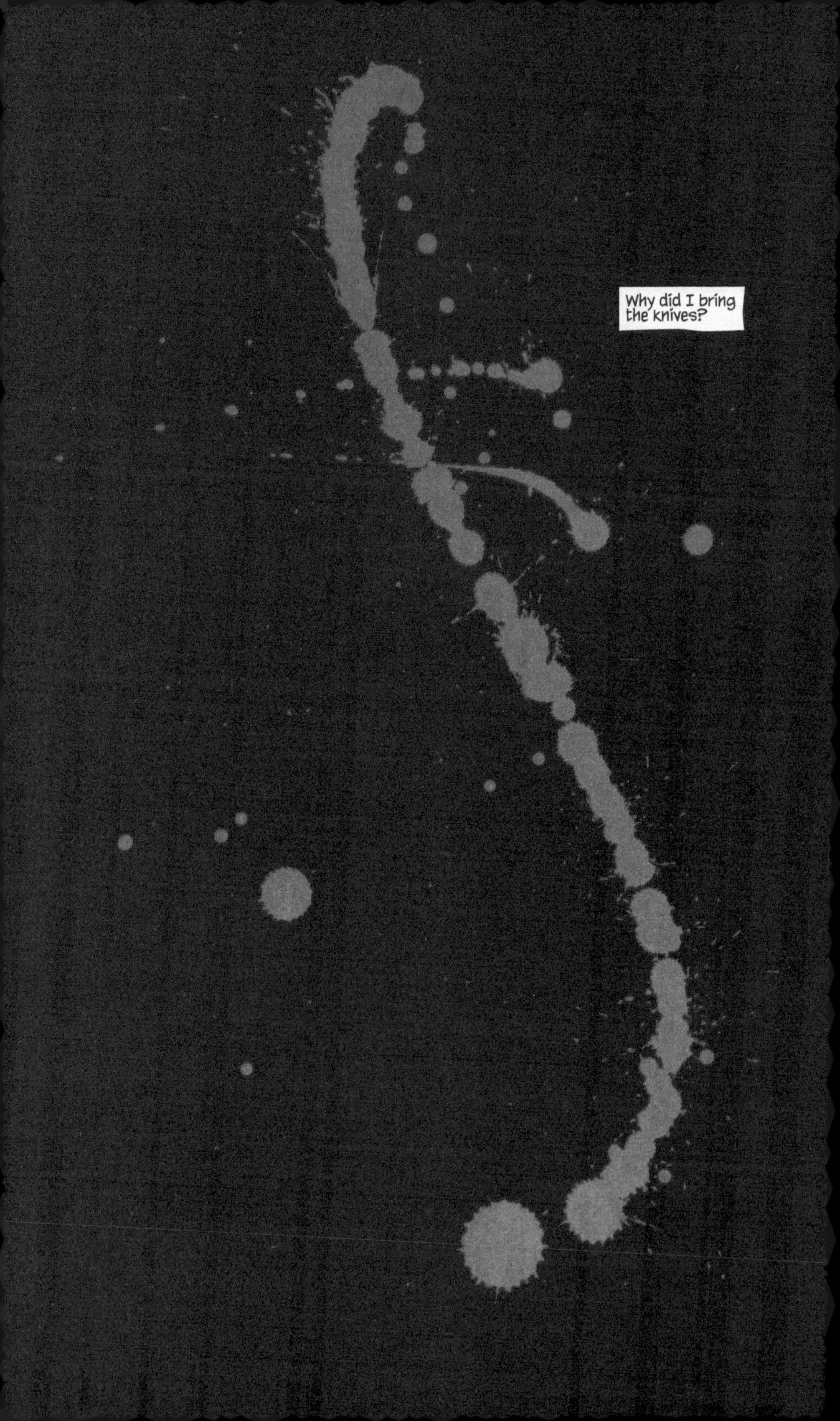
Why did I bring the knives?

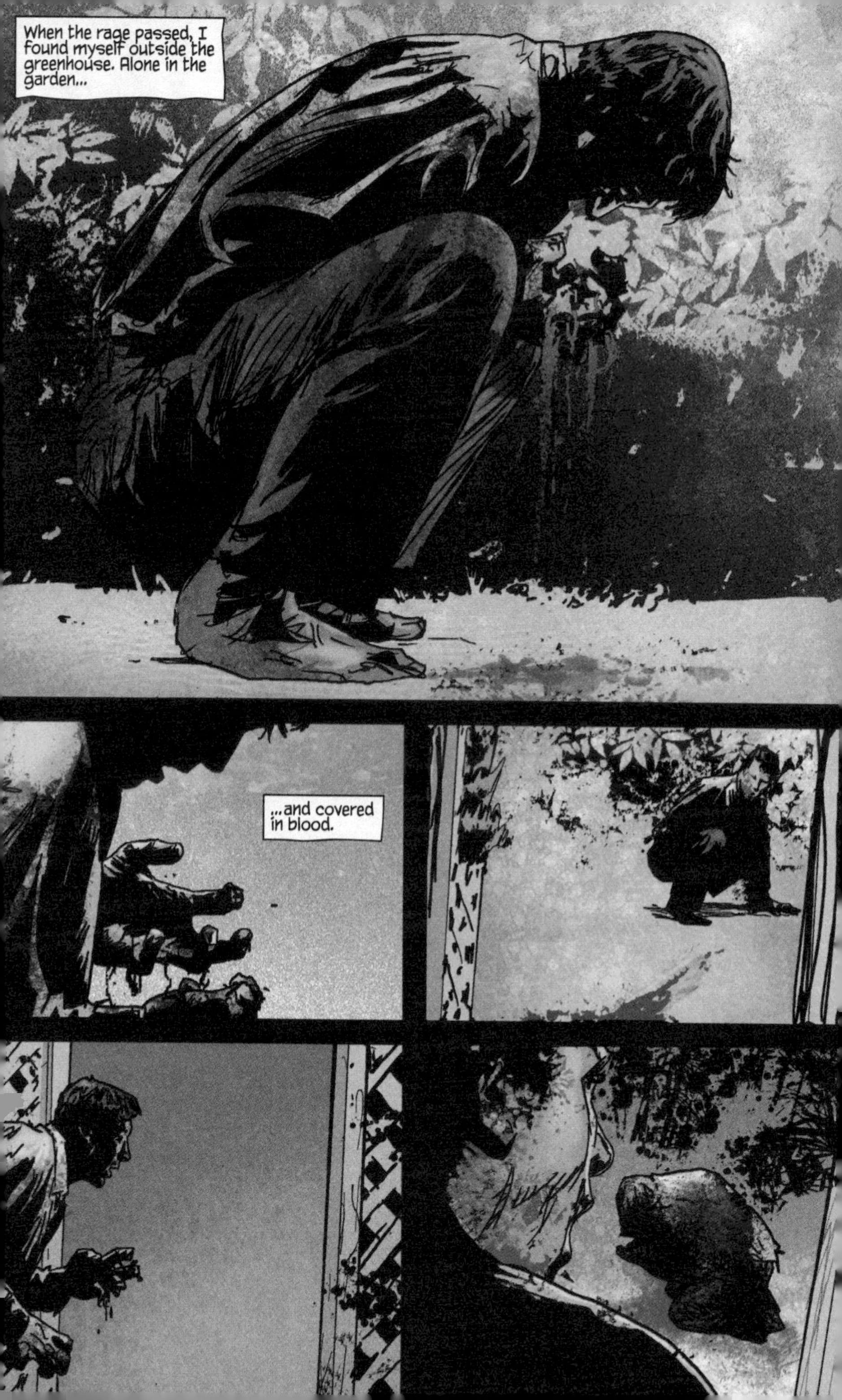
When the rage passed, I found myself outside the greenhouse. Alone in the garden...
...and covered in blood.

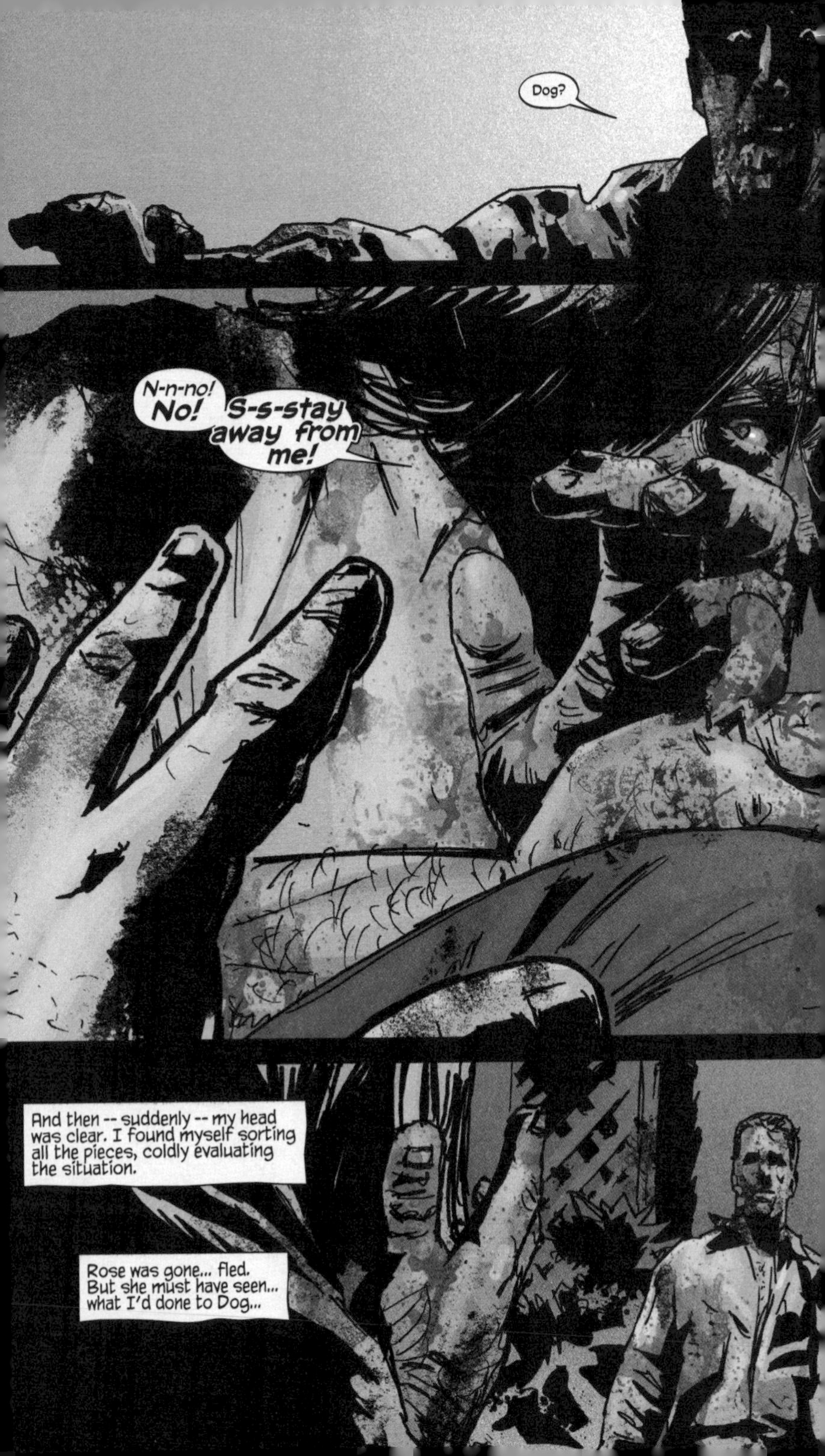
Dog?
N-n-no! No!
S-s-stay away from me!
And then -- suddenly -- my head was clear. I found myself sorting all the pieces, coldly evaluating the situation.
Rose was gone... fled. But she must have seen... what I'd done to Dog...

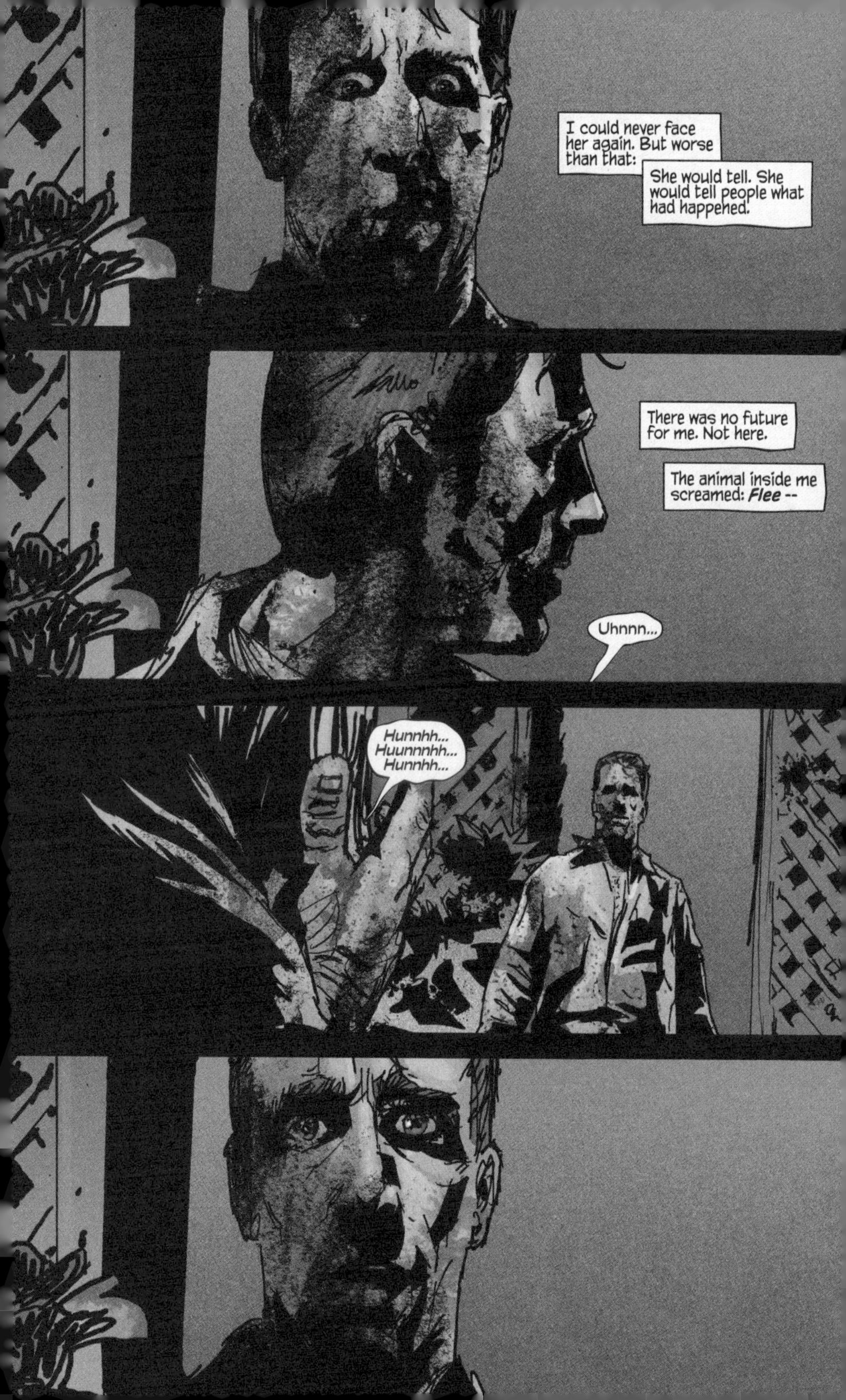
I could never face her again. But worse than that:
She would tell. She would tell people what had happened.
There was no future for me. Not here.
The animal inside me screamed: ***Flee*** --
Uhnnn...
Hunnhh...
Huunnnhh...
Hunnhh...

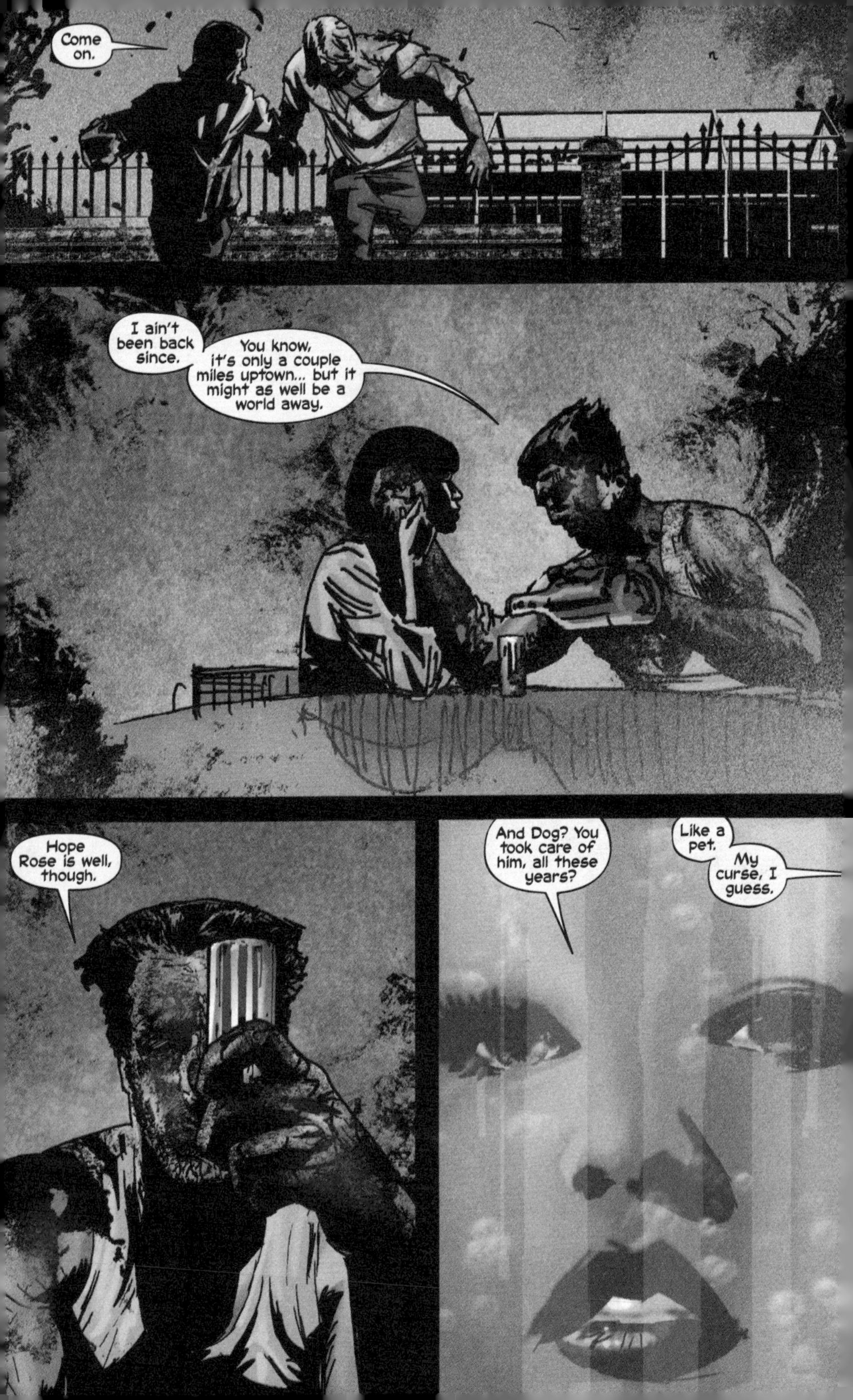
Come on.
I ain't been back since.
You know, it's only a couple miles uptown... but it might as well be a world away.
Hope Rose is well, though.
And Dog? You took care of him, all these years?
Like a pet.
My curse, I guess.

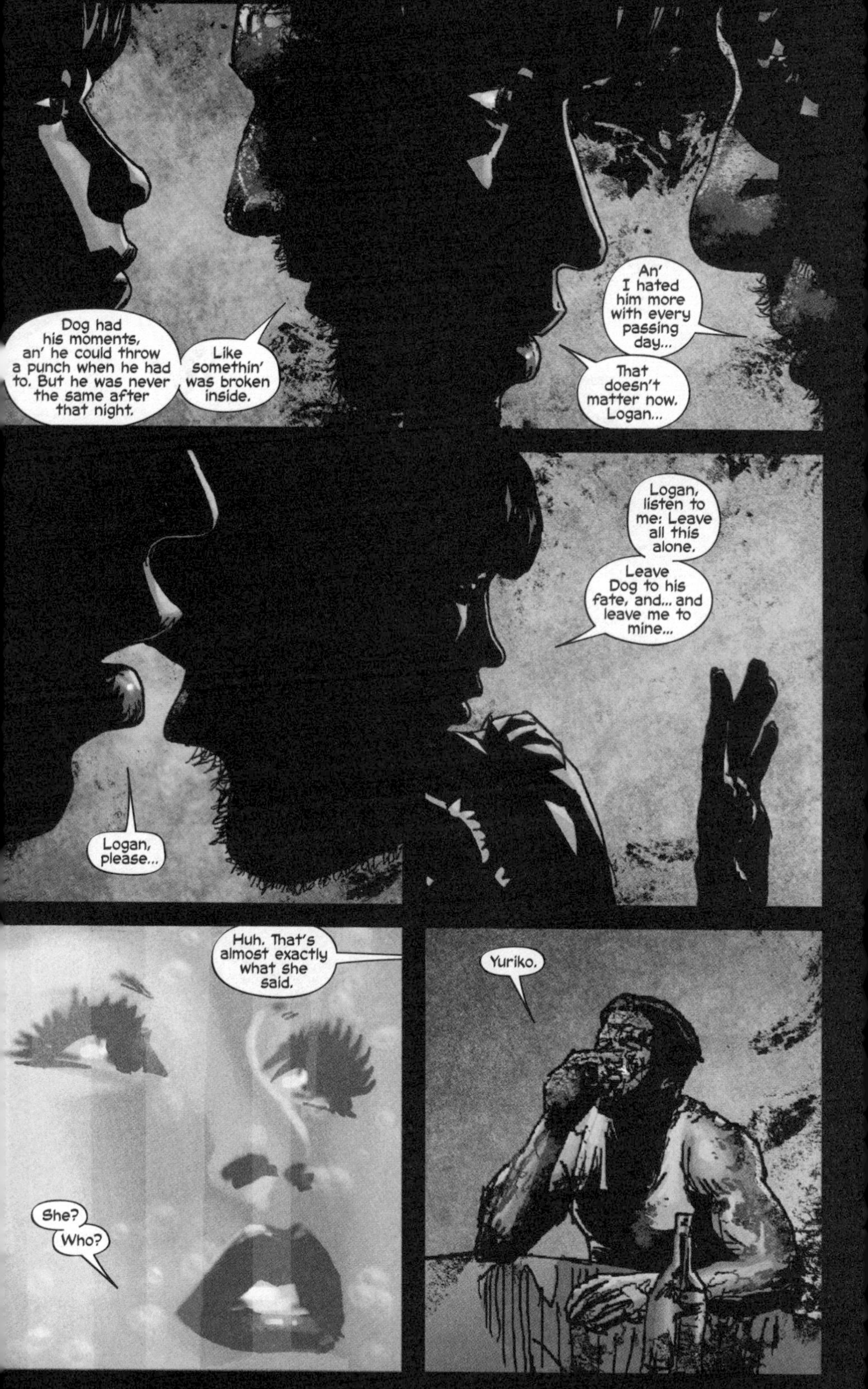
Dog had his moments, an' he could throw a punch when he had to. But he was never the same after that night.
Like somethin' was broken inside.
An' I hated him more with every passing day...
That doesn't matter now, Logan...
Logan, please...
Logan, listen to me: Leave all this alone.
Leave Dog to his fate, and... and leave me to mine...
Huh. That's almost exactly what she said.
She?
Who?
Yuriko.

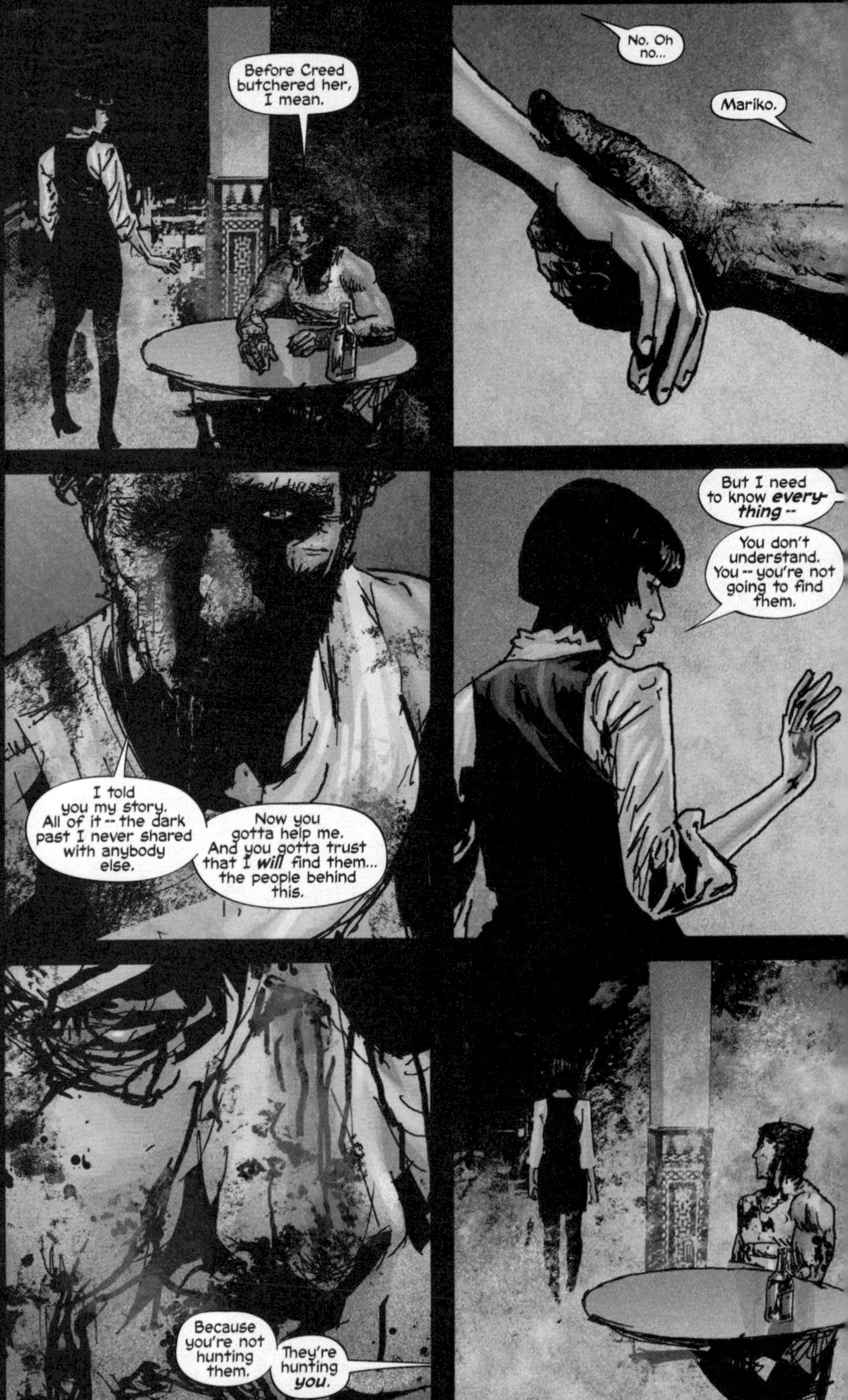

Before Creed butchered her, I mean.
No. Oh no...
Mariko.
I told you my story. All of it -- the dark past I never shared with anybody else.
Now you gotta help me. And you gotta trust that I *will* find them... the people behind this.
But I need to know *every-thing* --
You don't understand. You -- you're not going to find them.
Because you're not hunting them.
They're hunting *you*.

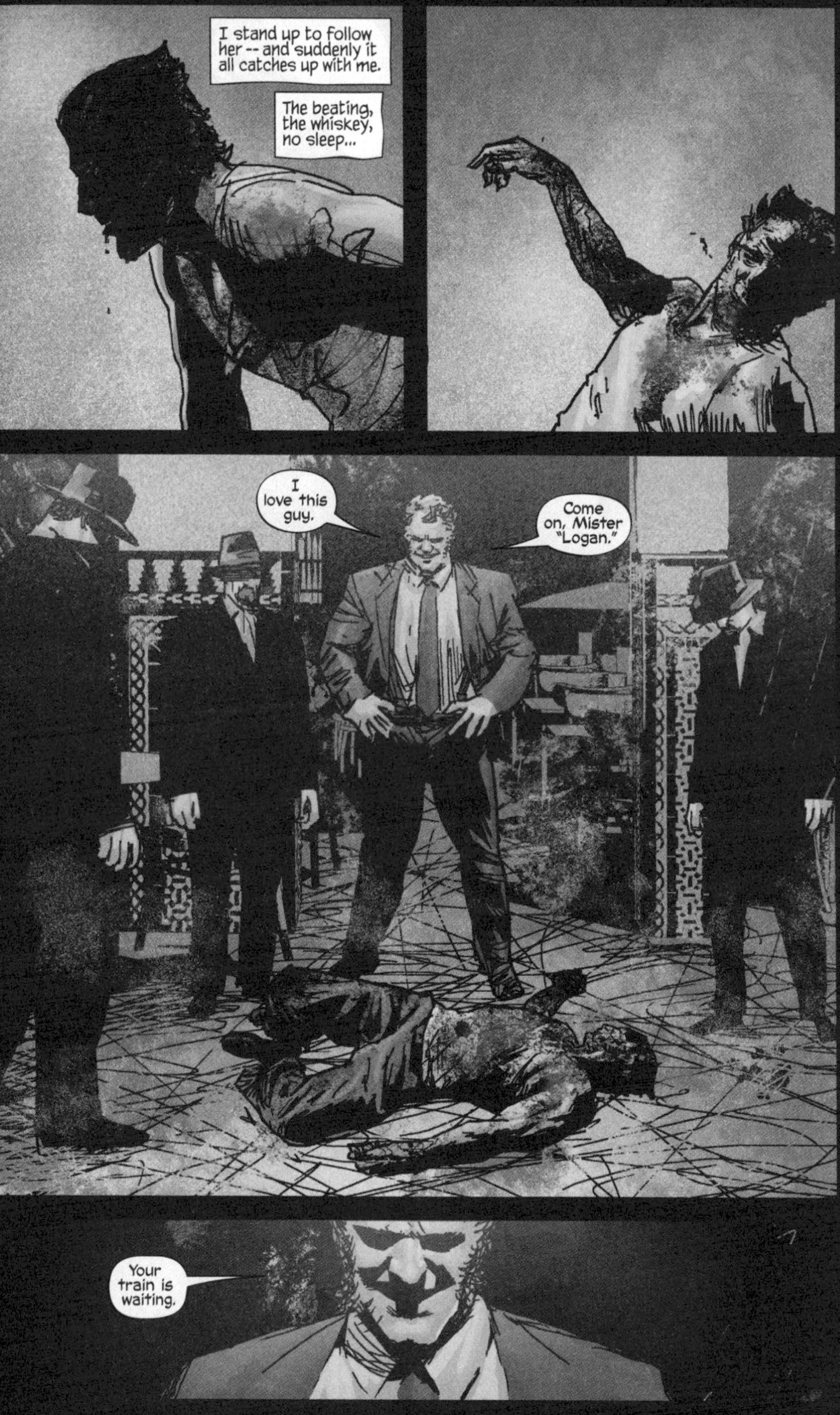
I stand up to follow her -- and suddenly it all catches up with me.
The beating, the whiskey, no sleep...
I love this guy.
Come on, Mister "Logan."
Your train is waiting.

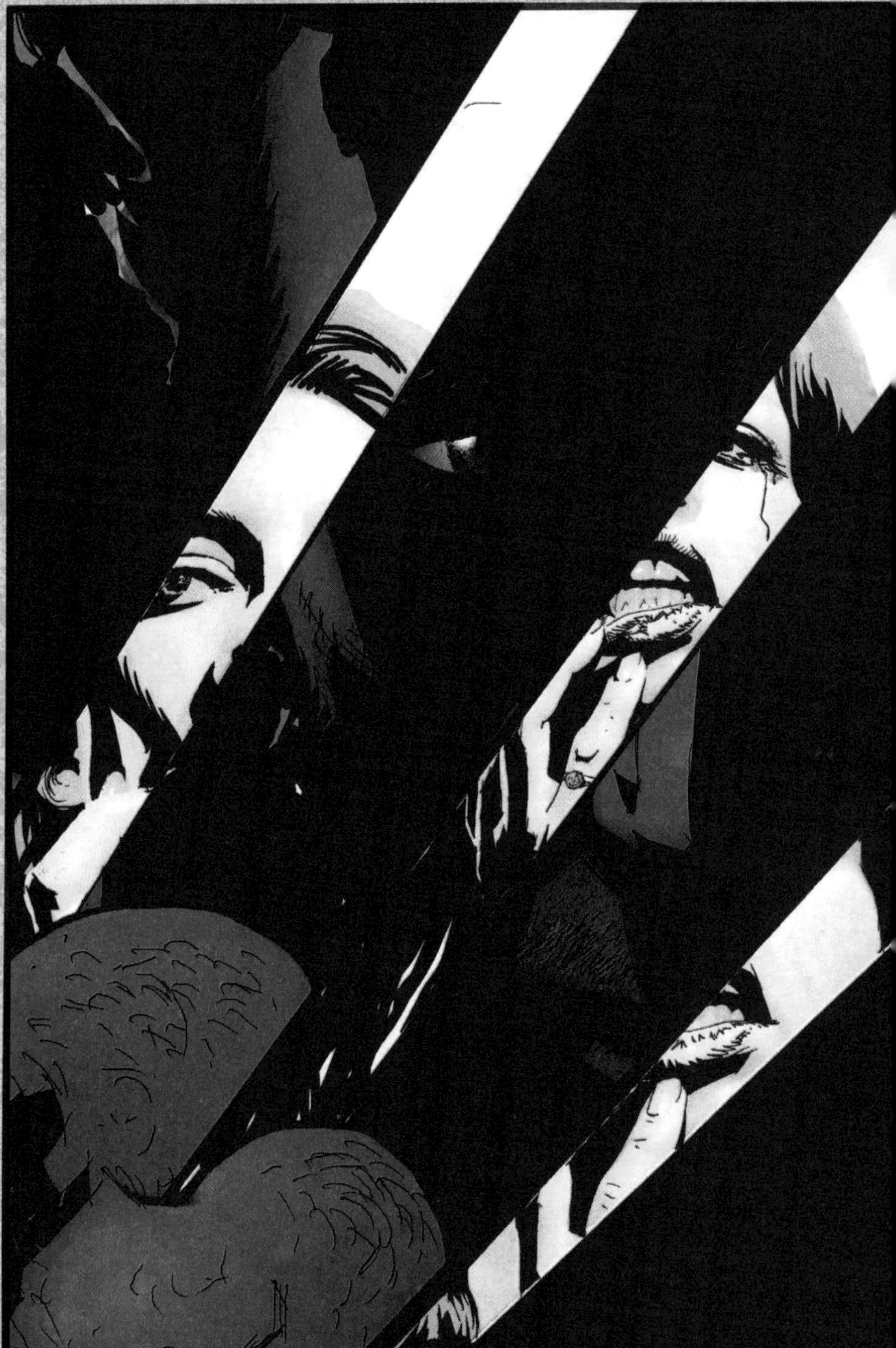

FOUR

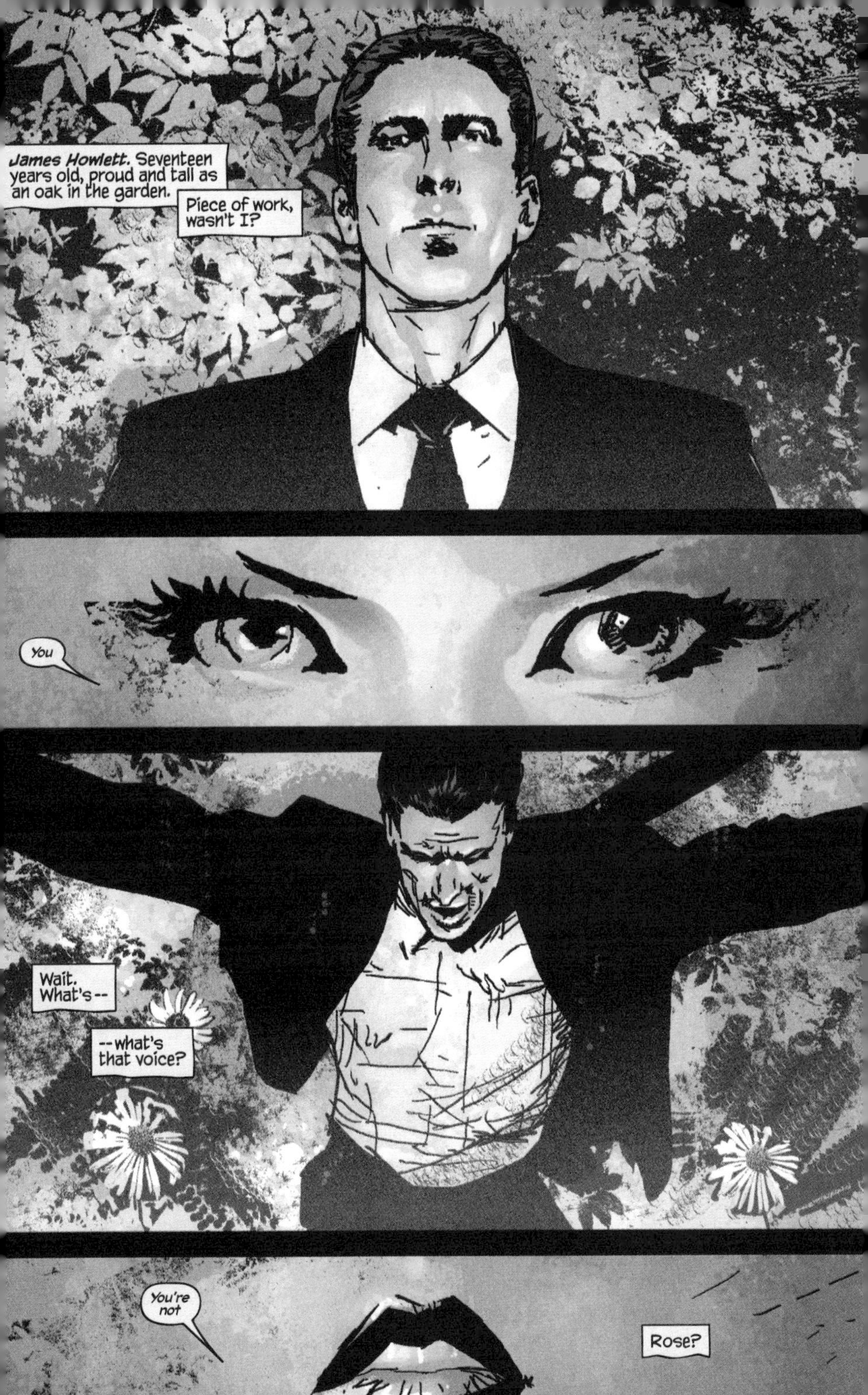
James Howlett. Seventeen years old, proud and tall as an oak in the garden.
Piece of work, wasn't I?
You
Wait. What's--
--what's that voice?
You're not
Rose?

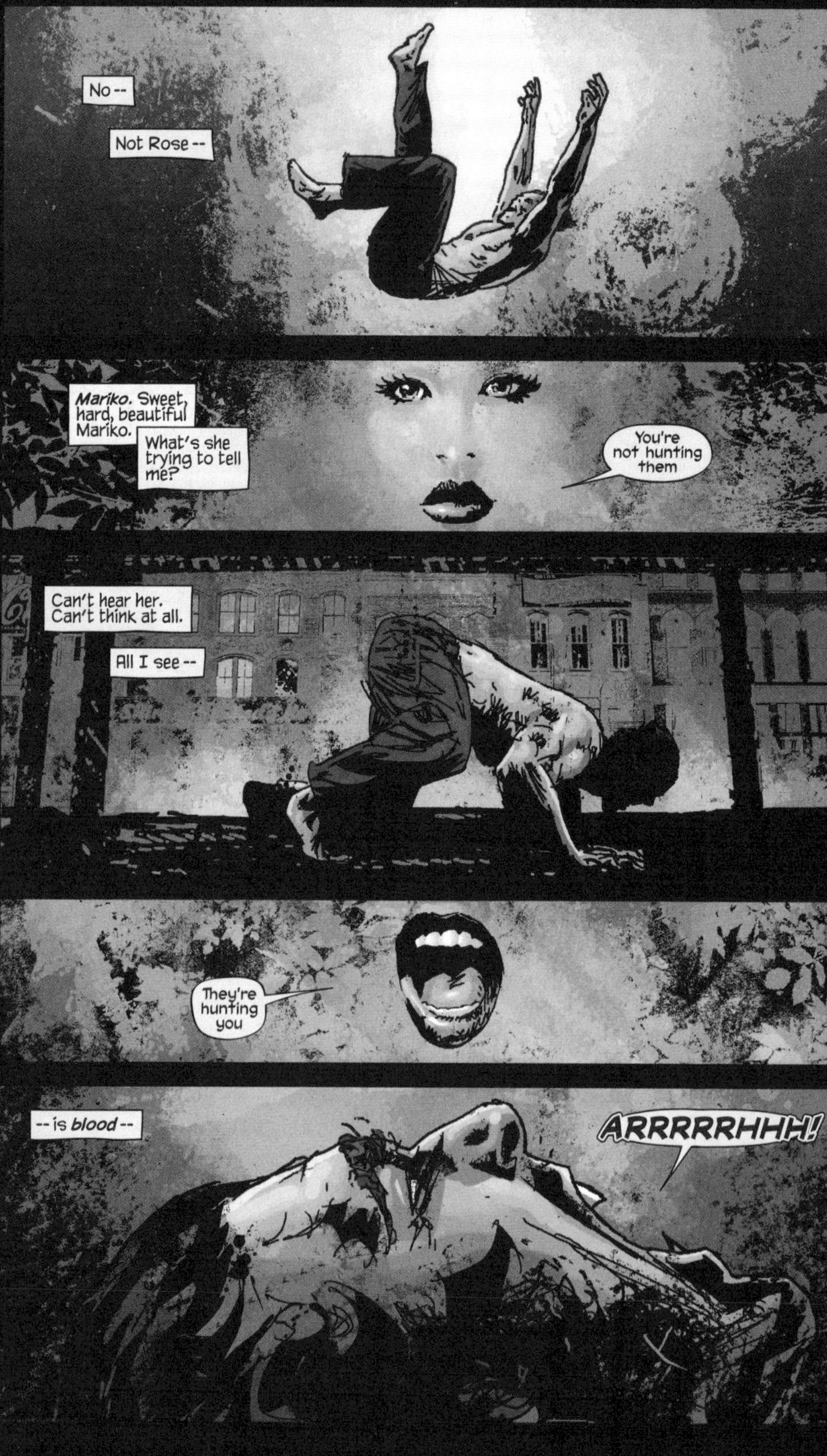
No --
Not Rose --
Mariko. Sweet, hard, beautiful Mariko.
What's she trying to tell me?
You're not hunting them
Can't hear her. Can't think at all.
All I see --
They're hunting you
-- is *blood* --
ARRRRRHHH!

WOLVERINE NOIR

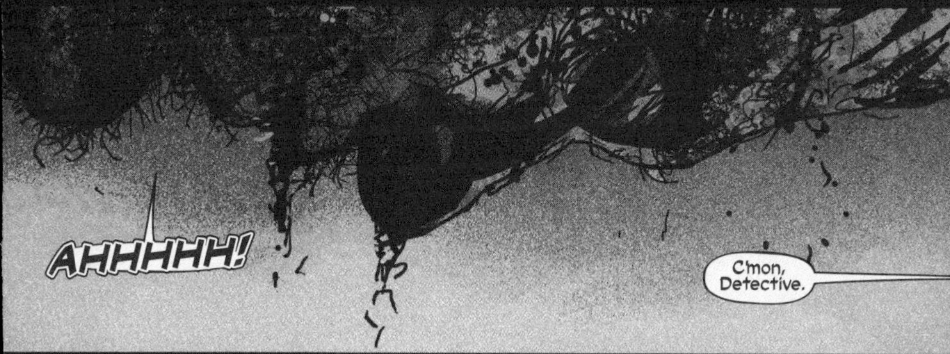

AHHHHH!
C'mon, Detective.

4: IN THE GARDEN

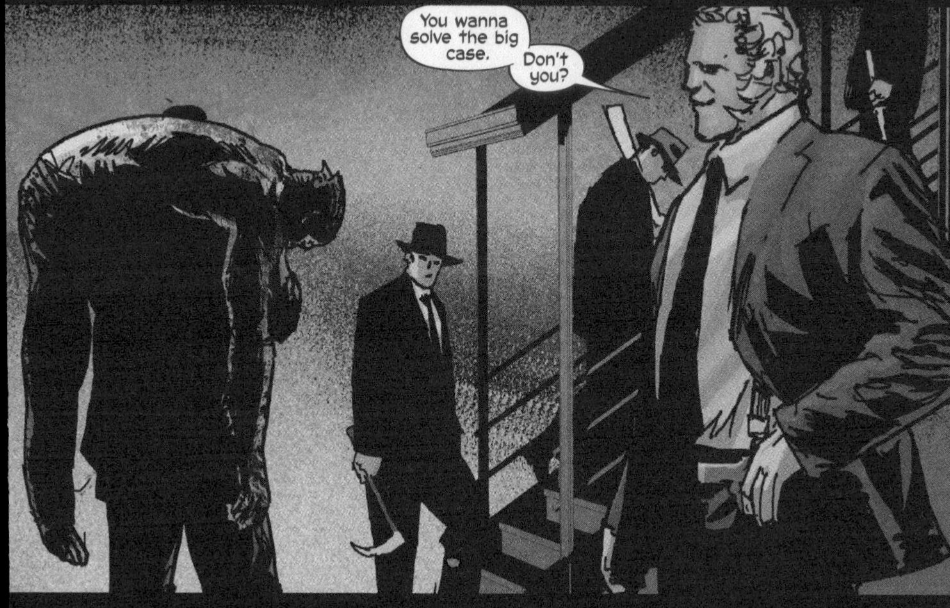

You wanna solve the big case.
Don't you?

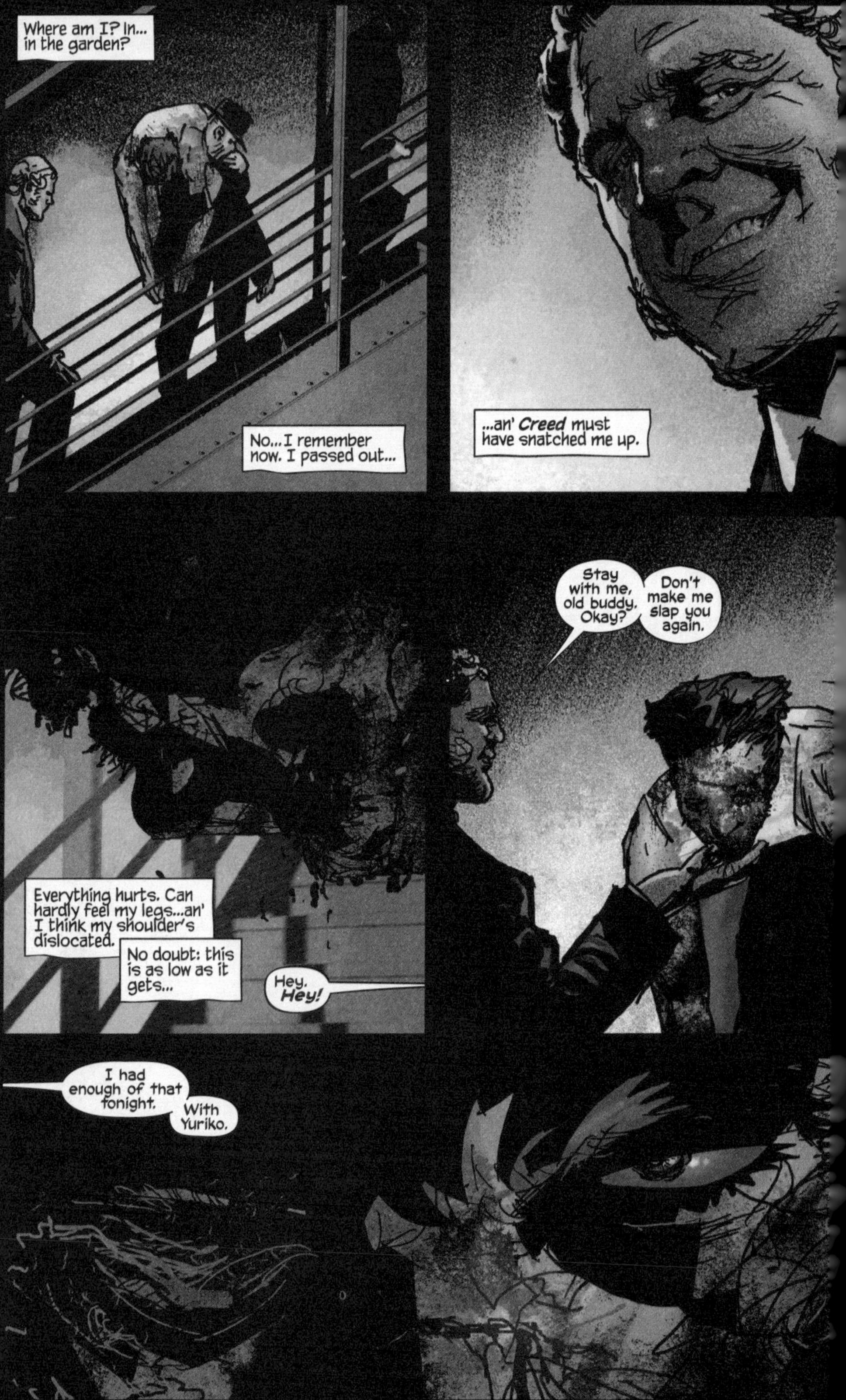
Where am I? In... in the garden?
No...I remember now. I passed out...
...an' Creed must have snatched me up.
Everything hurts. Can hardly feel my legs...an' I think my shoulder's dislocated.
No doubt: this is as low as it gets...
Hey. Hey!
Stay with me, old buddy. Okay?
Don't make me slap you again.
I had enough of that tonight.
With Yuriko.

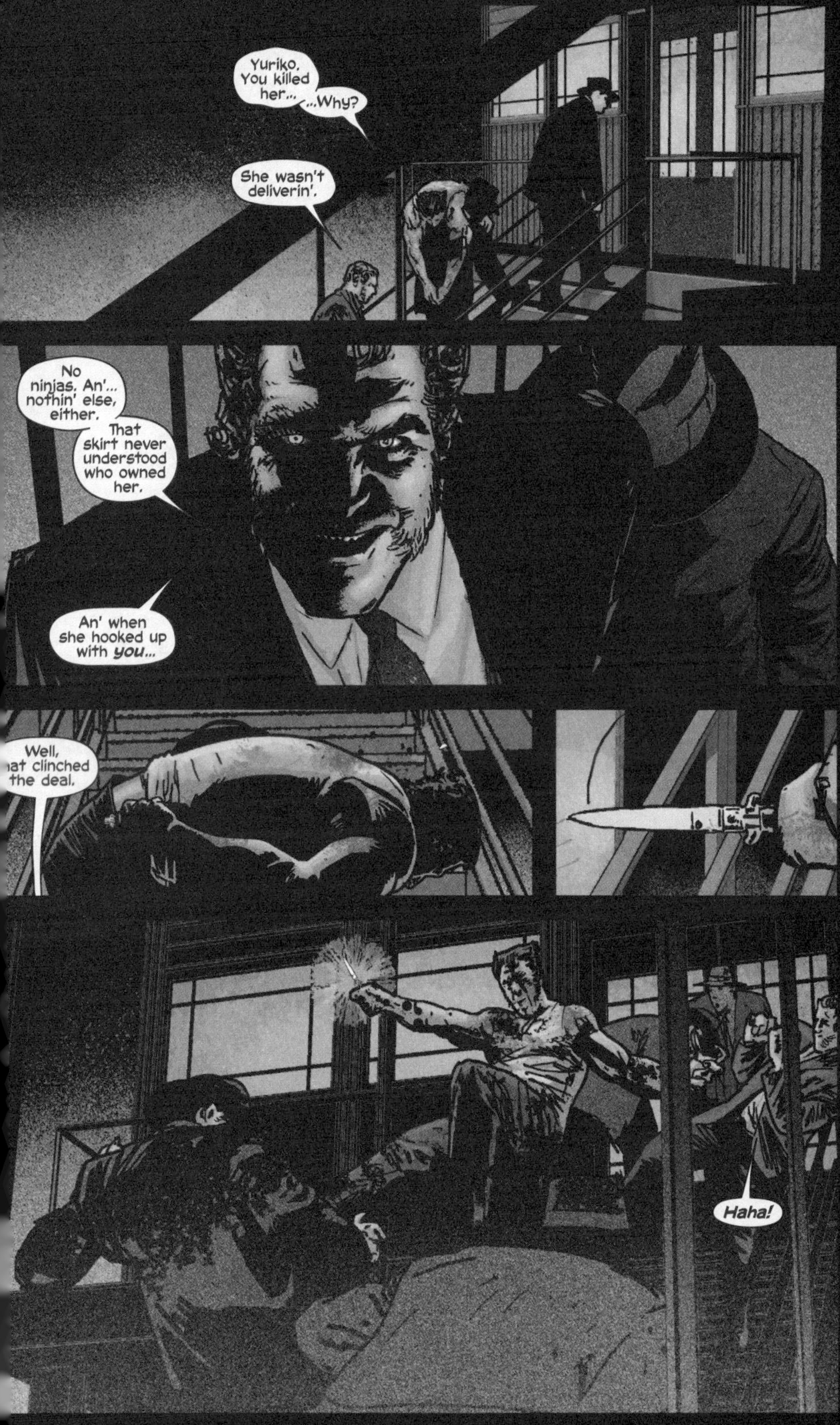
Yuriko. You killed her...
...Why?
She wasn't deliverin'.
No ninjas. An'... nothin' else, either.
That skirt never understood who owned her.
An' when she hooked up with *you*...
Well, hat clinched the deal.
Haha!

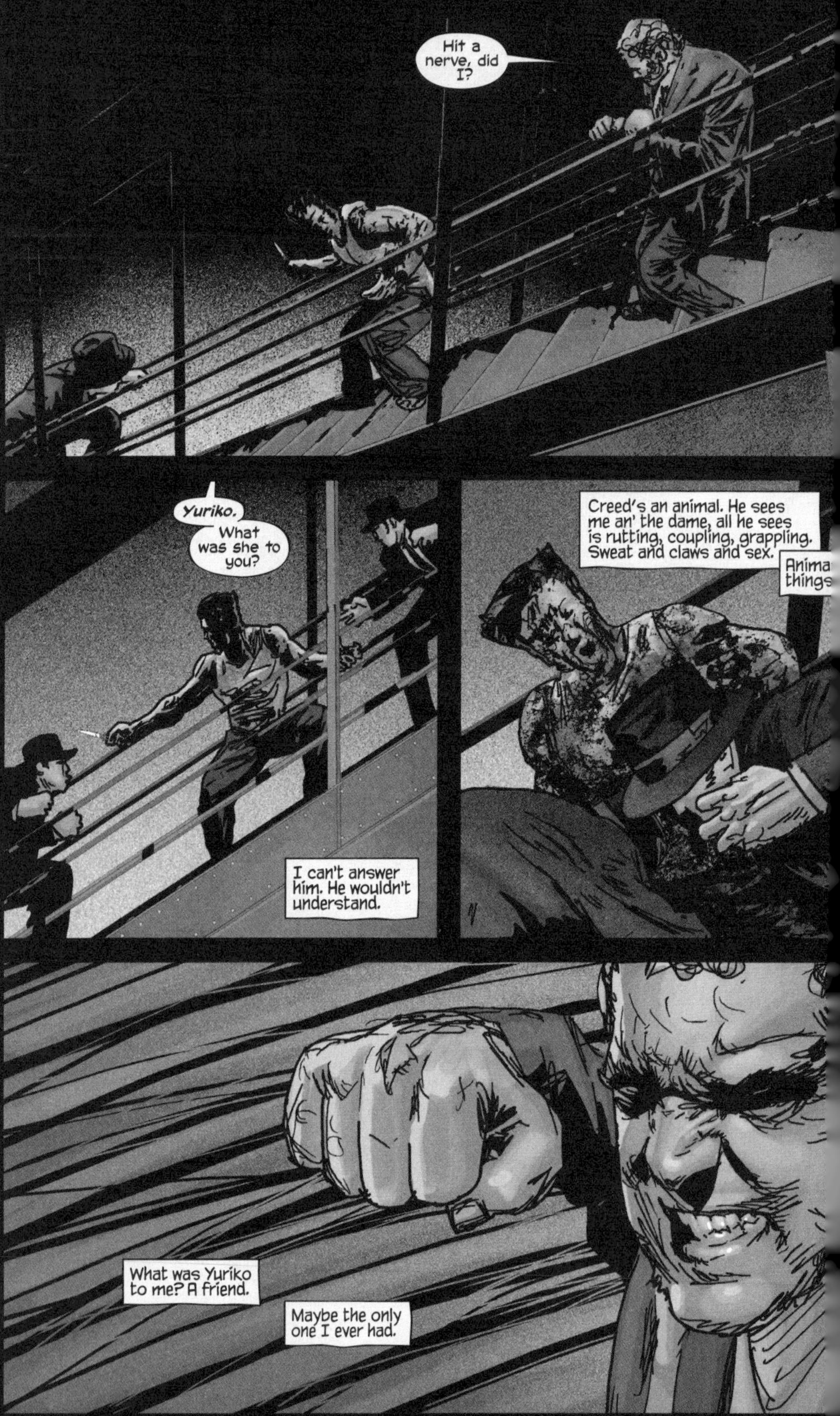
Hit a nerve, did I?
Yuriko. What was she to you?
I can't answer him. He wouldn't understand.
Creed's an animal. He sees me an' the dame, all he sees is rutting, coupling, grappling. Sweat and claws and sex.
What was Yuriko to me? A friend.
Maybe the only one I ever had.

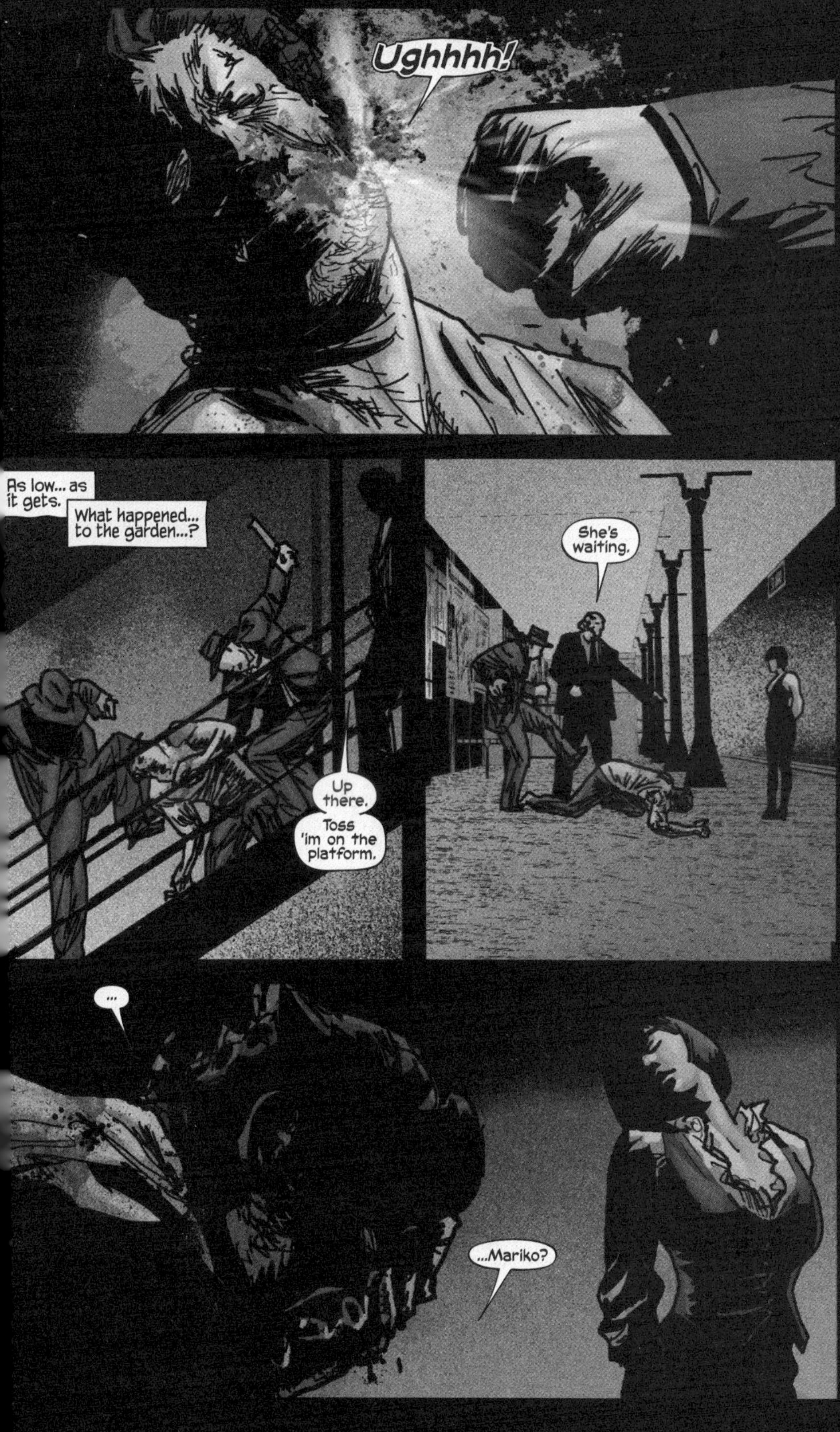

Ughhhh!
As low... as it gets.
What happened... to the garden...?
Up there.
Toss 'im on the platform.
She's waiting.
...
...Mariko?

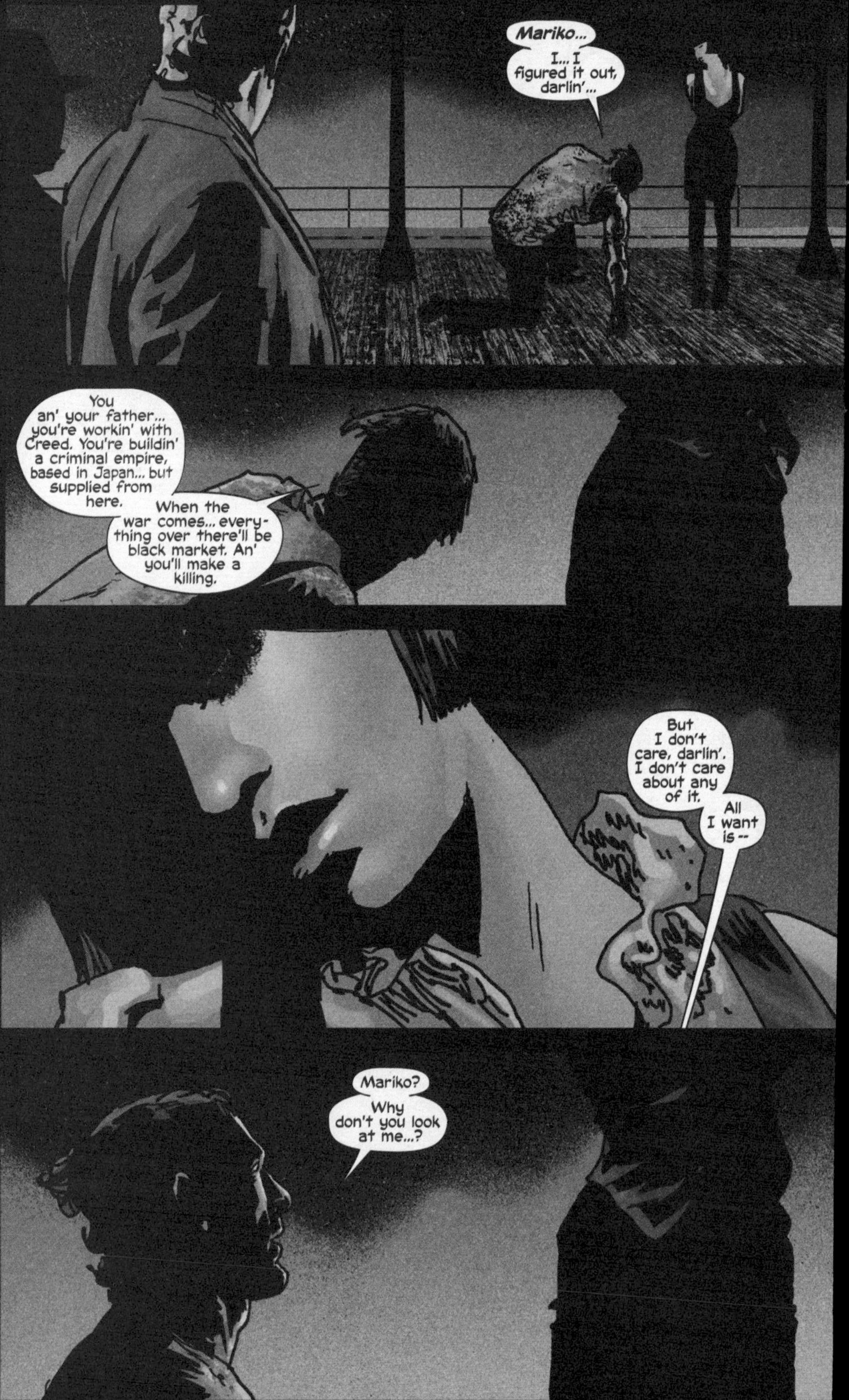
Mariko...
I... I figured it out, darlin'...
You an' your father... you're workin' with Creed. You're buildin' a criminal empire, based in Japan... but supplied from here.
When the war comes... every-thing over there'll be black market. An' you'll make a killing.
But I don't care, darlin'. I don't care about any of it.
All I want is --
Mariko?
Why don't you look at me...?

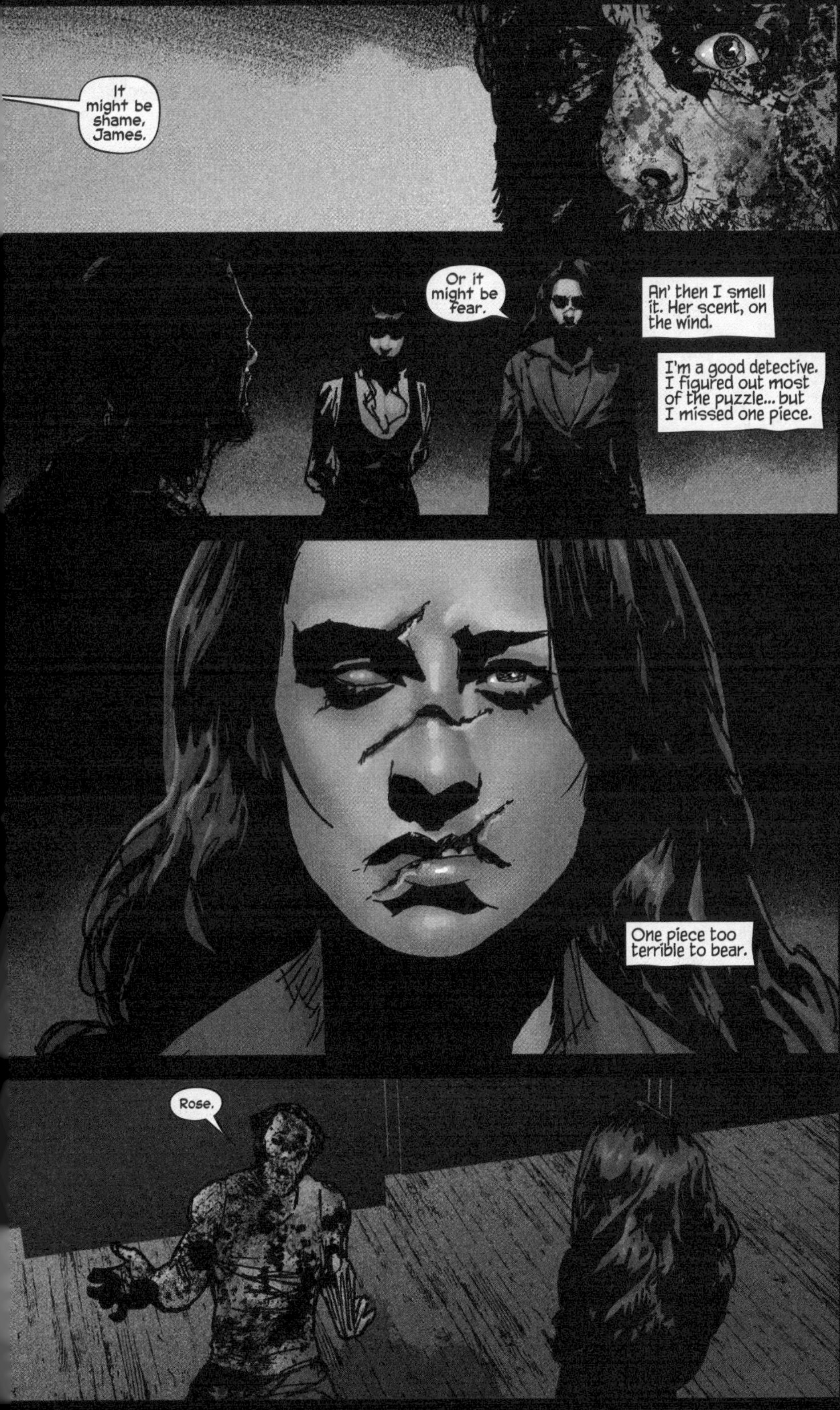
It might be shame, James.
Or it might be fear.
An' then I smell it. Her scent, on the wind.
I'm a good detective. I figured out most of the puzzle... but I missed one piece.
One piece too terrible to bear.
Rose.

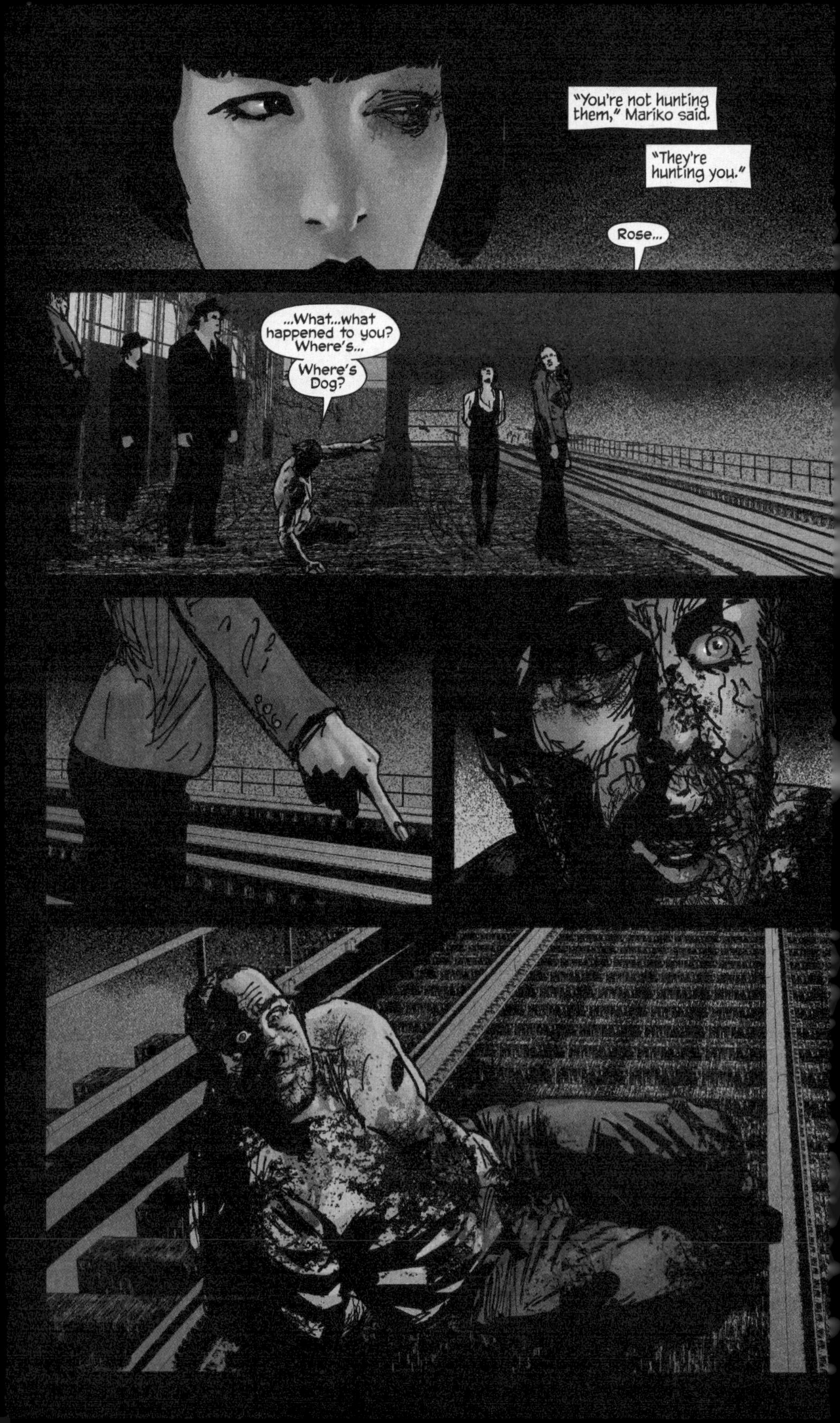
"You're not hunting them," Mariko said.
"They're hunting you."
Rose...
...What...what happened to you? Where's...
Where's Dog?

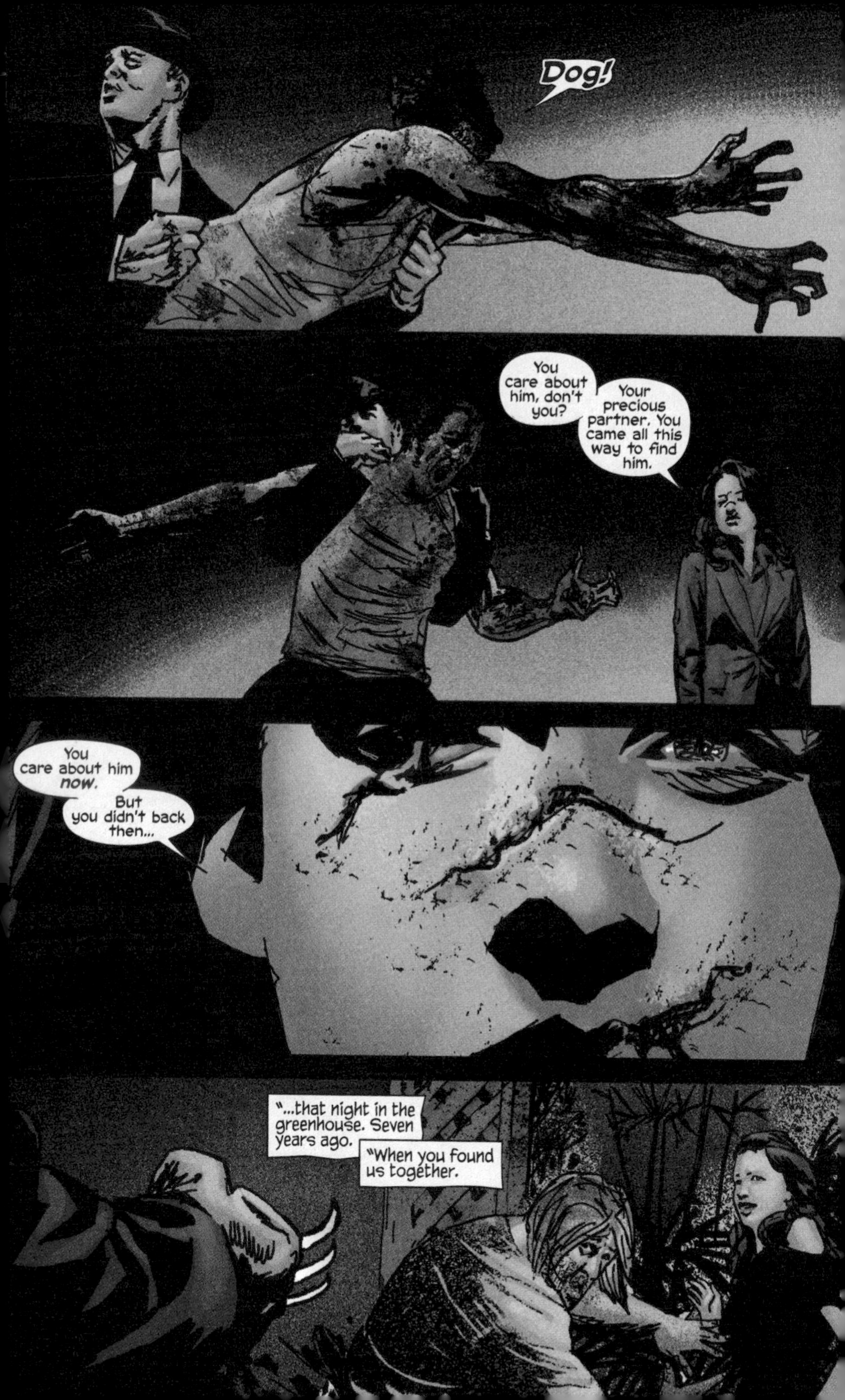
Dog!
You care about him, don't you?
Your precious partner. You came all this way to find him.
You care about him *now*.
But you didn't back then...
"...that night in the greenhouse. Seven years ago.
"When you found us together.

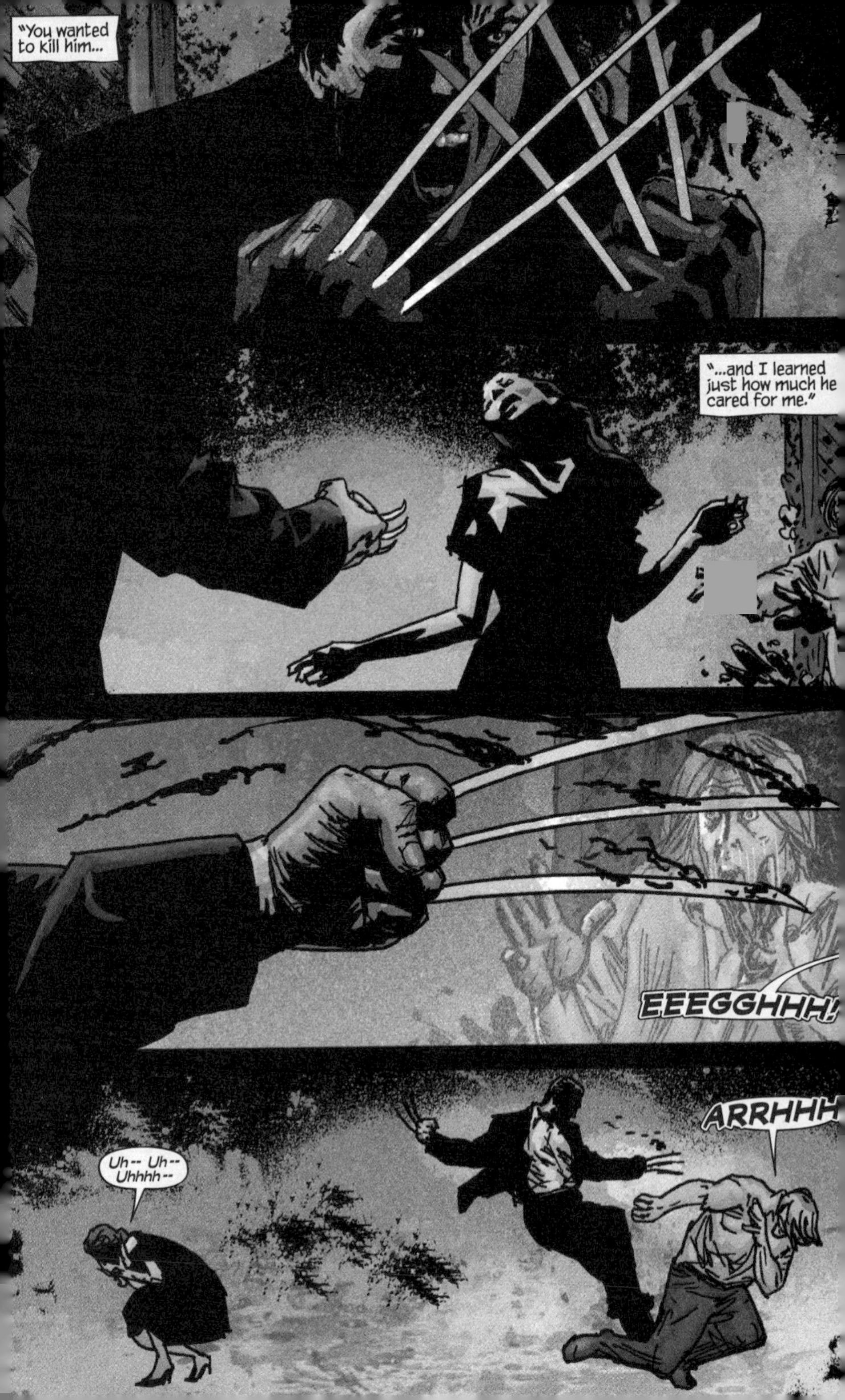
"You wanted to kill him...
"...and I learned just how much he cared for me."
EEEGGHHH!
ARRHHH
Uh-- Uh-- Uhhhh--

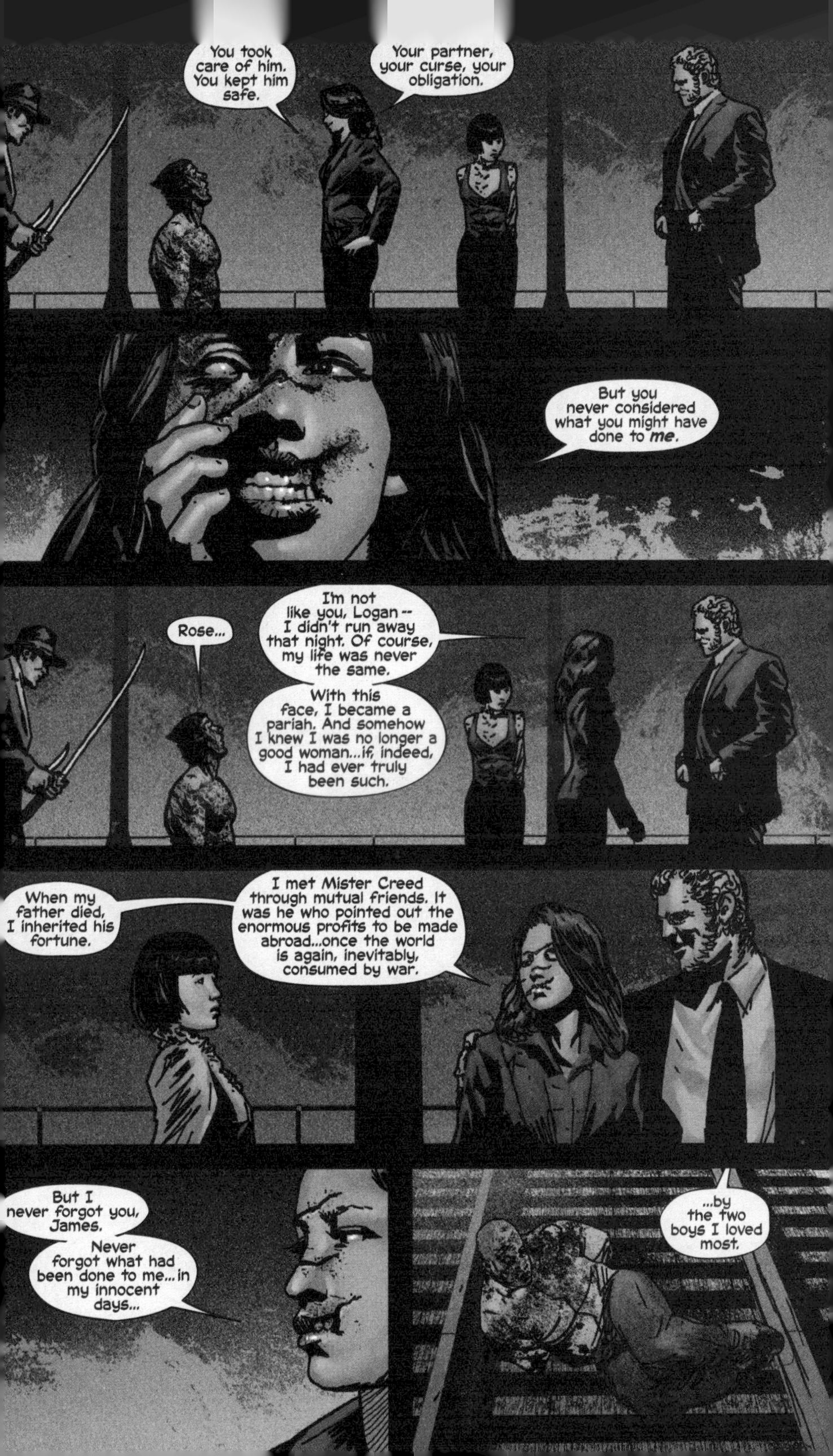

You took care of him. You kept him safe.
Your partner, your curse, your obligation.
But you never considered what you might have done to *me*.
Rose...
I'm not like you, Logan -- I didn't run away that night. Of course, my life was never the same.
With this face, I became a pariah. And somehow I knew I was no longer a good woman...if, indeed, I had ever truly been such.
When my father died, I inherited his fortune.
I met Mister Creed through mutual friends. It was he who pointed out the enormous profits to be made abroad...once the world is again, inevitably, consumed by war.
But I never forgot you, James.
Never forgot what had been done to me...in my innocent days...
...by the two boys I loved most.

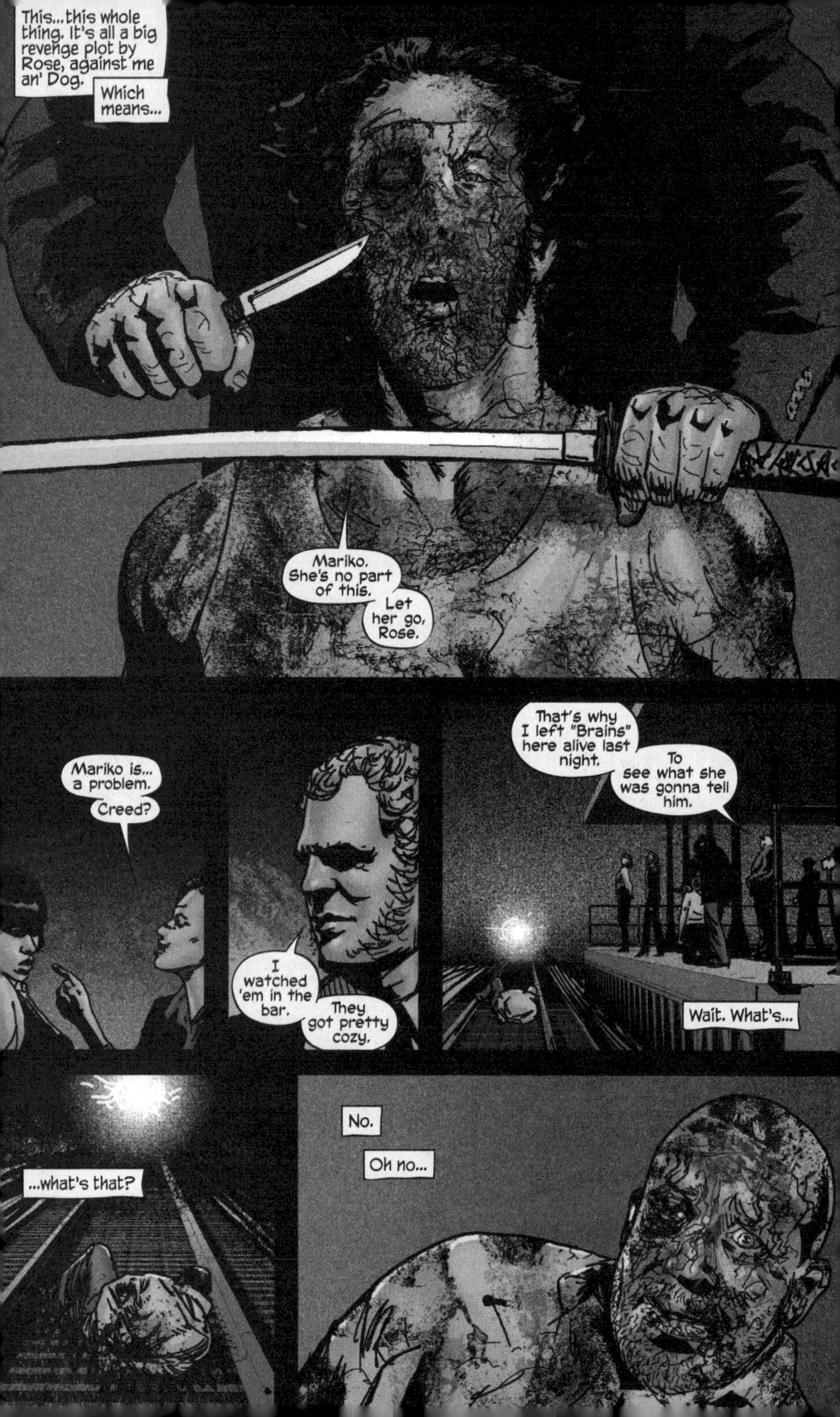

This...this whole thing. It's all a big revenge plot by Rose, against me an' Dog.
Which means...
Mariko. She's no part of this.
Let her go, Rose.
Mariko is... a problem.
Creed?
I watched 'em in the bar.
They got pretty cozy.
That's why I left "Brains" here alive last night.
To see what she was gonna tell him.
Wait. What's...
...what's that?
No.
Oh no...

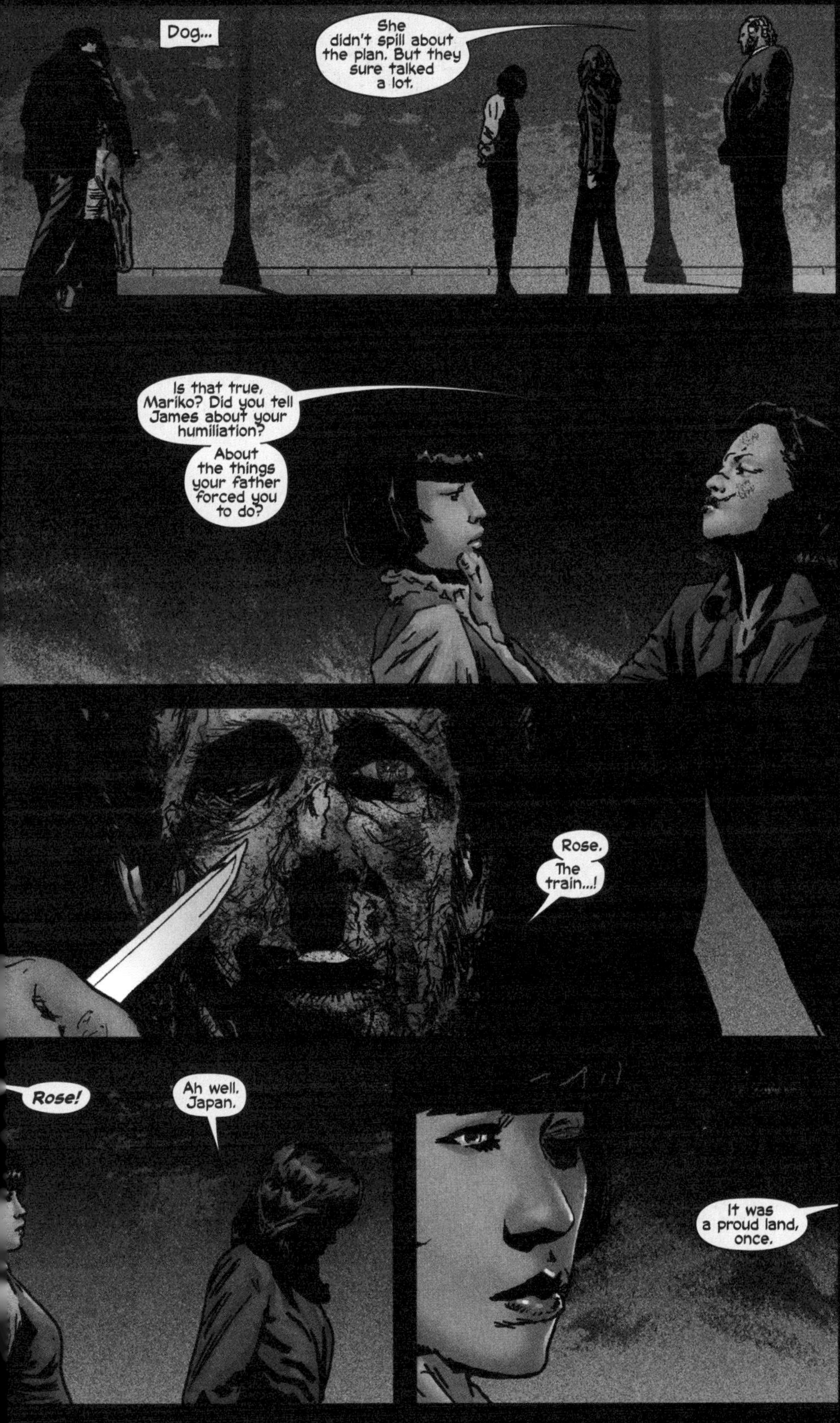
Dog...
She didn't spill about the plan. But they sure talked a lot.
Is that true, Mariko? Did you tell James about your humiliation?
About the things your father forced you to do?
Rose.
The train...!
Rose!
Ah well. Japan.
It was a proud land, once.

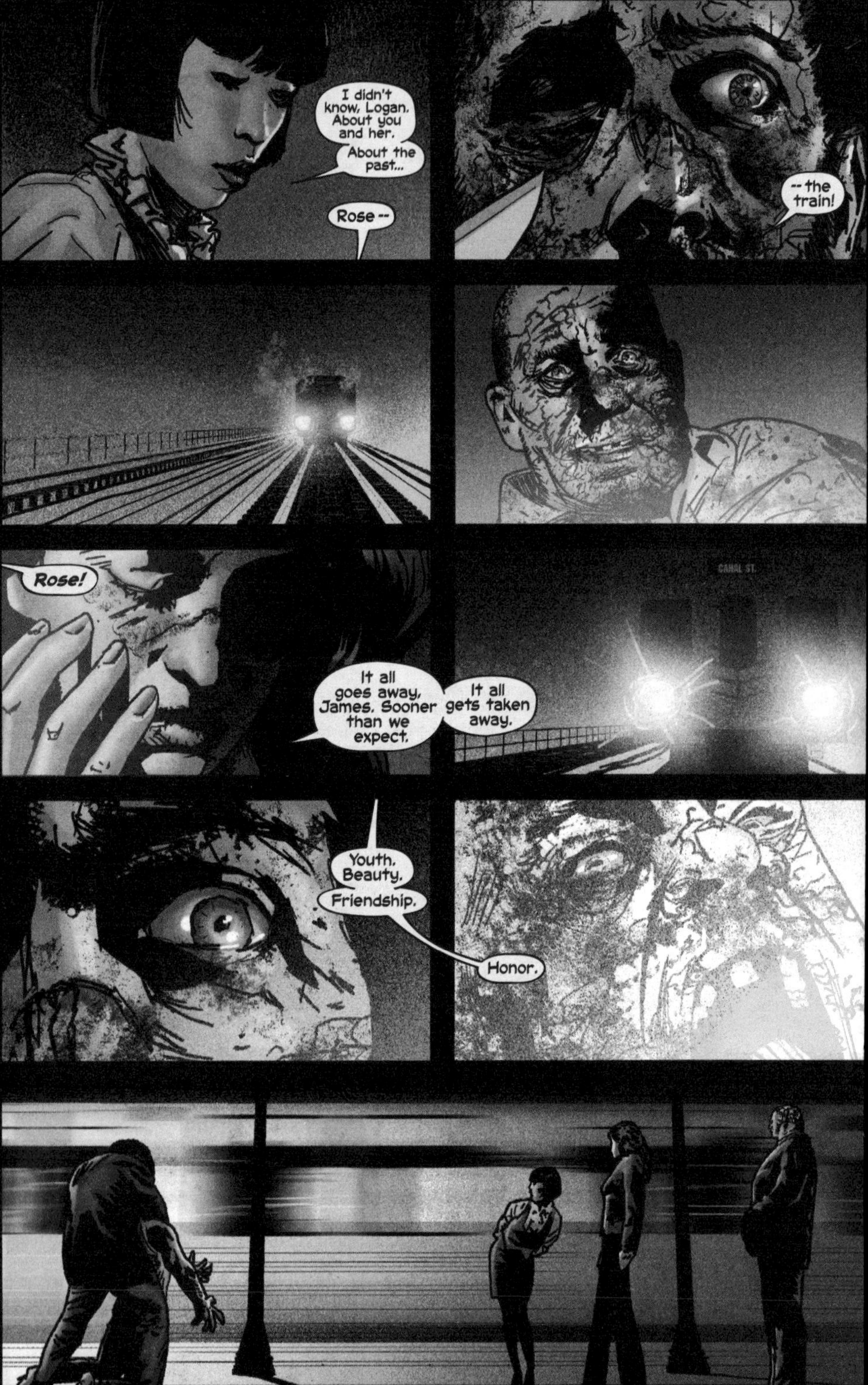

I didn't know, Logan. About you and her.
About the past...
Rose --
-- the train!
Rose!
CANAL ST.
It all goes away, James. Sooner than we expect.
It all gets taken away.
Youth.
Beauty.
Friendship.
Honor.

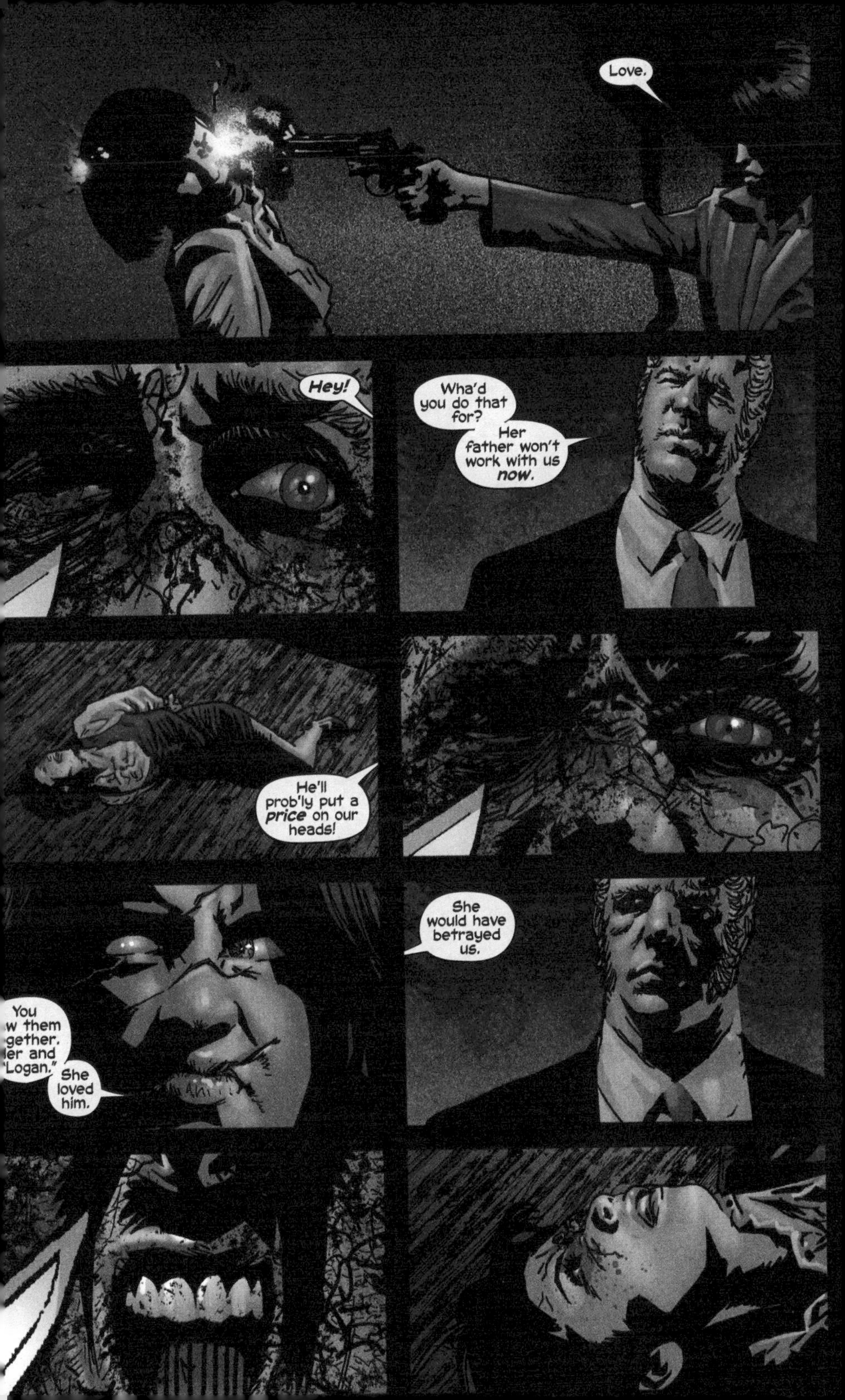

Love.
Hey!
Wha'd you do that for?
Her father won't work with us *now*.
He'll prob'ly put a *price* on our heads!
She would have betrayed us.
You w them gether. ler and "Logan."
She loved him.

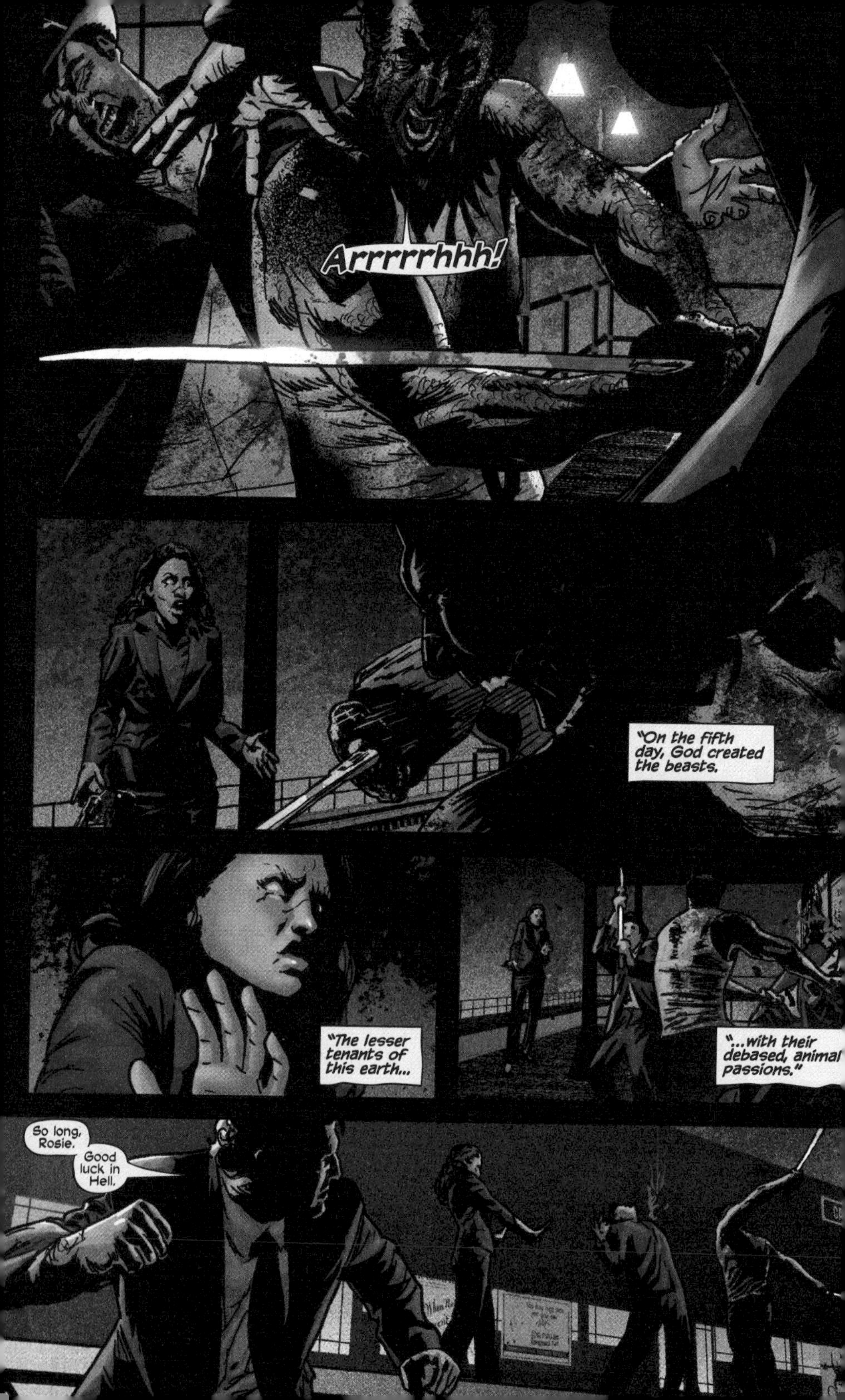
Arrrrrhhh!
"On the fifth day, God created the beasts.
"The lesser tenants of this earth...
"...with their debased, animal passions."
So long, Rosie.
Good luck in Hell.

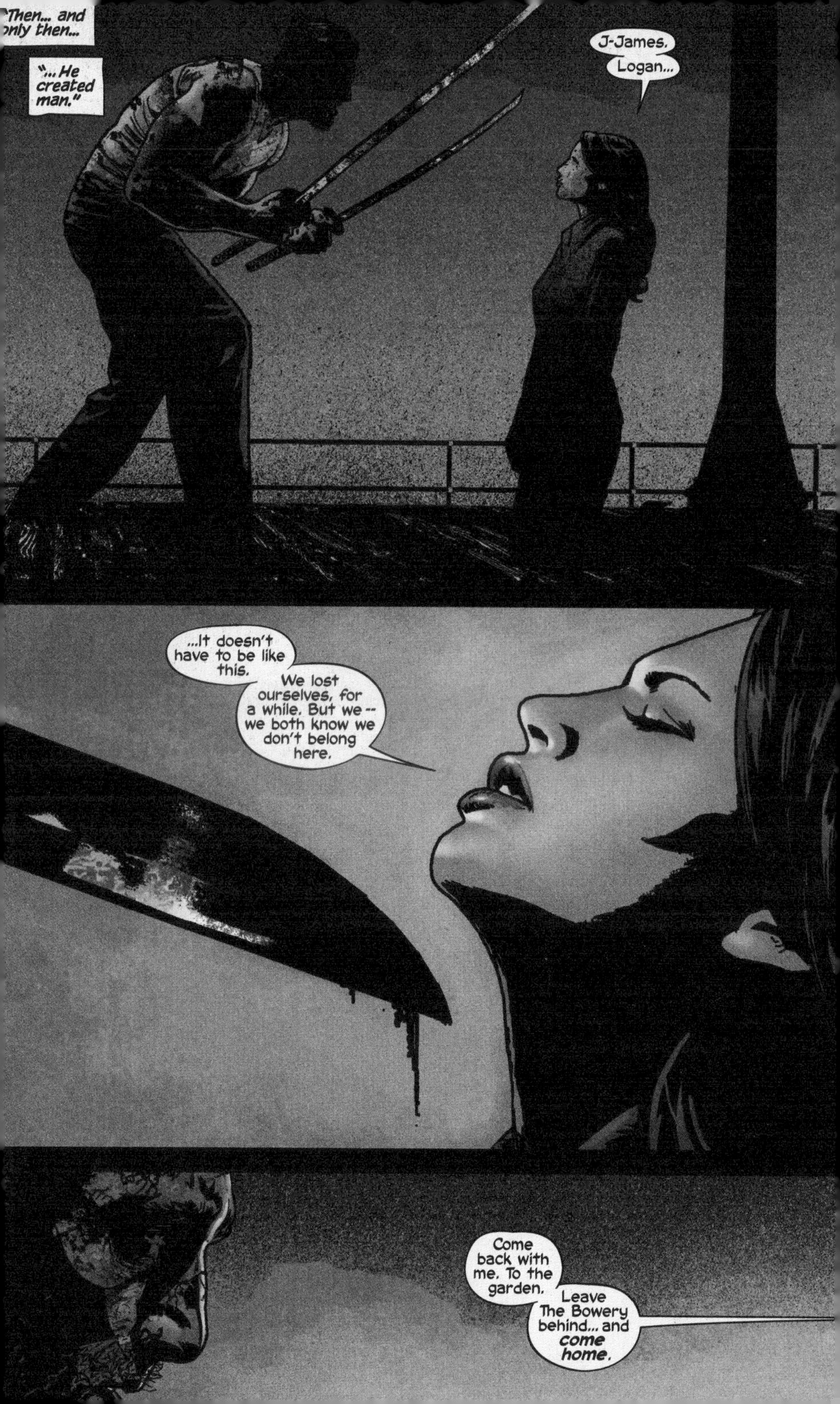
"Then... and only then...
"...He created man."
J-James. Logan...
...It doesn't have to be like this.
We lost ourselves, for a while. But we -- we both know we don't belong here.
Come back with me. To the garden.
Leave The Bowery behind... and *come home*.

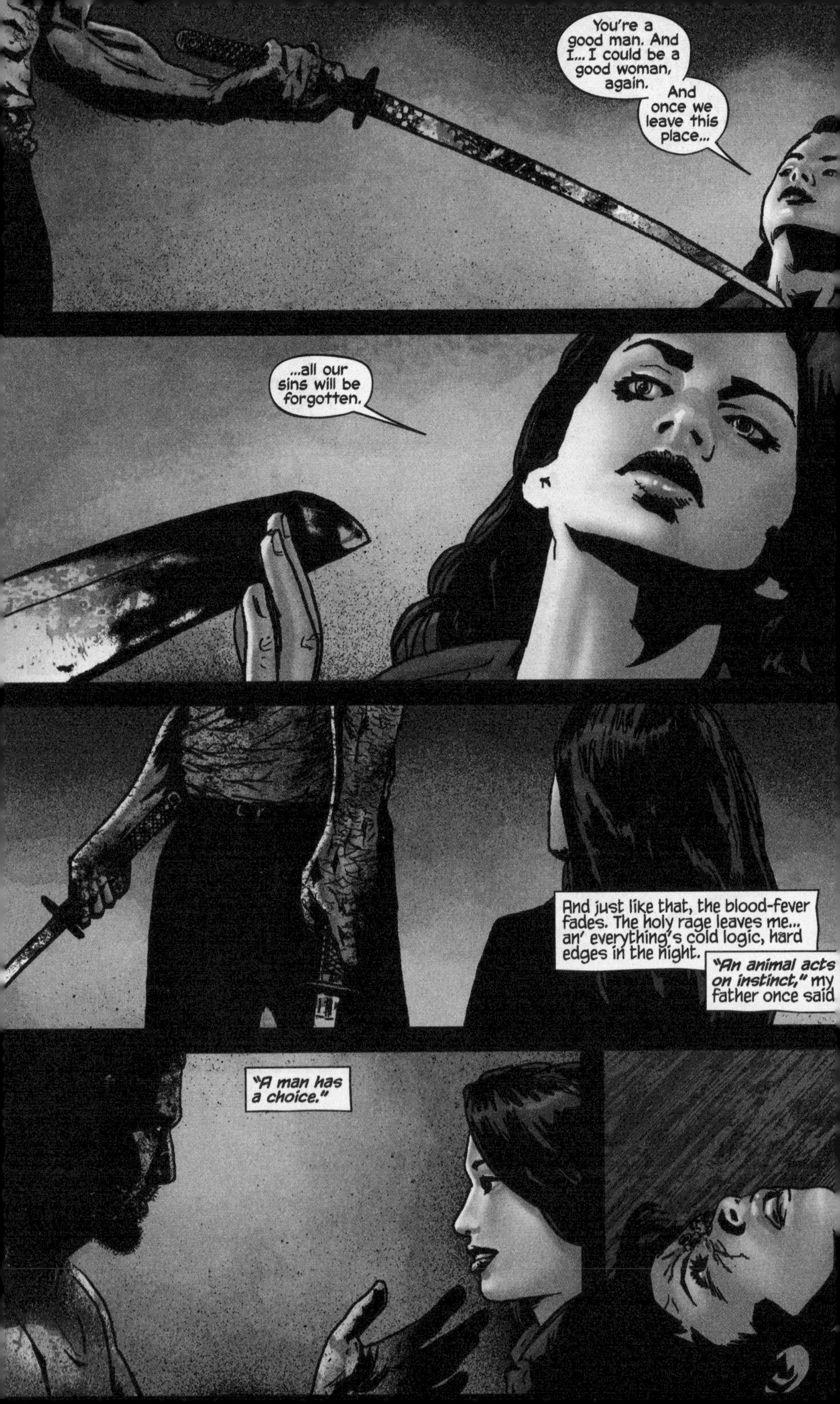
You're a good man. And I... I could be a good woman, again.
And once we leave this place...
...all our sins will be forgotten.
And just like that, the blood-fever fades. The holy rage leaves me... an' everything's cold logic, hard edges in the night.
"An animal acts on instinct," my father once said
"A man has a choice."

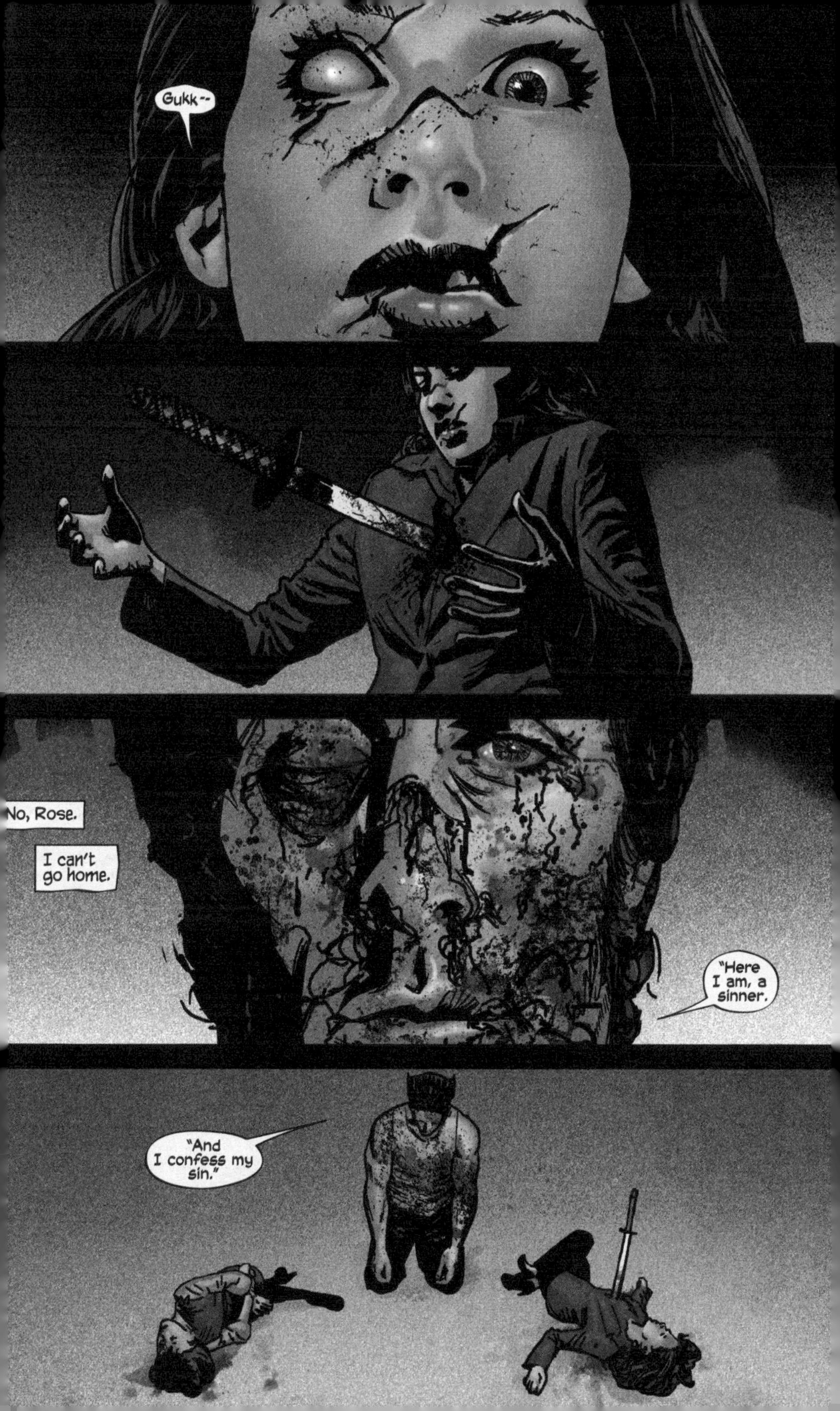
Gukk--
No, Rose.
I can't go home.
"Here I am, a sinner.
"And I confess my sin."

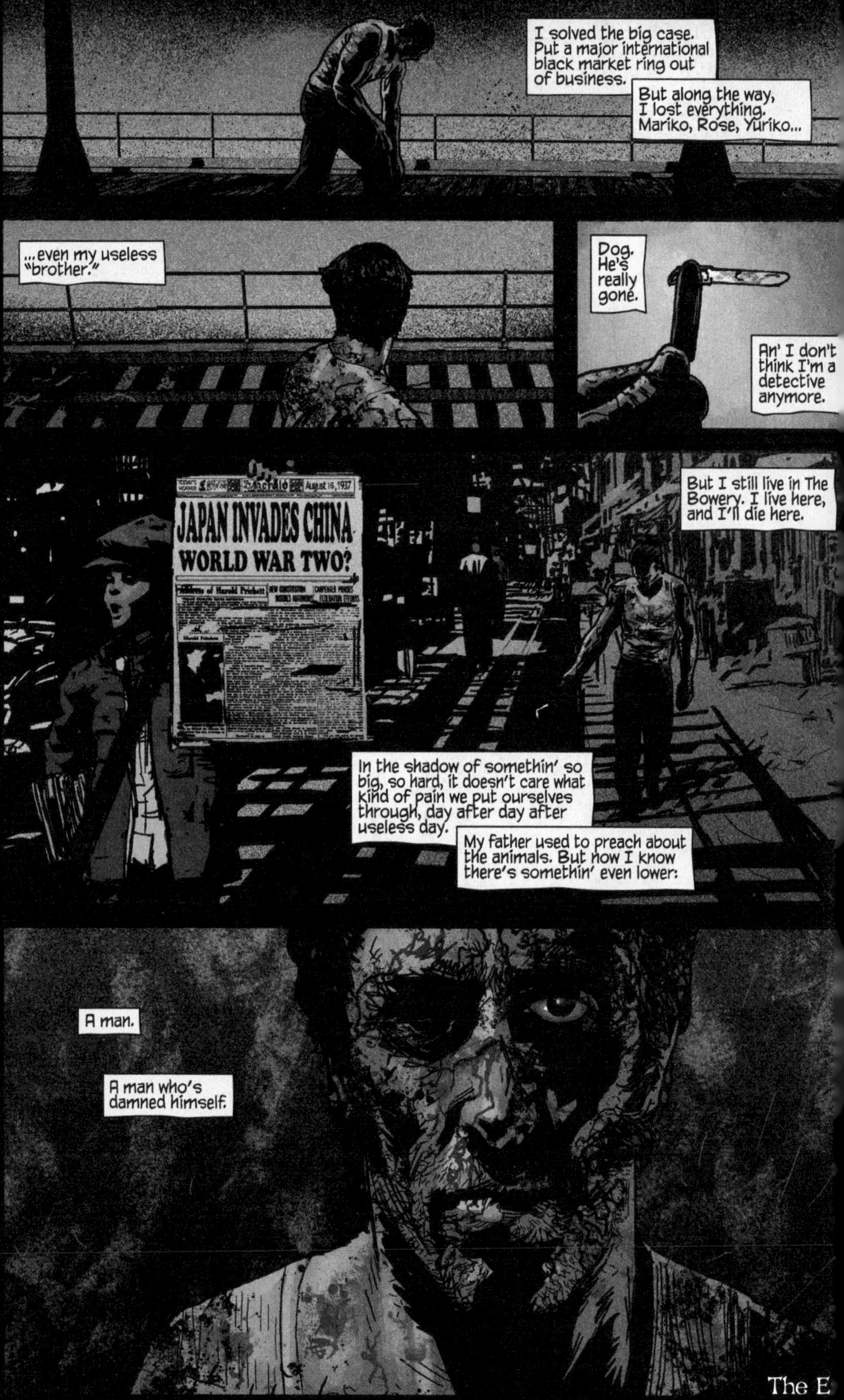
I solved the big case. Put a major international black market ring out of business.
But along the way, I lost everything. Mariko, Rose, Yuriko...
...even my useless "brother."
Dog. He's really gone.
An' I don't think I'm a detective anymore.
August 16, 1937
JAPAN INVADES CHINA
WORLD WAR TWO?
But I still live in The Bowery. I live here, and I'll die here.
In the shadow of somethin' so big, so hard, it doesn't care what kind of pain we put ourselves through, day after day after useless day.
My father used to preach about the animals. But now I know there's somethin' even lower:
A man.
A man who's damned himself.
The E

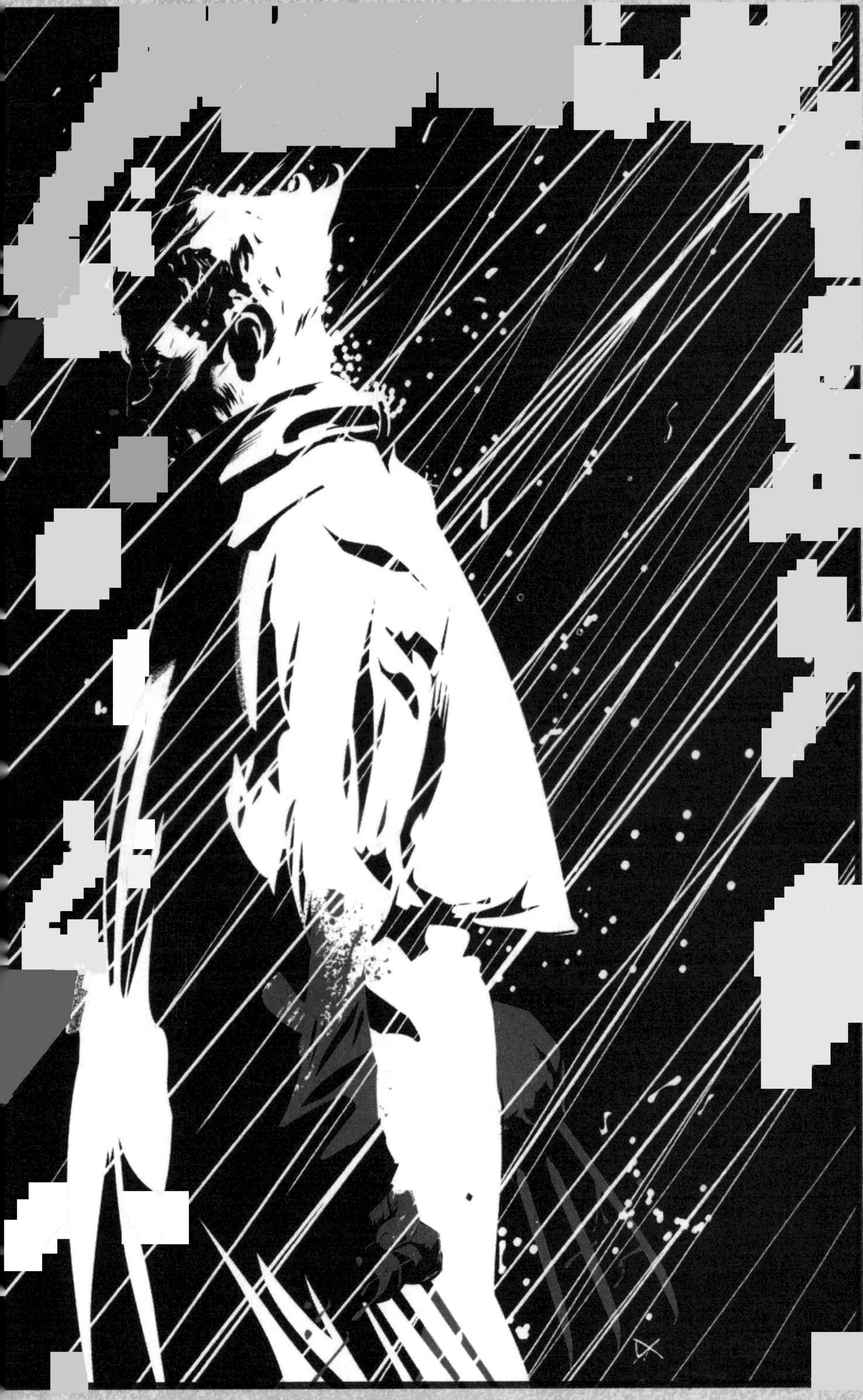

#1 VARIANT BY DENNIS CALERO

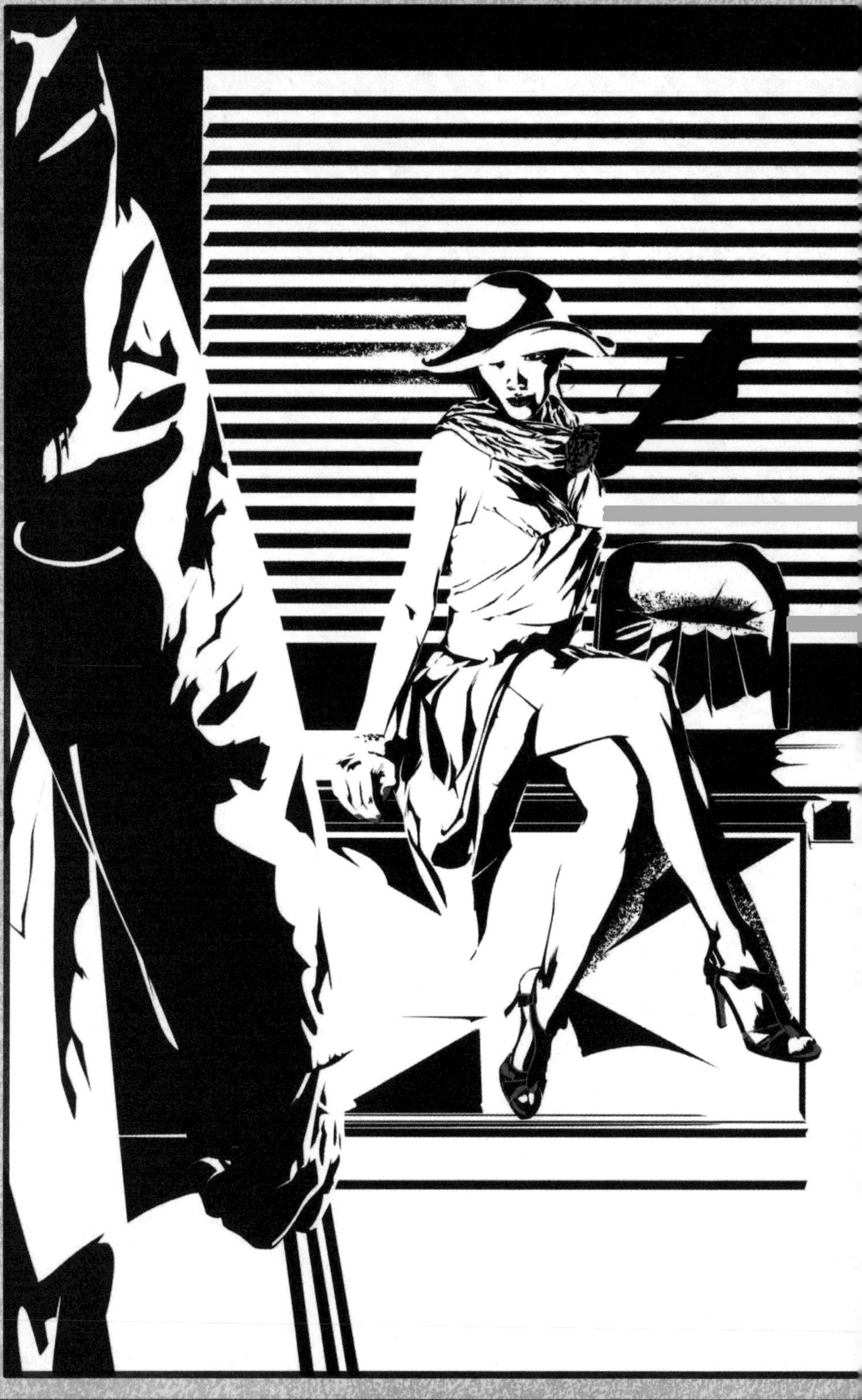

#2 VARIANT BY DENNIS CALERO

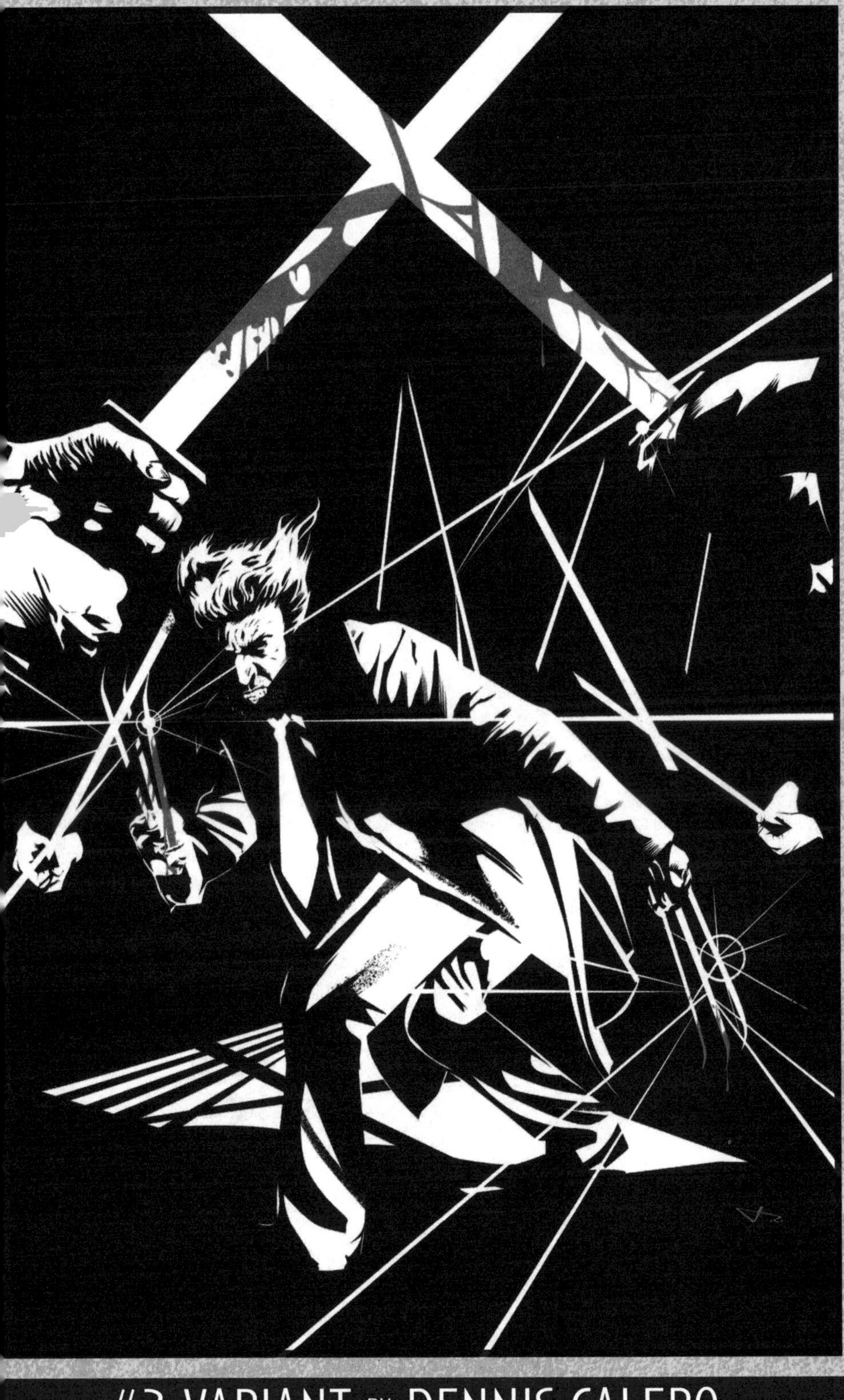

#3 VARIANT BY DENNIS CALERO

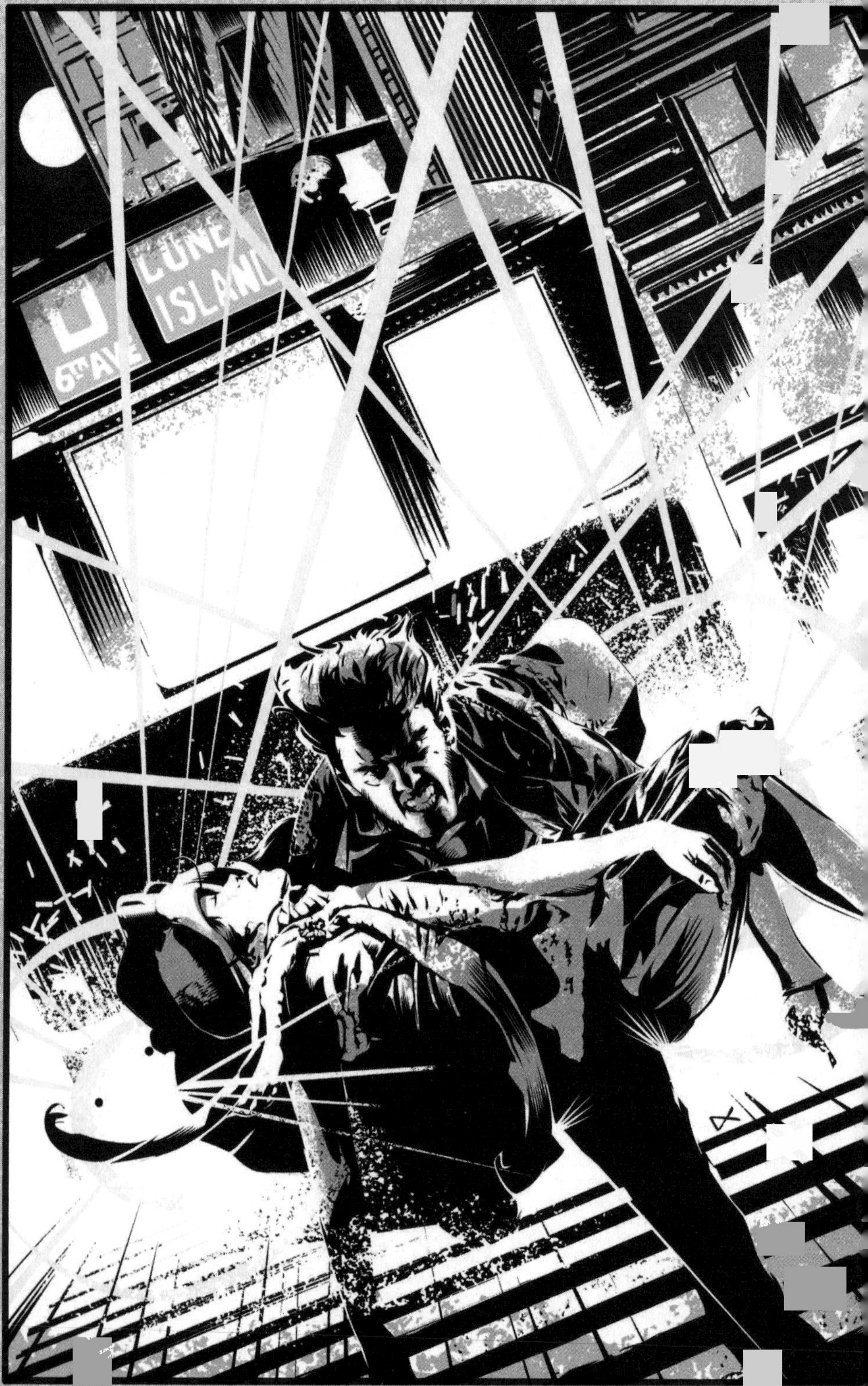
6TH AVE
ISLAND

#4 VARIANT BY DENNIS CALERO

Panel 1: Tight on a newspaper held in a grimy hand.

1 CAPTION: MY FATHER USED TO SAY: "A MAN KNOWS WHAT HELL IS.

2 CAPTION: "THAT'S WHAT SEPARATES US FROM THE ANIMALS."

NEWSPAPER TEXT: August 12, 1937
TENSIONS RISE IN ASIA
Japan, China still at odds over
"Marco Polo Incident"

Panel 2: Big panoramic shot. A period street scene: skid row to the nth degree. Lots of cheap, cut-rate men's clothing stores; plenty of bars, including the one where we find Logan in X-MEN NOIR (which we'll see again at the end of this miniseries). Some Chinese lettering on the buildings, but mostly English…AUCTIONS AND APPRAISALS, ROOMS, GAS LIGHTING, ads for seltzer, smoke shops, a charity mission, maybe one of the now-vanished flophouses.

Homeless and down-and-out men sit, stand, and trudge everywhere, many of them in the remains of suits and hats. A couple of young hoods in cheap suits -- Jack Rollers, who'll be important later -- eye passersby; one leans over an unconscious drunk on the sidewalk, rifling through his jacket. And in the center of the panel, a ragged man in tattered clothes holds up the newspaper, hawking it to passersby, who pay him no attention.

Above it all: The Third Avenue Railway runs along both sides of the street. It's day, but the rail casts the sidewalks into perpetual shadow. I'll provide a Flickr page full of reference photos.

3 CAPTION: I DON'T KNOW MUCH ABOUT HELL.

4 CAPTION: BUT I KNOW A LOT ABOUT THE BOWERY.

Panel 3: The rail. The train screeches by, spitting sparks and pitch from its wheels.

5 CAPTION: THEY SAY THIS WAS A CLASSY NEIGHBORHOOD ONCE. BEFORE THE ELEVATED RAILWAY CAME IN…SCREECHING AND ROARING ITS WAY THROUGH THE SKY, BLOTTING OUT THE SUN, SPITTIN' RED-HOT ASH AND OIL ON THE DAMNED SOULS BELOW.

Panel 4: Street level. A ragged man with a guitar sits on the sidewalk, shielding himself from the hot ash and sparks falling from above. He's propped up against a small, rundown storefront with visible letters on the window.

6 CAPTION: WE ALL LIVE IN THE SHADOW OF SOMETHING. SOMETHIN' BIG AND UNCARING AND SCARY AS HELL.

7 CAPTION: BUT THIS PLACE?

WINDOW: LOGAN & LOGAN
"The Best There Is at What We Do"

Panel 5: And a small closeup on the window, with the lettering larger now.

8 CAPTION: THIS IS ABOUT AS LOW AS A MAN CAN SINK.

Panel 1: I'm envisioning this page as a series of page-wide panels with black strips in between for the credits…but as usual, CP, do whatever you think works best. We're inside the office now, looking straight at Logan. He's dressed in period P.I. garb, and sitting at a plain wooden desk with a few knicknacks on it, papers strewn around. Logan's got an uncapped bottle of whiskey on the desk, mostly empty…and he's staring very intensely at something off-panel that we can't see.

The room is dark, cooled by bare metal fans, smoke hanging in the air. Behind Logan, the name of the detective agency is visible, reversed, on the window.

1 CAPTION: MY NAME'S JIM LOGAN. I'M A PRIVATE DETECTIVE.

WOLVERINE NOIR #1: JACK ROLLER SCRIPT

2 CAPTION: AND FOR ABOUT THE EIGHTIETH TIME TODAY…

Black strip one: title.

3 TITLE: WOLVERINE NOIR

Panel 2: Over Logan's shoulder. He's staring at a man named Dog, an almost-idiot who sits at a desk like Logan's, only smaller. Dog's hair is greasy and unkempt, his clothes are like Logan's only with more patches. And there's something wrong with his face -- let's not make it anything as obvious as a scar; more as if the flesh was ripped apart and grew back together not quite right. He's tossing a small toy knife back and forth from one hand to the other…smiling at it like it's the most delightful thing in the world. Let's make the toy knife distinctive…maybe give it an etched logo like RUFF FITER or something.

NO DIALOGUE

Black strip two: chapter title.

4 TITLE: 1: JACK ROLLER

Panel 3: And just a very intense slice shot of Logan's eyes, glaring out at us with dull, slightly drunken hatred.

5 CAPTION: …I'M THINKIN' ABOUT KILLING MY PARTNER.

Black strip three: credits.

6 CREDITS

PAGE THREE

Panel 1: On Dog. He's dirty, with bad teeth. He smiles nastily at a cockroach crawling across his desk, holding up his toy knife for the kill.

1 CAPTION: HE'S CALLED DOG. HE'S GOT THE BRAINS OF A BEDBUG AND THE MANNERS OF A GUTTER RAT.

2 CAPTION: A WHORE ON THE CORNER THREATENED TO CUT 'IM YESTERDAY. I THINK HE TRIED TO SNIFF HER GARTERS.

Panel 2: Logan takes a big swig from the whiskey bottle. Behind him, we see the backwards signage on the window: LOGAN & LOGAN.

3 CAPTION: EVERYONE THINKS HE'S MY BROTHER.

4 CAPTION: FIRST LIE I COULD COME UP WITH.

Panel 3: Dog stabs down at the desk with his knife, which lands dully -- missing the cockroach, which skitters off. Logan turns away in disgust, wiping the whiskey from his mouth.

5 CAPTION: I WISH I COULD. KILL HIM, I MEAN.

6 CAPTION: THEN I'D NEVER HAVE TO WATCH HIM PLAY WITH THAT BLASTED TOY KNIFE AGAIN --

Panel 4: Logan and Dog both turn, surprised, at the off-panel noise.

7 SFX: nok nok

PAGE FOUR

Panel 1: Big panel. On MARIKO YASHIDA, standing in the doorway, backlit by sunlight from outside. She wears an elegant '30s-style woman's suit with a few Japanese flourishes -- sticks in the hair, maybe -- and an expensive-looking wrap or boa. Very upscale and classy, a complete contrast to her seedy surroundings. She looks out at us, a bit haughty.

1 CAPTION: CLASSY DAME. LIKE A RAY OF SUNSHINE AT MIDNIGHT.

2 CAPTION: LIKE DIAMONDS IN A COAL MINE.

Panel 2: First of three small panels. Closeup Dog, his mouth hanging open. Slack-jawed with lust.

3 CAPTION: WHAT THE HELL IS SHE DOING HERE?

Panel 3: Closeup Logan, watching with half-drunken interest.

4 CAPTION: AND WHAT DOES SHE --

5 DOG: C-CAN I TOUCH YOUR TA-TAS?

Panel 4: Same as panel 2, but Dog speaks up.

6 LOGAN: EXCUSE MY PARTNER, MISS. HE AIN'T QUITE HOUSEBROKEN.

Panel 5: Wide. Unfazed, Mariko crosses the room past Dog, toward Logan. He watches her calmly.

7 MARIKO: THAT'S QUITE ALL RIGHT.

8 MARIKO: NEITHER AM I.

Panel 6: Now she perches, sexy, on the edge of Logan's desk, and looks down at him.

9 MARIKO: MY NAME IS MARIKO YASHIDA.

10 MARIKO: AND I'M LOOKING TO HIRE A DETECTIVE.

PAGE FIVE

Panel 1: Dog lurches between the two of them, smiling and leering at Mariko. She's cool... doesn't flinch at all. Logan glares at him.

1 DOG: W-WE'RE DETECTIVES.

2 DOG: IS THIS A CH-CH-CHINESE THING?

3 LOGAN: SHE'S JAPANESE, YOU IDIOT.

4 LOGAN: FROM A RICH FAMILY, I'M THINKIN'.

Panel 2: Just Mariko, smiling down at Logan. A superior smile.

5 MARIKO: YOU ARE A DETECTIVE, MISTER LOGAN.

6 MARIKO: AND YOU'RE CORRECT. IN FACT, I'M IN NEW YORK ON BUSINESS FOR MY FATHER.

7 MARIKO: UNFORTUNATELY, THERE ARE PEOPLE WHO WOULD PREVENT ME FROM CARRYING OUT THAT BUSINESS.

Panel 3: Wide. Mariko hands Logan a small slip of paper. Frowning, Dog watches their hands touch.

8 LOGAN: AND THIS BUSINESS WOULD BE...?

9 MARIKO: THE PAST FEW DAYS, I'VE BEEN FOLLOWED BY MEN FROM THIS HOTEL.

10 MARIKO: I BELIEVE IT'S ONE OF THE CHARMING "FLOPHOUSES" THAT INFEST THIS PART OF YOUR CITY.

11 ON PAPER (handwritten): Puritan Hotel

                    Klondike 5 4623

Panel 4: Downshot on Logan as he frowns at the paper.

12 CAPTION: SHE DIDN'T ANSWER THE QUESTION...

13 MARIKO (off): I HAVE MONEY. AND I'D VERY MUCH LIKE TO HIRE YOU TO LOOK INTO THIS FOR ME.

14 LOGAN: WHAT'S THIS NUMBER HERE?

Panel 5: Side angle -- maybe a silhouette -- as she leans over the desk, her lips parted. Sexy.

15 MARIKO: THAT, MISTER LOGAN, IS MY TELEPHONE NUMBER.

16 MARIKO: IN CASE YOU NEED ME.

PAGE SIX

Panel 1: Strutting tall, Mariko crosses casually back toward the door -- laying a big wad of bills right in front of Dog, who stares at it. Logan frowns, calling after her.

1 LOGAN: IF WE TAKE THE CASE, MISS YASHIDA -- OUR NORMAL FEE IS --

2 MARIKO: HERE'S A THOUSAND IN CASH.

3 MARIKO: KEEP ME APPRISED OF YOUR EXPENSES.

Panel 2: Just Logan, glaring hard at her (us).

4 LOGAN: MISS YASHIDA.

Panel 3: Wide. She stops at the door, turns back. Logan just sits at his desk, looking at her. Dog holds up the money now, rifling through it in amazement.

5 LOGAN: THIS IS A ROUGH NEIGHBORHOOD. WATCH OUT FOR THE JACK ROLLERS.

6 LOGAN: THEY'RE JUST CREEPS WITH KNIVES...THEY PROBABLY WON'T BOTHER YOU. THE DRUNKS IN THE GUTTER ARE EASIER PICKIN'S.

7 LOGAN: JUST TRY NOT TO LOOK TOO RICH.

Panel 4: Mariko pauses at the door, turns back with a slight smile.

8 MARIKO: I HAVEN'T MUCH EXPERIENCE IN THAT AREA, MISTER LOGAN.

Panel 5: As the door slams after her, Logan looks at it...intrigued but suspicious. Dog gapes at it.

9 MARIKO: BUT I WILL TRY.

PAGE SEVEN

Panel 1: Small. Logan holds up the piece of paper, frowning at it again.

1 CAPTION: A THOUSAND DOLLARS. TEN C-NOTES.

2 CAPTION: ENOUGH TO COVER A LOT OF LIES.

Panel 2: Same angle, but Logan looks up in surprise as Dog's hand snatches the paper away from him.

NO DIALOGUE

Panel 3: Past Dog as, clutching the paper and grinning, he runs toward the door. Behind him, Logan takes another long drink from the whiskey bottle.

3 DOG: I G-GOT THIS ONE.

4 DOG: I'M A DETECTIVE TOO, Y-Y-YOU KNOW.

Panel 4:

5 LOGAN: HA!

6 LOGAN: YEAH, SURE. DO YOUR BEST.

Panel 5: Setting down the bottle, Logan frowns at the pile of money sitting on Dog's desk. A dark, intense look.

7 LOGAN: DON'T GET KILLED OR ANYTHING.

PAGE EIGHT

Panel 1: Across the top of the page. A brooding head-shot of Logan melds into another shot of the elevated railway...the train rushing by, dirty, spilling coal ashes down below. And on the right, this melds again into a head-shot of young Jim Howlett -- a sickly boy of sixteen or so, acne pocking his face, his expression attentive, unsure. A big contrast to his older self. Color him the same as the flashbacks (see next panel).

1 CAPTION: WE ALL LIVE IN THE SHADOW OF SOMETHING. SOMETHING SO VAST IT DOESN'T CARE IF WE LIVE OR DIE.

2 CAPTION: THAT'S WHAT MY FATHER USED TO PREACH.

Panel 2: And into flashback. In a well-appointed study, Reverend Howlett -- James's father -- stands up at a practice lectern, launching into a fire and brimstone sermon. He's maybe forty-five, bushy sideburns and a very severe look. Focus on him in this panel. Across the room, in a single chair, young James sits, eyes wide, watching uncomfortably.

I'd suggest a sepia palette for the flashback scenes.

3 CAPTION: OR, AT LEAST, THAT'S HOW I HEARD IT.

4 REV HOWLETT: ON THE FIFTH DAY...GOD CREATED THE BEASTS.

5 REV HOWLETT: THE CRAWLING INSECTS...THE GRAZING CATTLE...THE CHATTERING APES. THE LESSER TENANTS OF THIS EARTH, WITH THEIR DEBASED, ANIMAL PASSIONS.

Panel 3: On James, just starting to stand and move toward the door.

6 REV (off):   THEN...AND ONLY THEN...HE CREATED MAN.

7 CAPTION: FATHER LIKED TO PRACTICE HIS SERMONS ON ME. HE SAID THAT IF HE COULD SWAY A SICK, HOPELESS SOUL LIKE MINE, HE COULD SAVE ANYONE.

8 CAPTION: BUT THERE ALWAYS CAME A POINT WHEN HE WAS POSSESSED BY THE RAPTURE -- WHEN HE DIDN'T EVEN NOTICE IF ANYONE ELSE WAS IN THE ROOM.

Panel 4: Now James runs furtively down the high-ceilinged hall of the house. Opulent furnishings, elaborate chandeliers. He's approaching a corner -- he can't see around it.

9 CAPTION: THEN I COULD ESCAPE.

10 REV (small, no tail):   IN ANCIENT TIMES, MAN WAS THE UNDISPUTED MASTER OF THE BEASTS. SUCH IS THE NATURAL ORDER.

11 LINKED (small): BUT TODAY -- AH, MY FRIENDS, TODAY --

PAGE NINE

Panel 1: Rounding the corner, James collides awkwardly with a beautiful, red-haired, teenage girl in upper-class period dress. She's carrying a metal bowl; a bit of ice spills from it at the impact. James panics at the sight of her.

1 REV HOWLETT: -- MAN HAS FALLEN.

2 JAMES: AAHHH!

3 GIRL: OH!

Panel 2: Scary upshot closeup on the Reverend Howlett, in full fire-and-brimstone mode, as he points an accusatory finger straight at us.

NO DIALOGUE

Panel 3: In the hallway. Rose bends down casually to pick up the fallen ice. James watches, nervous, painfully shy. Give us a good shot of her: She's absolutely beautiful here, a young man's dream girl.

4 JAMES:　　　　　R-ROSE…

5 ROSE:　　　　　DID I STARTLE YOU, JAMES? I'M DREADFULLY SORRY.

6 ROSE:　　　　　I SIMPLY CAME NEXT DOOR TO BORROW SOME ICE FOR MY MOTHER.

Panel 4: Past James at Rose, who smiles at him, holding a piece of ice.

7 ROSE:　　　　　OH, JAMES.

8 ROSE:　　　　　YOUR FACE IS FLUSHED.

Panel 5: Tight on him as she touches the ice to his forehead. He watches, sweating, excited.

9 ROSE:　　　　　MAY I?

PAGE TEN

Panel 1: Pull back. Rose and James both turn, her hand still holding the ice to his forehead, to see teenaged Dog watching them. His face is dirty, his clothes ragged; he looks hungry, lustful…but shrewder and sharper than he looks today, his skin smooth and unmarked. Before something bad happened to him.

1 DOG:　　　　　IF Y'GOT ANY MORE O'THAT HANDY, ROSIE…

2 DOG:　　　　　…I FEEL A BIT FLUSHED MYSELF.

Panel 2: James watches, angry and frightened, as Dog leers at Rose, his face very close to hers. She cocks her head, amused…not angry.

3 CAPTION:　　　YOUNG DOG WAS THE SON OF OUR MAINTENANCE MAN. MY FATHER WOULD HAVE HORSEWHIPPED HIM FOR SUCH A REMARK.

4 CAPTION:　　　BUT I WAS AFRAID OF HIM.

Panel 3: Rose strides away now, smiling, holding her ice bowl. Dog leers after her, and James watches her with naked longing.

5 CAPTION:　　　ROSE WASN'T.

6 ROSE:　　　　　I BELIEVE I'LL LET YOU TWO GENTLEMEN CARRY ON.

7 ROSE:　　　　　MY ICE IS MELTING.

8 DOG:　　　　　I'LL BET…

Panel 4: On James, helpless as he watches Dog follow Rose down the hallway.

9 CAPTION:　　　DOG BARELY NOTICED MY PRESENCE.

10 CAPTION:　　　AND AS I WATCHED HIM FOLLOW AFTER ROSE, I HEARD MY FATHER'S SERMON ONCE AGAIN…ECHOING THROUGH THE WALLS..

11 REV (small, no tail):　　BEWARE YOUR ANIMAL PASSIONS, MY FRIENDS.

12 REV (small, linked):　　BEWARE THE DEVIL'S SHROUD…

Panel 5: Just James, his face screwed up with anger and fear.

13 CAPTION:　　　AND I FELT A SHARP, STABBING MOMENT OF FEAR. FEAR THAT I WAS NOT A MAN AT ALL…

14 CAPTION:　　　…BUT AN ANIMAL.

15 REV (small, no tail):　　…THE SHROUD THAT HANGS O'ER US ALL…

PAGE ELEVEN

Panel 1: Out of flashback -- back to normal palette. Exterior the Puritan Hotel (see reference). Day.

1 CAPTION: DOG. MY PARTNER.

2 CAPTION: ONE THING'S FOR SURE:

3 DOG: AC-C-CORDING TO MY INVESTIG-GATIONS...TH-THIS HOTEL IS OWNED BY A MAN CALLED CREED.

Panel 2: Interior -- lobby of the hotel. Adult-Dog leans in to an impassive manager behind a cage, questioning him. A group of men sit in the lobby, bored, watching him: a few old guys, a vet in a wheelchair, three young Jack Rollers in cheap suits (as on page 1). One guy furtively eating a chocolate bar, toes poking through his ragged shoes. An old man pushes a mop. (Probably all would be Caucasian at this time period.)

I'll provide some reference shots of flophouse lobbies. These are modern photos, so adjust clothes and furnishings accordingly -- no fluorescent lights or TV!

4 DOG: CAN I S-SEE HIM, PLEASE?

5 CAPTION: HE AIN'T THE MAN HE USED TO BE.

Panel 3: Shot of the bored manager behind the cage, glaring at us.

NO DIALOGUE

Panel 4: On a couple of the men in the lobby. A Jack Roller stands, hand in his jacket pocket. Old vet in the wheelchair sits. The other old man holds his mop. All eyes are on Dog.

NO DIALOGUE

Panel 5: Zoom in on the Roller's hand as he pulls a sharp-looking knife just a little way out of his pocket.

NO DIALOGUE

Panel 6: Close-up Dog, his face screwed up in frustration.

NO DIALOGUE

PAGE TWELVE

Panel 1: Wide. Dog suddenly smacks the old man (the one with the mop) hard across the face, knocking him to the ground. Not an awkward move; a brutal act. The watchers eye the drama, a bit startled.

1 DOG: YOU THINK I'M SCREWIN' AROUND?

2 DOG (big):   I WANT CREED!

3 GUY: UHHHH!

Panel 2: Still impassive, the manager walks out from the cage, motions to Dog. The old man lies propped up on the floor, frightened, wincing.

4 MANAGER: NO NEED FOR THAT, SIR.

5 MANAGER: I'LL TAKE YOU.

Panel 3: Past the Jack Rollers...standing now, watching as the Manager leads Dog down the hallway out of the lobby.

NO DIALOGUE

Panel 4: Manager stands before an open door labelled 5B, motioning Dog inside. Manager's calm as always; Dog still looks angry.

6 MANAGER: IN HERE…

Panel 5: Tight on the door as it slams shut…the number 5B very prominent.

NO DIALOGUE

PAGE THIRTEEN

Panel 1: Back into flashback. Close-up young James, looking out at us, nervous but determined.

1 FROM OFF: IN ANCIENT TIMES, A NOVICE SAMURAI WOULD BE DRESSED UP ALL NICE, PLOPPED DOWN ON A MOCK-BATTLEFIELD, AN' HANDED HIS FIRST REAL SWORD.

2 LINKED: THEN HE'D BE A WARRIOR.

Panel 2: Pull back. We're in a kind of greenhouse or enclosed arboretum on the grounds. James stands, facing SMITTY -- the family gardener -- a World War I veteran who stands, facing him in combat stance. They're both holding rattan sticks -- mock knives, one in each hand, notched and marked to indicate a "live edge." Smitty smiles at Logan, a challenging smile.

This is Smitty's workshop as well. Various scythes, hoes, and primitive gardening implements line the walls -- along with a glass case full of real knives.

3 SMITTY: BUT IF WE DID THAT, YOUR FATHER WOULD SKIN ME LIKE A RABBIT.

4 SMITTY: SO WE'LL HAVE TO USE RATTAN STICKS INSTEAD.

Panel 3: Over Smitty's shoulder at James, focused and determined, holding up his mock knives in defensive posture.

CP: YOU PROBABLY KNOW MUCH MORE ABOUT SWORD AND KNIFE COMBAT THAN I DO, SO I'M JUST GOING TO SUGGEST THE BARE BONES OF ACTIONS AND LET YOU RUN WITH IT.

5 CAPTION: I LEARNED AS MUCH FROM SMITTY, OUR GARDENER, AS I EVER DID FROM MY FATHER.

6 CAPTION: SMITTY'D BEEN IN THE GREAT WAR. FOUGHT OVERSEAS.

Panel 4: Reverse angle…focus on Smitty. He holds his "knives" casually, eyes narrowed to study the boy as they circle each other.

7 CAPTION: AFTER THE ARMISTICE, HE TRAVELLED AROUND FOR A WHILE. CHINA, THEN JAPAN.

8 CAPTION: THAT'S WHERE HE LEARNED ABOUT KNIVES.

PAGE FOURTEEN

Panel 1: James lunges awkwardly toward Smitty, who sidesteps easily.

1 SMITTY: FOCUS, BOY. MAINTAIN YOUR BALANCE.

2 SMITTY: THE BLADE ISN'T JUST A WEAPON. USED CORRECTLY, IT'S THE PATH TO SEISHEN TANREN -- MORAL AND SPIRITUAL PERFECTION.

Panel 2: Still calm, Smitty grabs James by one arm, twisting and forcing him to drop one of the mock knives.

3 SMITTY: THE SAMURAI USED BOTH SWORD AND KNIFE -- LONG BLADE AND SHORT, IN PERFECT HARMONY.

4 JAMES: UHH!

5 SMITTY: MAYBE IT'S THE IRISHMAN IN ME --

Panel 3: Very tight. Smiling wolfishly, Smitty holds James in a headlock near his own head. James's eyes go wide, blood-rage rising.

6 SMITTY: -- BUT I'VE ALWAYS PREFERRED THE KNIFE.

Panel 4: Still holding one "knife," James breaks free, backing up toward the case of knives now -- which are very old-looking and elegant, a mix of designs, some of them very distinctive. If you can manage it, show us at least two of them clearly here; if not, we can see them on page 16. James looks wild now, savage.

7 CAPTION: I KNEW WHAT HE MEANT. THESE SPARRING SESSIONS WERE THE ONLY TIMES I FELT ALIVE.

8 CAPTION: AS I LUNGED FORWARD, MY BLOOD BOILED...MY FACE GREW FLUSH WITH AN ANCIENT RAGE...

Panel 5: James leaps through the air, Wolverine-style, his remaining knife raised. Smitty watches him come, a little worried for the first time.

9 CAPTION: ...AND THE KNIVES DANCED THEIR DARK, HOLY DANCE.

PAGE FIFTEEN

Panel 1: In full fury, James lands on Smitty, knocking him to the ground on his back.

1 CAPTION: IT MIGHT NOT HAVE BEEN SPIRITUAL PERFECTION -- BUT IT FELT RIGHT. IT FELT LIKE ME.

2 CAPTION: AND THEN -- JUST AS I WAS GETTING THE ADVANTAGE OVER SMITTY, FOR THE FIRST TIME EVER --

Panel 2: Near the door. Rose slips in, watching the fight with awe. Dog follows, frowning at her.

3 CAPTION: -- ROSE ENTERED THE GREENHOUSE.

4 CAPTION: DOG, TOO. NO DOUBT SNIFFING AFTER HER AGAIN.

Panel 3: James and Smitty grapple now; Smitty's recovered his balance, and they're holding each other's knives at bay. James looks like he's going through some internal struggle.

5 CAPTION: I REMEMBER THINKING: I MUST ACHIEVE THAT PURITY. THE SEISHEN TANREN.

6 CAPTION: FOR HER.

Panel 4: Dog points toward the display case with the knives. Rose turns to watch Dog, interested, her attention diverted from the fight.

NO DIALOGUE

Panel 5: Close-up Rose, her eyes wide with excitement.

7 CAPTION: TO BE WORTHY OF HER.

PAGE SIXTEEN

Panel 1: Close-up Smitty, still locked in combat with James. Smitty whirls his head around in outrage.

NO DIALOGUE

Panel 2: Smitty brutally "slices" James in the stomach with one mock knife, knocking him away -- while flinging the other knife off into the distance.

1 JAMES: UHH!

Panel 3: At the display case, now opened. Smitty's mock knife hits Dog painfully in the hand -- just as he's reaching out to grab a real knife from the case. Show us a couple of the knives with distinctive handles and designs, clearly here, so we'll recognize them later on when Logan uses them. Rose shrinks back.

2 DOG: AAAH!

Panel 4: Wide. Smitty points accusingly at Dog, who grasps his hand in pain. James lies propped up on the floor now, holding his stomach...and Rose turns to look at him now.

3 SMITTY: PATHETIC CUR-CHILD! STEAL MY PRICELESS JAPANESE KNIFE SET, WOULD YE?

4 SMITTY: AND FOR WHAT?

Panel 5: Just Dog, looking up -- trapped, humiliated.

5 SMITTY (off):   TO IMPRESS A GIRL?

PAGE SEVENTEEN

Panel 1: Dog and James stand now, facing each other...James uncertain, Dog glaring straight at James, for the first time, with hatred. Rose watches them both, and Smitty slams down the lid of his knife case.

1 SMITTY: COUNT YOURSELF LUCKY, BOY.

2 SMITTY: THE ANCIENT SAMURAI USED TO HUNT DOWN DOGS, SHOOTING THEM WITH ARROWS. FOR SPORT.

3 DOG (small):   YOU. MASTER JAMES.

4 DOG (small):   YOU PLANNED THIS...

Panel 2: Still angry, Smitty tosses the toy knife we've seen in the 1937 sequences to Dog, who grabs it, surprised.

5 SMITTY: LESSON'S OVER, YOUNG JAMES.

6 SMITTY: AS FOR YOU, LITTLE DOG -- TIME TO GO CRAWLING BACK TO YOUR FATHER.

Panel 3: Over Dog's shoulder as he stares at the toy knife. Give us a good look at it.

7 SMITTY: AND HERE: TAKE THIS WOODEN TOY.

Panel 4:

8 SMITTY: IT'S THE ONLY KNIFE YOU'LL EVER DESERVE.

Panel 5: Rose watches Dog run out the door, and James smiles tentatively at Rose.

NO DIALOGUE

Panel 6:

9 JAMES: HE'S...

10 JAMES: HE'S NOT LIKE US, IS HE, ROSE?

Panel 7: Wide. Rose watches the door, an odd, blank expression on her face. James stands with her. Behind them, Smitty angrily waters some plants.

11 ROSE: NO, JAMES.

12 ROSE: HE IS NOT.

PAGE EIGHTEEN

Panel 1: Lobby of the Puritan hotel. Logan, in full fury, holds the manager slammed up against the outside of his cage, threatening him. The other men watch, some bored, some alarmed.

1 CAPTION: EIGHT YEARS AND TWENTY-NINE HOURS LATER:

2 LOGAN (big):   WHERE IS HE?

Panel 2: Zoom in tight. Teeth gritted, Logan leans in very close to the manager's facen.

3 LOGAN: MY PARTNER. MASH-FACED LITTLE WEASEL WITH A SEVENTY-EIGHT-RPM STUTTER.

4 LOGAN: HE AIN'T CHECKED IN FOR MORE THAN A DAY. AND I KNOW HE WAS HERE.

Panel 3:

5 MANAGER: F-FIVE-B...

Panel 4: Dropping the manager on the floor, Logan stalks off down the hallway. The young guys in suits stand to follow him, just like with Dog on page 12, panel 3.

NO DIALOGUE

Panel 5:

NO DIALOGUE

Panel 6: Now Logan holds up a hand to the door labelled 5B. Hesitating.

6 CAPTION: SUDDENLY I GOT A VERY BAD FEELING ABOUT THIS.

7 CAPTION: LIKE THERE'S SOMETHING BEHIND THAT DOOR I DON'T WANT TO SEE.

PAGE NINETEEN

Panel 1: From behind Logan, still in the hallway. He whirls to see the three young men standing in a block, facing him, clearly hostile. Some of them are starting to pull out knives -- ordinary ones, but deadly-looking.

NO DIALOGUE

Panel 2: Close-up Logan, frowning: Something's not right.

1 CAPTION: THEY LOOK LIKE JACK ROLLERS. CHEAP HOODS WITH KNIVES.

2 CAPTION: BUT AS THEY START FORWARD, I REALIZE:

Panel 3: Big. The men launch themselves through the air at Logan, kicking and slicing with knives and truncheons. The exact moves of ninja, but with young, Caucasian men. Logan falls back into a defensive stance, pulling out an ornate knife.

3 CAPTION: NO JACK ROLLER EVER HAD MOVES LIKE THIS.

PAGE TWENTY

Panel 1: Logan faces the first enemy, who screams toward him, wielding two knives.

1 CAPTION: I ONLY EVER KNEW ONE MAN WHO FOUGHT THIS WAY.

2 CAPTION: SMITTY.

Panel 2: Logan counters, avoiding the attack and driving his own knife straight into the man's gut -- just as the other two men move toward him.

3 CAPTION: FORTUNATELY, HE TAUGHT ME SOME TRICKS.

Panel 3: On Logan, bloodlust on his face, as he pulls the blood-drenched knife out again -- and draws a second one. Now we can see: They're two of the knives from the display case, as seen on pages 14 and 16.

4 CAPTION: LEFT ME A FEW KEEPSAKES, TOO.

Panel 4: Big and bloody. Logan wades into the other two combatants, avoiding their kicks and knives, slashing and killing.

5 CAPTION: AND IN THE ROTTING HEART OF THE BOWERY -- IN THE SHADOW OF THAT ANCIENT RAGE --

6 CAPTION: -- THE KNIVES DANCE AGAIN.

PAGE TWENTY-ONE

Panel 1: Logan stands in the hall, facing away from the men -- who now lie dead on the floor. He stares at the doorway labelled 5B.

1 CAPTION: THEY DIDN'T WANT ME TO GO IN THERE.

2 CAPTION: I DON'T WANT TO GO IN THERE --

Panel 2: Teeth gritted, he kicks open the door, splintering it off its hinges.

NO DIALOGUE

Panel 3: Over his shoulder as he steps into the small room. Inside: just a cot covered with blood, and something small and metallic in the center of it.

3 CAPTION: BLOOD. AND SOMETHIN' ELSE, TOO...

Panel 4: Upshot on Logan, dread on his face as he reaches down toward the cot.

NO DIALOGUE

Panel 5: Over his shoulder as he holds up Dog's toy knife, covered with blood.

Note: I'm not sure if the caption here is necessary...consider it optional.

4 CAPTION: DOG'S TOY KNIFE.

PAGE TWENTY-TWO

Panel 1: Now he sits on the edge of the bloody cot, eyes wide and haunted. Still holding the toy knife.

1 CAPTION: OH GOD. OH MY GOD.

2 CAPTION: HOW MANY TIMES HAVE I WISHED HIM DEAD?

Panel 2: Zoom in tighter as he stares at the knife.

3 CAPTION: I HATE HIM MORE THAN ANYONE I'VE EVER KNOWN. AND YET...EVEN SO...

4 CAPTION: ...I'VE CARED FOR HIM ALL THESE YEARS. BECAUSE I CAN NEVER MAKE UP FOR WHAT HAPPENED.

Panel 3: Now Logan stands, walking toward the door. Blood on his hands and clothes.

5 CAPTION: THERE'S A LOT OF BLOOD. HE MIGHT BE DEAD.

6 CAPTION: MAYBE. MAYBE NOT.

7 CAPTION: BUT EITHER WAY...I'VE GOTTA FIND HIM.

Panel 4: Now he walks through the lobby. The manager and old men watch him go, keeping their distance.

8 CAPTION: BECAUSE HE'S MY PARTNER. BECAUSE IT LOOKS LIKE SOME FLASHY DAME THREW HIM TO THE WOLVES.

9 CAPTION: AND BECAUSE EVEN HERE...IN THE LOWEST PLACE ON EARTH A MAN CAN SINK...

Panel 5: And a final shot of Logan walking down the twilight Bowery street. Winos, bums, and cheap bars. Like he says: Hell on Earth...and he looks like he really belongs.

10 CAPTION: ...I STILL OWE HIM.

11 CAPTION: TO BE CONTINUED